THE WINONA LETTERS
BOOK ONE

RICHARD N. WILLIAMSON

THE WINONA LETTERS • BOOK ONE
IN THE *LETTERS FROM THE RECTOR* SERIES

THE COLLECTED WORKS ✦ VOLUME II

© 2019 BRN Associates, Inc.
All rights reserved.

ISBN (paper) 9781940306018
ISBN (Kindle) 9781940306056
ISBN (ePub) 9781940306063
ISBN (PDF) 9781940306070

For more information,
or for additional titles, contact:

Marcel Editions
An Imprint of the St. Marcel Initiative
www.stmarcelinitiative.com
c/o BRN Associates, Inc.
9051 Watson Rd., Suite 279
St. Louis, MO 63126
(855) 289-9226

St. Louis, Missouri ❧ 2019

CONTENTS

NO. 63 | AUGUST 1, 1988 Rome Relentlessly Conciliar	1
NO. 64 | SEPTEMBER 1, 1988 Aftermath of the Consecrations	7
NO. 65 | OCTOBER 1, 1988 Irreconcilability of Tradition & Vatican II	13
NO. 66 | NOVEMBER 1, 1988 The Arguments of *Ecclesia Dei*	19
NO. 67 | DECEMBER 1, 1988 Obedience Must Be to Tradition	24
NO. 68 | JANUARY 1, 1989 Southern Africa, Down Under, Hawaii	29
NO. 69 | FEBRUARY 1, 1989 Rome and the Fraternity of St. Peter	36
NO. 70 | MARCH 1, 1989 Paul, An African Catholic	42
NO. 71 | APRIL 1, 1989 Picasso, Art, and Morality	46
NO. 72 | JUNE 1, 1989 *Ecclesia Dei* – Impossible Halfway House	51
NO. 73 | JULY 1, 1989 Tradition Miraculously Protected in Nimes	58

| NO. 74 \| AUGUST 1, 1989 | 63 |

Ecclesia Dei Playing Softball

| NO. 75 \| SEPTEMBER 7, 1989 | 68 |

Asian Tour

| NO. 76 \| OCTOBER 1, 1989 | 73 |

Traditional Bishops Absolutely Necessary

| NO. 77 \| NOVEMBER 1, 1989 | 77 |

Women in Arms

| NO. 78 \| DECEMBER 1, 1989 | 82 |

Indult Masses & Fatima

| NO. 79 \| JANUARY 1, 1990 | 87 |

Coming Decade Calls for Heroes

| NO. 80 \| FEBRUARY 1, 1990 | 92 |

Is Communism Dead?

| NO. 81 \| MARCH 1, 1990 | 101 |

Our Lady of Akita

| NO. 82 \| APRIL 1, 1990 | 106 |

Sedevacantism Not Obligatory

| NO. 83 \| MAY 4, 1990 | 111 |

Rome Puts Out Feelers

| NO. 84 \| JUNE 4, 1990 | 117 |

The Modernist Church Self-Destructing

| NO. 85 \| JULY 1, 1990 | 122 |

Sedevacantism Fails to Grasp Modern Mind-Rot

| NO. 86 \| AUGUST 1, 1990 | 132 |

Archbishop Lefebvre Charged with Racism

| NO. 87 \| OCTOBER 1, 1990 | 136 |

Principles with Wolves' Teeth

| NO. 88 \| NOVEMBER 1, 1990 | 140 |

SSPX Celebrates 20 years

| NO. 89 \| DECEMBER 1, 1990 | 143 |

The Death of Malcolm Muggeridge

| NO. 90 \| FEBRUARY 1, 1991 | 148 |

Gulf War I

NO. 91 | MARCH 1, 1991	154
Visit to Latin America	
NO. 92 | APRIL 1, 1991	160
Death of Archbishop Lefebvre	
NO. 93 | MAY 9, 1991	166
Death of Bishop de Castro Mayer	
NO. 94 | JUNE 10, 1991	170
Unity and Perseverance in Tradition	
NO. 95 | JULY 1, 1991	175
Should Abortionists be Assassinated?	
NO. 96 | AUGUST 1, 1991	180
Consecration of Monsignor Rangel	
NO. 97 | SEPTEMBER 1, 1991	185
Slacks I	
NO. 97 | SEPTEMBER 1, 1991	191
The SSPX as Pilot-Light	
NO. 99 | NOVEMBER 3, 1991	196
Slacks II	
NO. 100 | DECEMBER 1, 1991	202
Why Rome Must Take Out the SSPX	
NO. 101 | JANUARY 1, 1992	207
Young Mothers, Keep Mothering!	
NO. 102 | FEBRUARY 1, 1992	212
Cardinal Oddi's Visit to Ecône	
NO. 103 | MARCH 5, 1992	217
Sedevacantism: Too Simplistic, Too Absolute	
NO. 104 | APRIL 1, 1992	224
"JFK"	
NO. 105 | MAY 8, 1992	228
Reasonableness of Garabandal	
NO. 106 | JUNE 5, 1992	237
500th Anniversary of Columbus' Landing	
NO. 107 | AUGUST 1, 1992	242
The Slaughter-Fields of Verdun	

NO. 108 | SEPTEMBER 13, 1992	249
The Cardinal Lienart Question	
NO. 109 | OCTOBER 6, 1992	255
Schism, By Shifted Goal Posts	
NO. 110 | NOVEMBER 5, 1992	260
Columbus Commemoration in Argentina	
NO. 111 | DECEMBER 1, 1992	265
The Sadness of Johannes Brahms	
NO. 112 | JANUARY 1, 1993	271
Accompanying Slacks III	
NO. 113 | FEBRUARY 4, 1993	278
The American Patriot's Catechism	
NO. 114 | MARCH 1, 1993	285
Pope John Paul II's Voodoo Scandal	
NO. 115 | APRIL 2, 1993	293
Death of Fr. Barrielle	
NO. 116 | MAY 4, 1993	299
Importance of the Family Rosary	
NO. 117 | JUNE 4, 1993	305
Architects of Neo-Modernism	
NO. 118 | JULY 4, 1993	318
The New Testament Priesthood	
NO. 119 | SEPTEMBER 1, 1993	323
Executives of Neo-Modernism	
NO. 120 | OCTOBER 1, 1993	335
The Humble Rosary	
NO. 121 | NOVEMBER 6, 1993	340
A Discerning Young Man	
NO. 122 | DECEMBER 11, 1993	345
A Trip Through Africa	
NO. 123 | JANUARY 1, 1994	352
Slacks IV, or Dinosaur's Delight	
NO. 124 | FEBRUARY 3, 1994	359
St. Agnes & St. Emerentiana	

NO. 125 | MARCH 1, 1994   366
Pope John Paul II's Encyclical *Veritatis Splendor*

NO. 126 | APRIL 2, 1994   377
Impressions of Ordinations

NO. 127 | MAY 1, 1994   382
Confusing Human Dignity and Human Liberty

NO. 128 | JUNE 7, 1994   387
The SSPX's General Chapter

NO. 129 | JULY 1, 1994   392
The Human Frailty of the SSPX

NO. 130 | AUGUST 12, 1994   398
Bishop Fellay Elected Superior General

INDEX   403

NO. 63 | AUGUST 1, 1988

Rome Relentlessly Conciliar

So Archbishop Lefebvre has consecrated four bishops, with Rome's approval in principle on May 5, but without its permission in practice for June 30. The enclosed *Verbum* would have been in color to commemorate the occasion, had *The Angelus* not anticipated us with its consecrations issue containing pictures and documents, which you must not miss!

A great number of you are overjoyed at having four new bishops for Tradition, with good reason. Let me here thank all of you that sent congratulations, gifts or the promise of (much needed) prayers. As for the "excommunications" from Rome, easily most of you are not upset, on the contrary. Judging by your letters, I think many of you would have liked also to sign the "Open Letter" sent to Cardinal Gantin on July 6 by all the leading priests of the Society gathered at Ecône, in which they invited him to "excommunicate" them also, as a badge of honor and of orthodoxy!

However, a certain number of you prayed so earnestly for a reconciliation to take place between Rome and the Society, that you were puzzled or disappointed when your prayers were seemingly unanswered. Why did the Archbishop not stay with the May 5 agreement and work from there?

Richard N. Williamson

Rome conceded one bishop for August 15, why ruin everything for mere details such as one bishop or three, August 15 or June 30? For an answer, it is best (as usual) to listen to the Archbishop himself, speaking in private in mid-June:

> It is not true that between ourselves and Rome it is just a question of details to negotiate. The basic problem is always there – Rome's liberalism and modernism. They mean to bring us and all our works round to the Council while leaving us a little Tradition. Thus Cardinal Ratzinger said in the negotiations that Tradition is the Church and the Church is Vatican II, so by leading us to the Council he thinks he is saving our Tradition! When we signed the agreement he also put before me a letter to the Pope that I should sign, apologizing for my errors! But it is we that should be questioning them on their faith. We should be demanding of them to pronounce the Anti-Modernist Oath, and to accept papal documents such as the anti-liberal *Quanta Cura* and the anti-modernist *Lamentabili*, but whenever I bring up their liberalism and modernism, they never reply. They just persist in their errors.
>
> The more you think about it, the more you realize their intentions are not good. The problem is not a few negotiable details. They remain what they are. We can't put ourselves into their hands. To think they would do anything other than eat us up little by little is an illusion. With the kind of agreement they were proposing we would not have lasted a year. Dom Gerard (of Le Barroux) thinks an agreement would open up an immense apostolate for us. Yes, but in a half-Catholic, half non-Catholic environment which would in the end corrupt us. Ah, they say, but union with Rome would bring us in many more vocations. Maybe, but vocations coming to us because we were "with" Rome would bridle at a single word being spoken "against" Rome, our seminaries would immediately be split in two. As we are now, vocations are self-sifting before they come to us.
>
> Similarly, in the wake of such an agreement the mainstream bishops would say, "Now we are 'together,' you

The Winona Letters ✦ Book One

must mix with us!" Slowly the mixture of Novus Ordo and Tradition would take place, the Society would split down the middle, everything would become a source of division. Take for example the Archbishop of Lyons' offer to our Father L. of a traditional parish in the archdiocese on condition he quit the Society. They mean to pick up our people and bring them round to the Council. (Editor's note – compare the massive campaign launched since June 30 by the Vatican to draw away Traditionalists from Tradition – more anon). By prudently stepping back from such an agreement we are saving the Society of St. Pius X and Catholic Tradition. We made an honest attempt to continue under Rome's protection, but it did not work out. Their intentions were not good. They never intended to secure a place for Tradition within the Church. Their intentions in all these negotiations were quite different from ours. I entered these negotiations because Rome's reactions in the second half of last year had raised in me a faint hope that these churchmen had changed. They have not changed, except for the worse. Look at Casaroli in Moscow! They have spiritual AIDS, they have no grace, their immunity defense system is gone.

I do not think one can say that Rome has not lost the Faith. As for an eventual "excommunication," its disagreeableness diminishes with time. Simple Catholics understand. It is the clergy who will come down hard on us. But then witnesses for the Faith, the martyrs, have always had to choose between the Faith and the authorities. We are reliving the trial of Joan of Arc, only with us it is lasting not twenty days but twenty years.

Altogether, the Archbishop is convinced that it was by a grace of Our Lady that he was impelled on May 6 to go no further with the agreement he had signed on May 5. Not that he retracted his signature of May 5, but that at the very moment of signing, Rome showed its wholly different understanding of what was being signed by, for instance, immediately prevaricating over the practical date for the consecration of the one bishop in theory agreed to. And when some three weeks later, a date of August 15 for this bishop's consecration was conceded by them, they promptly refused all three candidates proposed by the Archbishop. Clearly, Rome would only have approved a candidate of whom they knew he would help them to bring the Society and Traditionalists back into the Conciliar Church.

Dear Friends and Benefactors, not one breath of all your prayers was wasted – unless you wished to follow Vatican II!

Vital question – are these Romans in good faith? When Catholic common sense judges their poisoned fruits, obvious to all, of destruction of the Faith and of the Church, the answer is a resounding No – how could they not know what they are doing? How could God let them not know, when they are destroying His Church? Has not God raised Archbishop Lefebvre (amongst others) precisely to show them what they are doing? Yet they appear so sincere that down the years they succeed in persuading one group of Traditionalists after another to rejoin them! How is it possible?

Merely the latest in a long line of such groups from within the Society is one you may have read about in the papers: some (to date) dozen Society priests and fifteen seminarians (none yet from Winona), led by the Society's former Second Assistant, forming a Society of St. Peter (who else?), modeled on the SSPX, promised pontifical status by Rome, but already so divided over the Mass that they have reportedly almost come to blows and two groups of them have had to negotiate separately with Rome's Cardinal Mayer! Of course this "Society of St. Peter" will swiftly disintegrate, like the seminary Mater Ecclesiae, and its members will likewise dissolve individually back into the Conciliar Church. But how could these Romans deceive yet another group of Society priests? It is a vital question, because who can guarantee that he will not be the next one to succumb to such an apparently powerful recurring temptation?

I think the answer lies in the history of modernism. Liberals and Modernists are dreamers, dreaming the modern world's great naturalist dream of solving all mans' ills without need of, or recourse to, penance, grace or the Cross. Unless one loves the truth, this dream is, firstly, most seductive. Secondly, it has by 1988 become all but universal, for with Vatican II even the Church of Truth slipped into it, so that today virtually everyone is confirming everyone else in thinking that truth is the dream and the dream is true. So the whole dreaming world applauds the now dreaming Romans, and they have themselves convinced they are serving the truth when they are in fact trampling on it. As Our Lord says to His Apostles, "They will put you out of the synagogues: yea, the hour cometh that whosoever killeth you, will think that he doth a service to God. And these things they will do to you, because they have not known the Father, nor Me." (Jn. 16: 2-3) However, the Romans' universally induced conviction that they are serving the truth enables them to play most convincingly – conviction convinces – the part of sincere churchmen, and the dream marches on. Only the facts give it the lie.

Two simple facts: the six bishops of June 30 and all who follow them are neither schismatic nor excommunicated. One reason they are not schismatic is because as the Dean of the Canon Law Faculty at Paris' Catholic Institute (nothing to do with the Society) said on July 4, what constitutes schism is not one bishop consecrating another without permission (even if that gravely offends against Church discipline), but the subsequent conferring upon him of an apostolic mission, i.e., jurisdiction. But upon the bishops of June 30 Archbishop Lefebvre pretended to confer no jurisdiction – they are merely his auxiliary bishops, at the service of the Society, and under orders of its Superior General, principally to confirm and ordain (in the USA prepare for a tour of Confirmations in the spring).

Nor are they excommunicated, firstly because a Church censure like excommunication to be valid requires a real offence (c. 1321, #1, New Code), and by consecrating bishops in the line of refusal of the novelties of Vatican II, Archbishop Lefebvre has offended against neither the doctrine nor the unity of the true Church nor against true obedience (our flyer is on its way). Secondly, because whoever breaks a law because of an emergency (c. 1323, #4, NC) or because he sincerely thinks there is an emergency (c. 1323, #7, NC), incurs no penalty, and Archbishop Lefebvre knows, as do we all, that there has been a major emergency in the Church for the last 20 years, brought on by the willful blindness of the Roman authorities.

See the *L'Osservatore Romano*, English edition, July 4, 1983, page 12, for their truly incredible statement that it is the Archbishop who has purposely created the "emergency!" These poor Romans! Our Lord again: "Let them alone: they are blind and leaders of the blind. And if the blind lead the blind, both fall into the pit." (Mt. 15: 14)

Friends and Benefactors, you will be delighted to know that you have surprised the Archbishop himself by your steadiness under fire, this latest fire from Rome. You have a man to follow, and you are following in manly fashion. I beg you to continue your support in renovating Winona for his American and English-speaking seminarians.

With all my heart I send you the first episcopal blessing in this letter of your servant in Christ.

NO. 64 | SEPTEMBER 1, 1988

Aftermath of the Consecrations

WHEN ARCHBISHOP LEFEBVRE referred in his Consecrations Sermon of June 30 to a message of Our Lady from Quito, Ecuador, alongside her well known messages of La Salette (France, 1846) and Fatima (Portugal, 1917), a number of you were interested. The latter two messages were known to you, and their importance, but the former only some of you saw when a version of it was printed in *The Angelus* about a year ago. Here, firstly, is how the Archbishop referred to the message from Ecuador:

> It was not only the good Pope Leo XIII who said these things (e.g., how "The See of Peter would become the seat of iniquity"), but Our Lady prophesied them as well. Just recently, the Society's priest in charge of our Priory in Bogotá, Colombia, brought me a book concerning the apparition of Our Lady of "Buen Suceso," of Good Fortune," to whom a large church in Quito, Ecuador, was dedicated. They were received by a nun shortly after the Council of Trent, so you see, quite a few centuries ago. This apparition is thoroughly recognized by Rome and the ecclesiastical authorities; a

magnificent church was built for the Blessed Virgin Mary wherein the faithful of Ecuador venerate with great devotion a picture of Our Lady, whose face was made miraculously. The artist was in the process of painting it when he found the face of the Holy Virgin miraculously formed. And Our Lady prophesied for the twentieth century, saying explicitly that during the nineteenth century and most of the twentieth century, errors would become more and more widespread in Holy Church, placing the Church in a catastrophic situation. Morals would become corrupt and the Faith would disappear. It seems impossible not to see it happening today.

I excuse myself for continuing this account of the apparition but she speaks of a prelate who will absolutely oppose this wave of apostasy and impiety, saving the priesthood by forming good priests. I do not say that prophecy refers to me. You may draw your own conclusions. I was stupefied when reading these lines but I cannot deny them, since they are recorded and deposited in the archives of this apparition.

The text of the apparition itself is enclosed. We have marked out the passage referring to the prelate saving the priesthood, of whom the Archbishop says it may or may not be himself. Certainly it is getting a little late in the 20th Century (to which Our Lady explicitly refers) for any other prelate to be seen as doing anything like saving the Catholic priesthood!

And now the Archbishop has been "excommunicated" for his pains. Of course the excommunication is of no significance. By refusing the uncatholic novelties of Vatican II the Archbishop has committed no offence against Catholic doctrine; nor then against Catholic obedience by refusing orders to follow these novelties; nor against Catholic unity by not being at one with those who do follow them; from which it also follows that in no Catholic sense of the word is he schismatic, any more than Our Lord was schismatic when by telling the truth He so antagonized and divided the Jews of His day. Now common sense and Church law (c. 1321, #1, New Code) say that where there is no offense, there is no penalty. So the apparent excommunication is no excommunication at all. However, what has been the fall-out?

The Archbishop himself is in good health, I learn, maybe better than he expected. It might not be surprising if God, having given him to apprehend his departure from this life in order to incite him to consecrate auxiliary bishops, was now to keep him in good health for a while yet. For when this crisis is over and the Church has to be rebuilt, which of today's churchmen with any experience will then have any credit with Catholics? (The protestations of large numbers in the swollen victory parade that they were with Tradition all along, may not convince everyone). But which of today's churchmen earning credit in the action will, even by then, have had anywhere near the administrative experience necessary to rebuild the Church? For the combination of prestige and experience which will be needed, myself I can, humanly speaking, see only one candidate. In any case the Archbishop is at present actively at work and continuing to guide events. *Deo Gratias.*

As for Cardinal Ratzinger, we know that within weeks of the consecrations he addressed the bishops of Chile on the "positive elements" in Archbishop Lefebvre's movement, responding to deficiencies in the post-Vatican II Church, e.g., an entertainment liturgy, the super-dogmatising of Vatican II and the ecumenical dilution of Catholic belief! Very true, dear Cardinal! Then why did you excommunicate him? Because, as the Cardinal himself told an Italian paper before the consecrations, "We cannot have a body inside the Church refusing to join the main movement of the Church." Ah, dear Cardinal,

Richard N. Williamson

I hope you were not surprised if you saw some of the Chilean bishops faintly grinning as you addressed them on the sins of Vatican II – your actions against the Archbishop speak louder than your words for him!

The Cardinal may have been happier when Dom Gerard, Prior of the well-known Traditional Benedictine Monastery of Le Barroux in France, and a world-renowned Traditionalist leader, accepted in July Rome's terms for rejoining the mainstream Church, which Archbishop Lefebvre had turned down in May. Dom Gerard was granted for his monastery by Cardinal Ratzinger the lifting of all suspensions for his community, reconciliation with the Holy See, the Tridentine liturgy of 1962, ordinations by a bishop "in good standing," free contact between the faithful and his monks, and reintegration in the mainstream Confederation of Benedictine communities. And in return? Merely the undertaking no more to resort to Archbishop Lefebvre (or any of his auxiliaries) for episcopal services to the monastery. It looks like a good bargain, does it not?

Most of Dom Gerard's intellectual following has accordingly approved of it, but not the "little" Catholics. So many of these have protested or withdrawn their support that to defend his action Dom Gerard has felt obliged to issue a Declaration, of which he had me sent a copy. He makes the opening towards Rome look very attractive, but he will not mind if I differ in public, because the issues concern us all.

He lays out four main reasons for accepting what the Archbishop refused: Tradition should not be outlawed from the Church (of course); the traditional liturgy should not be outlawed from the Benedictine Order (of course); so long as the Faith and Sacraments are safeguarded, it is better to observe the Church's laws than break them (of course – but the whole problem is that these modernists in Rome have a 25-year track-record precisely for wrecking the Faith and the sacraments); fourthly, the opportunity should be seized that will enable Catholics freely to attend the True Mass (of course – but what price the opportunity?).

Dom Gerard comes to the conditions: no discrediting of Archbishop Lefebvre, and no doctrinal or liturgical compromise on the monastery's part, nor silencing of its anti-modernism. Is that all? Dom Gerard makes no mention of the cutting with Archbishop Lefebvre which was apparently the one condition required by Rome. Yet here is the rub. "Divide and rule" – one may well wonder how Dom Gerard will fare amidst the Roman foxes, once he is divided from Tradition's proven champion: "Who sups with the devil, needs a long spoon."

Yet Dom Gerard resents such distrust. He goes on to suggest that some traditionalists are setting up Tradition like a political party within the Church, with a leader elected by them to push them around as he likes, while they enjoy resisting for its own sake, and trample on charity in the process. Of which, all one can say is that if that is true of a few followers of Tradition, it is certainly not true of the mass of them, who would much rather be united with Rome, but not at the price of their Catholic Faith. Far from being pushed around like by a party politician, they freely follow the shepherd they have learned to trust will best defend their Faith.

Dom Gerard concludes with three wishes: firstly, let no one judge hastily, but wait for the fruits (but do we not know these Romans' fruits well enough by now to fear that if our friends sit down to sup with them, it may well already be too late?). Secondly, let all Traditionalists unite for Christ the King (of course, but should we unite with His proven enemies?). Thirdly, let all remember Our Lord's words that whoever is not against Him, is for Him (yes again, but is Dom Gerard willfully blind to all the fruits proving these Romans to be against Christ?).

Richard N. Williamson

Dom Gerard is letting himself be deceived by the honeyed words of these perfidious modernists, objectively perfidious even if we suppose them to be in such mental confusion as to have good intentions for the evil they do of crippling Tradition. We pray for Dom Gerard that he quickly get up from his supper with the devil! The Archbishop for his part is apparently refusing to reopen negotiations with Rome until they make a profession of Faith in accordance with the old catechisms. Exactly right. The Truth has done enough begging for respectability from people turning their backs on it.

From Winona, a few dates: Sept. 10, beginning of the school year; Sept. 24, arrival of the new seminarians, maybe fourteen in number; Oct. 7, Minor Orders for twelve; Oct. 8, Blessing of the Seminary and Official Opening – you are all invited to a Solemn High Mass at 10 a.m., followed by a buffet lunch and Solemn Vespers at 5 p.m. Nov. 1, Subdiaconate for seven seminarians; Dec. 21, Diaconate for four, and thus the ordinations will have been caught up.

We apologize if the latest set of the three audiotapes has taken a little time to reach you, but orders are being processed as swiftly as we are able. We will not fail to let you know as soon as a videotape of the Consecrations is available in the USA. Available now is the Mass flyer in Spanish. Order from us as many as you like, especially for the Sun Belt.

And "beware of false prophets that come to you in sheep's clothing, but inwardly they are ravenous wolves. By their fruits you shall know them." How many more "excommunications" does anyone need to recognize the wolves in Rome? Patience. The truth will prevail and is prevailing upon all of you that wish to keep the Catholic Faith.

The blessing of our Lord be on each of you.

NO. 65 | OCTOBER 1, 1988

Irreconcilability of Tradition & Vatican II

For Catholics with eyes to see, the very real division between Catholic Tradition and the Second Vatican Council has long been apparent. With the unauthorized consecrations of the four Society bishops at the end of June, this long existent split simply came still more sharply into focus. It is in fact the split between Jesus Christ and the world. But men do not like having to choose. They want to be on good terms with both. Ignoring Our Lord's warning that a man cannot serve two masters, they seek like Pontius Pilate a way out, a third way, a way of reconciling Christ and the world.

Accordingly what we have seen since July is an extra flurry of words and deeds on the part of those seeking to reconcile the Second Vatican Council with Catholic Tradition. Alas, whether it is well-intentioned Romans reaching out to Traditionalists, or more or less well-intentioned Traditionalists going begging to Rome, there is no way in which either of them are going to be able to make work a mixture of Catholicism and the Second Vatican Council. "For either he will hate the one, and love the other: or he will sustain the one, and despise the other" (Mt. 6: 24). To see in theory and in depth why the Council and Catholicism are irreconcilable, read a book like Archbishop Lefebvre's *They Have Uncrowned Him*, just published in the USA. To see the irreconcilability in practice, one need only observe current events:

On the one side, an example of a Roman reaching out to Traditionalists, is Cardinal Ratzinger (soon after the May-June negotiations broke down, one morning it is said he could not continue Mass for weeping). A friend of the Society living in Rome comments:

> As a moderate liberal, Cardinal Ratzinger absolutely wished for an alliance with the Traditionalists to help him stand up to the extreme liberals. The breakdown of negotiations has discredited this policy, and so weakened the moderates. It is their scalps that the extremists now want, and since the moderates refuse to take their stand on doctrine and truth, they have neither strength nor courage to stand up to the extremists, and they have lost the battle in advance.
>
> The extremists have also triumphed by getting Archbishop Lefebvre excommunicated on doctrinal grounds, for having – allegedly – a false notion of Tradition. For the first time the Archbishop has been condemned not just on disciplinary grounds. Henceforth, any opposition to the Council is schismatic! However, the Catholic world in general has reacted somewhat indifferently to the excommunication. This punishment, in itself terrifying, has not terrified, which again weakens the moderates' position. With what punishment can the Cardinal now threaten the radicals when they ordain women priests, or whatever? He must either let them do as they like, or risk splitting the Church into a thousand fragments. Either way he loses.
>
> Outwardly we have peace, but it is logical to foresee an explosion of schisms, the disintegration of the Church. The modern world is a gigantic corpse which can fall apart from one moment to the next. This status

quo of confusion belongs to the devil. Any gesture of truth, every outburst of truth is a germ of hope. The right word from Peter could turn the situation around, but this word he does not say.

These comments are surely accurate, because they make all the moderates' weakness flow from their departure from Catholic doctrine. It is because the "excommunications" had no basis in Catholic teaching that Catholics generally have been indifferent. Polled in early August, after a TV program in France opposing a supporter to an adversary of the consecrations, 65% of the viewers answered that Archbishop Lefebvre is more Catholic than Cardinal Lustiger, 66% thought the Archbishop was right to perform the consecrations, and 60% considered that the separation between Archbishop Lefebvre and Rome will not last long! Three cheers for Catholic common sense! God is not abandoning His people.

Yet in pursuit of that chimeric third way, on the other side from Roman conciliarists groping after Tradition, we still have the spectacle of Traditionalists going over to Conciliar Rome. An outstanding example of these "refugees" is Dom Gerard, Prior of the erstwhile Traditional Benedictine Monastery in the South of France, who, having accepted in July an offer of Rome similar to that turned down by Archbishop Lefebvre for the Society in May and June, must now, by his own choice, be meshing in with the Conciliar Church. By the terms of the July 25 letter to him from Cardinals Ratzinger and Mayer, the bishop of the diocese in which lies Dom Gerard's monastery can control its apostolic activity (c. 680, New Code), and even "for very grave cause" expel it from his diocese (c. 679, New Code).

Now the bishop in question, Bishop Bouchex of Avignon, has made clear in a mid-August letter how he understands the meshing-in will take place: rebuilding unity will be painful, he says, but "let us help one another along this path, all the while remaining firmly attached to Vatican II, to the Council in its entirety, which forms part of the Church's Tradition." So if Dom Gerard shares this evolutionary notion of Tradition, then he and Bishop Bouchex will get on famously, and Le Barroux will gently evolve into a fully Conciliar monastery. But if Dom Gerard still at all grasps like Archbishop Lefebvre and like the extreme Liberals of Vatican II, that the Council represented a radical break with Tradition, a 1789 or a French Revolution within the Church, then how is he going to mesh in with Bishop Bouchex? He must take his pick – either Conciliar "tradition" or Catholic Tradition, but he cannot have both.

Yet Tridentine priests have been, I have been told, "swarming" to Rome to obtain for their activities Rome's approval from the Commission to Recuperate Traditionalists set up by the Pope immediately after the consecrations of June 30. Yet the same source said that this Commission is "the biggest mess he ever walked into," a saying not elegant but probably accurate. For when in his Motu Proprio of July 2, "*Ecclesia Dei*," the Pope condemned what the Archbishop was doing and set up a Commission to do it in his place, how could such a Commission not reflect such confusion?

However, God does not abandon His Church. See firstly the magnificent Declaration enclosed of Dom Thomas Aquinas, O.S.B., who refused to follow Dom Gerard back into the Conciliar fold. And be consoled that ordinary Catholics are not as confused as so many of their leaders. An estimated 10 to 12,000 people took part in the Society's August 15 Marian Procession in the center of Paris, many more than in the two previous years. At a stopping-point for the procession in Lutetia's Arena, they were treated to the spectacle of a live lion in a cage, hired by Fr. Laguerie for the occasion, to put Catholics in mind of their illustrious forebears who used to make a close acquaintance with lions in arenas. However this lion raised a question vexing Parisian minds – since he took public part in a procession led by one of the four new bishops, was he or was he not excommunicated? Notwithstanding, the procession – and lion – were a roaring success.

Another up-rising of Catholic common sense took place in South Germany at the end of the same month. In Penk, a little village not far from the Society's German-speaking seminary in Zaitzkofen, Bavaria, a shooting association wished to celebrate its 30th anniversary, and invited 42 similar associations from the area to join in the celebration. The parish priest having refused to celebrate Mass for them, they turned to the Rector of Zaitzkofen, Fr. Natterer, who accepted. In the wake of the June consecrations, the local bishop threatened excommunications all around, but the laymen were not scared. Then the Vicar General turned round and proposed the auxiliary bishop to offer the Mass, but the shooters were now no more impressed by the blandishments than they had been by the threats. So on Sunday, August 28, between 5 and 6,000 Catholics attended the open air Mass in Penk, celebrated by Fr. Natterer. One may hope a number of these Catholics came to the ordination by Bishop Fellay at Zaitzkofen of three new priests for the Society on October l, within a week of Bishop Tissier de Mallerais' having ordained six at the French-speaking Seminary in Ecône. These ordinations were brought forward to replace the casualties fallen in the line of spiritual battle, but have no fear of the consecrations causing many more defections. Instead, join us in thanking the Mother of God for having secured for the Church the means of the Society's survival for one whole year every day all Society priests are in turn offering a Mass of thanksgiving for the consecrations.

A series of ordination ceremonies also began today at the Society's English speaking seminary, which is fitting into its new home in Winona like a hand fits into a glove. After years of neglect and months of builders' dust and dirt, the terrazzo floors are coming up gleaming, just like apparently they used to gleam under the Dominicans years ago. Each time I step into the corridor outside my room, I feel like singing "I dreamt I dwelt in marble halls." To these halls fifteen new candidate seminarians and five postulant brothers have just returned from their entry retreat in North Dakota. Your own unrivalled chance to dwell in marble halls may be the Spiritual Exercises or Ignatian Retreats which begin here for men the second week after Christmas. Send the yellow flyer here to sign up for the retreat here, to Canada for the retreat immediately after Christmas in Grand Forks, North Dakota, but to Ridgefield for any of the retreats now blessedly available all year round at St. Ignatius Retreat House in Connecticut. And if there are names of dead friends and relatives whose souls you would wish to benefit from the monthly Requiem Mass at the seminary, and whose names you have not already sent us, use the enclosed card which will be placed on the main altar for that Mass, and throughout the month of November.

Pray the Rosary especially faithfully during the month of October, month of the Holy Rosary. It is difficult for anyone who regularly prays the Rosary to lose the Catholic Faith. Each night of October, there will be Rosary and Benediction of the Blessed Sacrament at the seminary, including the prayer for the Pope.

Finally, thank you for your continual generosity to the seminary, continually necessary (we have $360,000 of debts and still two floors of one wing to finish renovating), and thank you especially for your prayers for a new bishop rapidly growing into an old bishop.

Yours most devotedly in Christ.

NO. 66 | NOVEMBER 1, 1988

The Arguments of *Ecclesia Dei*

ONE REMARKABLE FEATURE of this summer's condemnation by Rome of Archbishop Lefebvre was, as commented on in this letter last month, that for the first time Rome ventured to condemn the Archbishop on doctrinal and not just on disciplinary grounds. It will be interesting to see what those grounds were.

They are to be found in their most authoritative form in the Apostolic Letter of JP2, "*Ecclesia Dei*," given at Rome on July 2. Section 4 of the Letter is the doctrinal section. In it the Archbishop and those who think like him are accused of having "an incomplete and contradictory notion of Tradition."

The Pope seeks firstly to prove that the Archbishop's notion of Tradition is incomplete, "because it does not take sufficiently into account the living character of Tradition." In other words the Archbishop has a dead, or "fixist" notion, a too rigid notion of Tradition. To expound the supposedly true or living notion of Tradition, *Ecclesia Dei* gives an extensive quotation from the Second Vatican Council's Dogmatic Constitution, *Ver-*

bum Dei, Section 8. Here the Council says, (A) there is a progress of Tradition, (B) by a growth of insight, (C) by believers' contemplation and study, (D) by their intimate experience, and (E) by the bishops' preaching. Since the Pope hangs the whole first part of his argument on this text, maybe we should quote it in full:

> Tradition (A) "comes from the apostles and progresses in the Church with the help of the Holy Spirit. (B) There is a growth in insight into the realities and words that are being passed on. This comes about in various ways. (C) It comes through the contemplation and study of believers who ponder these things in their hearts. (D) It comes from the intimate sense of spiritual realities which they experience. (E) And it comes from the preaching of those who have received, along with their right of succession in the episcopate, the sure charism of truth."

Now at the time of the Council, Archbishop Lefebvre himself voted to approve *Verbum Dei*, so no doubt each of the five sentences above can be given a Catholic meaning, for instance: (A) with the passage of time there is a progress in Catholics' grasp of the abiding truths of the Faith. (B) They see deeper into these truths, (C) by contemplating and studying these truths, (D) by more deeply penetrating into them, and (E) by the bishops' preaching fresh aspects of these same truths.

That is undoubtedly the kind of interpretation that the Archbishop gave this text at that time. With such an interpretation, it would give him no problem, but it also could not serve to condemn him. If then the Pope is using the passage to condemn him, the Pope must be giving it a different interpretation, for instance: (A) Catholic truth lives and grows and changes with the passage of time. (B) Modern Catholics have more living insights than olden-day Catholics. (C) Modern Catholics' hearts studying their living needs discover new truths to believe in. (D) Modern Catholics' inner sense of their own religious experience creates new and living truths from within them. (E) Also Catholic truth is added on to with the novelties preached by the living bishops, because these bishops can say no wrong.

Now interpreted in some such way, no doubt the text condemns the Archbishop, and he in turn would find it reeking of modernism, which Pope St. Pius X stigmatized as "the synthesis of all heresies." But there is just one problem. With such an interpretation the Council's text is absolutely not Catholic. In which case, how can it serve as a basis of a Catholic condemnation? In other words, either the text is given a Catholic meaning, and then it in no way condemns the Archbishop; or it is given a non-Catholic meaning, and then it has no right to condemn him.

But, someone might object, it is totally unfair to the text to say it can bear such a modernist interpretation! Fine, is the reply. Let us suppose for the sake of argument that it cannot be given any modernist interpretation (that is a big supposition, but let that pass). Then if the text is only Catholic, it is capable of approving, and of being approved by, someone like the Archbishop. There is no way round the fact that in any Catholic sense the text does not condemn him, and in any non-Catholic sense it stands itself condemned! The reason for this is that one who thinks like the Archbishop takes his stand four-square on Catholic truth, and nobody will prove the contrary by casting in his teeth ambiguous texts of a two-tongued Council!

Is the second argument of *Ecclesia Dei* any better? The Pope seeks secondly to prove that the Archbishop's notion of Tradition is contradictory, because it pretends to set up Christ's Tradition against Christ's

Vicar. Now it is true that these two cannot contradict one another, as they are both of Christ. But to assume in the case of an apparent contradiction that the mistake is on the side of Tradition, without proving it, as is done here, is to assume that the Vicar of Christ has an infallibility which not even Peter himself had (Mt. 16: 23; Mt. 26: 69–75; Gal. 2: 11–14), which the Church has never taught the Pope to have had (his ordinary infallibility (DS 3011) is circumscribed within Tradition, his extraordinary infallibility (DS 3074) is strictly conditioned), and which history shows some Popes certainly not to have had (e.g., Pope Liberius excommunicated St. Athanasius (DS 138, 141, 142), and Pope Honorius (DS 563) "allowed the immaculate Faith to be stained").

Clearly, the Pope can make even grave mistakes. Then in the case of a clash he may not assume, but must prove, that he and the mass of bishops are right and the Archbishop is wrong. This he does not do in the rest of Section #4 of "*Ecclesia Dei*," so its second argument falls to the ground.

Now in defense of *Ecclesia Dei* it might be said that Sections #5 and #6 urge bishops, priests, and faithful, while steering clear of Archbishop Lefebvre, nevertheless to have more consideration for Catholic Tradition. But consider the following facts:

- On the very day after the issuing of "*Ecclesia Dei*," Bishop Poletti, the Vicar Apostolic of Rome, gave instructions at San Geronimo della Carita, the parish church in Rome where visiting priests have for years been able to celebrate in peace the Tridentine Mass, that henceforth every foreign priest must celebrate Mass in the vernacular, with the Novus Ordo Missal.

- Three times in the last two weeks Archbishop May of St. Louis has refused a Novus Ordo priest in his 50's permission to celebrate a Tridentine Requiem Mass for his own mother's funeral.

This October 22, just as the seminary of the Conciliar-protected "traditional" Fraternity of St. Peter was about to open in Wigratzbad in South Germany, the diocesan bishop (of Augsburg) required of Fr. Bisig a signature which Fr. Bisig felt unable to give. Exit in haste Fr. Bisig, probably to Rome. And maybe this time Rome will override Augsburg for him. But who cannot foresee an inexorable series of ultimately deadly harassments?

Dom Gerard's claim, that his July agreement with Cardinals Ratzinger and Mayer for a Rome-approved Traditional monastery, required of him no essential concessions in doctrine or Liturgy, was contradicted by Cardinal Mayer in an interview published in the October issue of *30 Days*. Said the Cardinal: "Dom Gerard's statement was not exact," and the journalist colloquially sums up the Cardinal's stand-point as follows – "Me, sell out the Council? You've got to be kidding!" (*30 Days* is not a Traditional monthly!).

And Tradition-loving Carmelites are being persecuted in New Jersey, and so on, and so on. Dear Friends and Benefactors, it is a long, hard road ahead of us, but since when did Our Lord promise it would be easy? However, He does give us encouragement.

Remember also the Holy Souls in November, including another young Society priest Fr. Denis Marehal, killed a few days ago in a car-crash in France. May his soul and the souls of all the faithful departed through the mercy of God rest in peace.

With all good wishes and blessings,
Most sincerely yours in Our Lord.

NO. 67 | DECEMBER 1, 1988

Obedience Must Be to Tradition

THE ORIGINAL PURPOSE of this monthly letter was to thank the seminary's regular benefactors. The end of the calendar year is a good time to think of what you have obtained for us.

Firstly, your prayers have obtained us many graces. For instance, the seminary this summer lost only one seminarian because of the consecrations. If the seminarians have kept their balance, this is not something that happens all on its own, it happens because someone is praying for them to become good servants of God. Please continue to pray for the perseverance of the seminarians we have, and for the vocation of those we need. We are in the thick of the battle with Satan, and there is no way we could have survived or are going to survive another year. The seminary is very happy in its new surroundings. When I was back in Ridgefield for two days in October, I could not imagine how the seminary used to fit in there, so small did the house seem, compared with the spaciousness here. Now all the figures are not yet in, but look at it which way you will, Winona was a "steal." With renovations, I guess the total cost will be around one million dollars for what every visitor recognizes to be a superb facility, only a small part of which could be constructed today for one million dollars if it had to be built new.

Interesting question – from whom was Winona "stolen"? Not from the layfolk who actually sold the building to us, because they paid a paltry $157,000 when they bought it from the Dominicans a few years ago. In that case the people who put such value into the building were the Catholic contributors who enabled the Dominicans to build this first-class priory back around 1950. Then it was, so to speak, these contributors who took the heavy loss when the Dominicans "unloaded" the building in the early 1980's. So if you Catholics today bought so much more than you paid for, it is because those Catholics yesterday put into the building so much more than it was sold for. In which case, so to speak, you "stole" from them! Consoling theft, both for the victims whose loss has turned into no loss, and for the "thieves" who turned a Catholic loss of their brothers in the Faith into a Catholic gain. "I believe…in the Holy Catholic Church, the communion of saints . . . " What a marvel, the Mystical Body of Christ!

We must also thank you for your sustained generosity each month that we have been here in Winona. Running expenses for the larger building are heavier than they were in Ridgefield, but we are beginning to get after our debts, standing now around $340,000. When I remember how you rid us in Ridgefield of a burdensome mortgage, this figure does not worry me, except for the vulnerability of the economy . . . Might it be wise today to transfer some assets from Wall Street to an account in heaven? In any case, many thanks for all of your help so far.

By way of return, please find enclosed a small Christmas present, the flyer on "obedience." It is a difficult subject to get into one small flyer, so the flyer is quite dense. It may repay study. As you open the flyer, it first seeks to establish that obedience is essentially relative. Obedience relates to who or what I am obeying. Hence, being fundamentally a faith, Catholic obedience cannot be conceived without reference to the Catholic Faith. That is in fact what Catholic obedience is for, and what it is about.

Now whatever be true of other faiths, the Catholic Faith is essentially a deposit of doctrinal and moral truths, coming from Our Lord Himself and entrusted by Him to His Apostles: "Teach ye all nations, teaching them to observe all things whatsoever I have commanded you" (Mt. 28: 19–20). Hence the Catholic expression, "the Deposit of Faith." This deposit, deposited by Our Lord with His Church, the Church has to hand down faithfully, unchanged – "whatsoever I have commanded you." The reason for this is because Our Lord Himself is only handing down to His Apostles what He himself has received from His Father, as He emphasizes again and again in Scripture – three of these quotes are in the flyer, but there are some two dozen in St. John's Gospel! So the Catholic Faith is essentially something handed down, from all eternity by Father to Son, and from Jesus by his Church to men down to the end of the world. (Mt. 28: 20)

Now the Latin word for handing down is trado, tradere, from which comes traditio, or tradition. If then the Faith is essentially handed down, it is essentially traditional, hence the expression, "Catholic Tradition." And so if Catholic obedience is essentially relative to the Faith, it is essentially relative to Tradition. And so just as an obedience outside of or contrary to the Faith would not be Catholic obedience, so any obedience outside of or contrary to Catholic Tradition will not be Catholic obedience either.

Hence Catholic Tradition sets the parameters of Catholic obedience. Proceeding then to the flyer's centerfold, we find that, as one can either overshoot or undershoot any given parameters, so one can in matters of the Faith either undershoot the parameters of Tradition by disobedience, or overshoot them by exaggerated, indiscreet or false obedience. Disobedience and false obedience you find both colored red, with large "STOP" signs, while the Catholic balance in between is colored green for "GO." Note on each of the seven white-separated lines beneath the centerfold pictures, how Catholic obedience is a balance of two parts each of which is contradicted in the red column next to it, and exaggerated in the red column farthest from it. True obedience is a balance, balanced by Faith, measured by Tradition.

Conclusion – final panel in blue – when the fruits of our priests, bishops and Pope are thoroughly good, we may give them "blind" obedience because those fruits make us sure that the churchmen are leading us in the Faith (actually, such obedience is not blind, it is seeing the fruits as Our Lord told us to do). But when we see the fruits turning thoroughly bad, as today, then the time for that kind of unquestioning obedience is over, and I must fall back on my Faith, measured by Tradition, to tell me when obedience is true and when it is false. For God can allow even the Pope to make grave mistakes. Apparently JP2 has just commemorated Assisi again by a meeting with 85 leaders of different religions in Santa Maria Trastevere in Rome. If that is so, may God one day give him to weep as He gave to Peter!

We have available here and now at the Seminary any number of these flyers, cost price about ten cents each, but you need not pay a cent. Order as many as you like. Enclosed also is a Seminary Continuous Support Fund card, which you can fill out and return to us if you would like to receive each month a return envelope to facilitate a regular donation. You will also then receive this letter by first-class mail, instead of by bulk mail.

Have a happy Christmas and, close by the crib, let nothing daunt you. For – Romans 8 – "if God be for us, who is against us? . . . For I am sure that neither death, nor life, nor angels, nor principalities, nor powers, nor things present, nor things to come, nor might, nor height, nor depth, nor any other creature, shall be able to separate us from the love of God, which is in Christ Jesus Our Lord." At the seminary, this year as last, we will celebrate a Christmas novena of Masses on the main altar for all your intentions.

With all good wishes and blessings for Advent and Christmas.

NO. 68 | JANUARY 1, 1989

Southern Africa, Down Under, Hawaii

ON DECEMBER 18TH I landed in the mainland United States back from a swift five-week visit to South Africa, Zimbabwe, Australia, New Zealand, and Hawaii. What traveler's tales do I have to tell? All around the world, in widely varying circumstances, God is raising up a remnant of Catholics to keep the Faith in the midst of a world giving itself over to the Devil.

The tour began at the southern end of Africa with confirmations in Windhoek, the capital of South-West Africa, a country whose fall into Communism is now being jointly engineered in Moscow and Washington. For while Russia gives some of her latest Mig-23 fighters to the Cubans in Angola, the American Congress imposes sanctions to paralyze South Africa, and the European bankers queue up to lend Russia billions in Western currencies to pay for the Mig-23's. Suicidal stupidity! Is anyone still surprised at the advance of Communism? In fact the Liberals rejoice in the birth of a new and better world – understand, without God – and beg the Communists to deceive them. The Communists naturally oblige, and tighten the noose around the liberals' necks, with rope, as Lenin foresaw, gladly paid for by the victims.

And where in this scene are the interests of God? While He lets the majority prepare a major scourge for their own backs to remind them that He is not mocked, He is turning a minority of Catholics more seriously to their Faith. In each of the main cities of southern Africa, Windhoek, Capetown, Port Elizabeth, Durban and Johannesburg a kernel of Catholics, most numerous in Durban and Johannesburg, is gathering with more and more conviction around the Tridentine Mass, celebrated for the most part by three Society priests, and these Catholics rejoice in being able to present their children for confirmation by a Society bishop. In Capetown a sedevacantist priest on the right and a diocesan bishop exploiting the Indult on the left – sounds familiar? – have unsettled the Society's mission, but with a regular Society priest this situation would soon stabilize.

Not that these Catholics take much interest in politics, not even in the "problem" of apartheid. For to those, black or white, who take heaven and hell seriously, racism and anti-racism pale into insignificance, as did slavery for the early Christians. In truth, apartheid, like the Boer War (1899–1902), is a problem engineered by the liberals to force the old-fashioned Calvinist Boer into step with their Brave New World. His strength was always his religion. His downfall will be neither Mig-23's, nor apartheid, still less sanctions, but his turning aside from his old-fashioned religion and morals to delight in the sinful pleasures of Western materialism. So unless he turns back, the turmoil of Revolution is inevitable.

However – lesson for ourselves – such turmoil need not be only harmful to the Faith and so need not only be feared. In Zimbabwe, formerly Rhodesia, the country immediately to the north of South Africa, the turmoil of a terrorist war ran from about 1966 to 1980 when the Communists gained control. Yet the SSPX has a priory in the capital city, Harare, and is right now finishing construction of a beautiful church to hold 250 people! The priests find their ministry often more rewarding in Zimbabwe than in South Africa, and the local laity are convinced there is amongst both whites and blacks a great apostolic opening for true priests, because the terrorist war was a chastening experience for everyone. One soul in Zimbabwe told me she reckoned that with all the shortages and inconveniences typical of communist rule, it was nevertheless easier now to save one's soul in deprived Zimbabwe than in prosperous and comfortable but materialistic South Africa. What God has to do to get our attention!

After the confirmations in Harare, a long flight across the southern Indian Ocean led to the next stop, in Sydney, southeast Australia, where the Society has its Australasian headquarters. Many Rhodesians and South Africans have taken this flight in recent years in order to escape from the past or future Revolution in Africa. However, spiritual problems do not have geographical solutions. It is true that in Australia the aborigines have proved too peaceful to serve the agitators' purposes of stirring up non-whites against whites, but the Revolution is nonetheless striding ahead amongst the whites with socialism and materialism. An interesting newsletter by a brave young man, Peter Sawyer, gave graphic details of huge new bunkers in Canberra and Melbourne, disguised at first as "telephone exchanges," but designed in fact to house vast interdepartmental governmental computer centers. The facilities for big Government to spy on every detail of citizens' lives, "Big Brother" in George Orwell's "1984," are being put in place, linked apparently with similar facilities in the USA and elsewhere...

Meanwhile the Society in Australia has large and thriving parishes with churches in both Sydney and Melbourne, a growing parish with a church in Brisbane, many outlying missions and a newly bought seminary building not far from Canberra where I was able to give tonsure to eight seminarians at the end of their first year of seminary studies. The building formerly of the Christian Brothers is much in need of repair, but lay helpers had already done a beautiful job of renovating the Chapel. Sound familiar? "For in one Spirit were we all baptized into one body, whether Jews or Gentiles, bond or free . . . and there are diversities of operations, but the same God, who worketh all in all" (I Cor. 12: 13, 6). Truly, Wisdom "reacheth from end to end" of the world "mightily and ordereth all things sweetly."

The highpoint of the visit to Australia was the ordaining of Winona seminarian Shane Johnson to the priesthood – see the enclosed Verbum. He is Australian, and will in a few week's time begin his ministry with the other Society priest in New Zealand, Fr. Ruben Gentili from the Argentine. At the Society's two main centers in New Zealand, Wellington and Auckland, there were numerous confirmations, although Archbishop Lefebvre's last visit had not been so long ago. And from New Zealand the Society priests make occasional visits to the island of Fiji, way out in the Pacific. "Yes, verily, their sound hath gone forth into all the earth, and their words into the ends of the whole world" (Ps. 18: 5; Rom. 10: 18). The only thing that stops the Society priests from going there more often is the airfare, and the same must be true for the farthest-flung islands in the Pacific!

In all these distant parts all over the world, Society priests find themselves full of admiration for the work done by Catholic missionaries of yesteryear. How well many of them did their work of planting the Faith! It is often there all ready to revive under the hand of the Society priests. What a crime, that Second Vatican Council, which paralyzed missionary effort by "re-evaluating" all the false religions! For "how shall they believe him, of whom they have not heard? And how shall they hear without a preacher? And how shall they preach unless they be sent." But who shall send anyone when Vatican II states (Unitatis Redintegratio, #3) that "the spirit of Christ has not refrained from using non-Catholic Churches and Communities as means of salvation"?

Between New Zealand and the mainland USA, it was easy to stop over for two days in Honolulu. The eight-island multi-racial state, a quarter of whose one million inhabitants are Catholic, is presently plagued with such a blatantly bad bishop as to make wholly likely the thesis of communist infiltrators in the episcopacy. Be that as it may, a group of Hawaii Catholics, quite independently of the SSPX, have got themselves together to defend their faith, with a weekly radio program and a monthly newspaper and the Tridentine Mass celebrated each Sunday by a "suspended" diocesan priest in a hall obtained with the backing of the Mayor of Honolulu who cannot stand the bishop! The bishop is very much aware of these Catholics, who cause him an annoyance – of the right kind – out of all proportion to their relatively insignificant numbers.

From me they asked for a day-long recollection concluding in a slightly improvised ceremony of some twenty confirmations and Mass, at which a piece of cord attached to a piece of string out of someone's trunk had to make do for the bishop's cincture! But what is that when compared with such attachment to the Faith? On the following day, Sunday Mass was attended by about a hundred souls. Stranded in mid-Pacific, they are tempted to think no one is concerned for their struggle for the Faith, but they should know they have close friends in the same combat all over the world, Hawaii, can you hear us? Keep up the good fight! All of us are behind you!

Richard N. Williamson

I arrived back in Winona just in time to ordain three deacons on the Feast of St. Thomas, Apostle. With Deacon Timothy Pfeiffer from Ecône, that would make four American priests to be ordained at Winona on the Feast of St. John the Baptist, June 24.

And what occurs for the New Year? Any of you in the Metropolitan New York area that have not yet thrown out your TV sets may be interested to watch WNBC-TV's religion special "Splitting Faith," because it will include shots taken last autumn of priests and laity from the Society's retreat house in Connecticut. Of course we expect nothing very good to come out of the media where for some interesting reason the liberals are in their element, while the conservatives are always swimming against the current. But a colleague recently pointed out to me the wisdom of President Reagan's handling of the media with patience and courtesy, despite all their antipathy for him. The same holds for the Catholic – even the Traditional Catholic – media. No names!

The American people have loved President Reagan for standing for sanity and against liberalism in many of its insane forms. Here he is on Communism: "Have you heard the Communists now have a million-dollar lottery for their people? The winner gets a dollar a year for a million years." On socialistic government: "Government's view of the economy? If it moves, tax it. If it keeps moving, regulate it. If it stops moving, subsidize it." On Congress: "If they want to bring the Panamanian economy to its knees, why don't they just go down there and run the country?" On Communism again: "If the Soviet Union let another political party come into existence, they would still be a one-party state, because everyone would join the other party."

Catholics will surely miss Reagan for many of his qualities, and we must pray for George Bush, who may pleasantly surprise us. We have the leaders we deserve, and the best of them will say they can do little good without the support of good people. And where does the goodness of good people come from? From their religion, or rather, from whatever is Catholic in their religion.

May God then give you all a New Year filled with an ever increasing knowledge and love of Himself and of your Catholic Faith.

Rome and the Fraternity of St. Peter

MANY CATHOLICS ARE presently pinning their hopes on the Society of St. Peter, founded last summer by ex-priests of the SSPX to combine Traditional beliefs and practices with Papal approval. So I know you will be interested in what Archbishop Lefebvre said in private a few weeks ago:

> Between ourselves and Rome right now there is complete silence, thank goodness. We will have to wait some 6 to 12 months. They are trying to destroy us by means of the Society of St. Peter. Rome is granting them all kinds of things, but it's a bluff – they're trifles, superficial things – it all has no basis. Besides, those joining them will have Novus Ordo habits, which will not make things easy for them.
>
> On our side I think the bleeding has stopped. They will be disappointed that the excommunications and so on have not demolished us, on the contrary we are continuing stronger than ever, and so when Rome comes under the inevitable pressure from the bishops, it will give way. For instance, Bishop Mamie of Fribourg in Switzerland told journalists recently, "There will be no

Society of St. Peter in my diocese, and on this point we bishops of Switzerland are agreed. This is because by the positions it takes, the Society of St. Peter is implicitly refusing the Novus Ordo Mass, which means refusing the Council. Likewise, insisting on the old catechism means refusing the new catechism, which also means refusing the Council. Now as far as I am concerned, there is the Council, the Council, and again the Council."

Archbishop Lefebvre continued:

> So Rome and the bishops are at loggerheads. Rome does not mind approving of the Society of St. Peter, because it is not on their hands, it is on the bishops' hands. However, the bishops want nothing to do with it. Rome will do nothing about our case until it has resolved the case of the Society of St. Peter, which is where there is now the open conflict. The bishops of Augsburg in Germany and Bourges in France refused to let Cardinal Mayer come into their dioceses to do ordinations for St. Peter's. The monastery of Fontgombault in France accepted. Then the bishop of Augsburg would not let the ceremony take place in Wigratzbad. However he did attend the ordination which finally took place in Rome.
>
> Who will win? Rome or the bishops? Rome cannot fight the bishops. And the bishops are right, because Rome promotes the Council, and Rome is now imposing on them what the Council forbade! Rome is between a rock and a hard place. And all this because of ourselves. Rome is at a loss what to do. Their ecumenism is now meaningless – the same ecumenists who made excommunication into a pre-historic relic, suddenly made it front-page news! As for the two Masses – their new Mass made them hound us for maintaining the old Mass which they now promote – they are in hopeless self-contradiction.
>
> As for ourselves however, there is no problem. We have undergone another purification making the de-

Richard N. Williamson

fense of Tradition more solid than ever. So if Rome wanted to re-open the dialogue, we would put the dogmatic problems in the fore-front. I was willing to deal on the disciplinary level in order to obtain bishops, but now that we have bishops, the disciplinary question is over. Now they must get the Council and the Decree on Religious Liberty into line with Tradition. Dogma first and foremost. But questions of dogma are far more difficult to arrange than questions of discipline. We can hope for no change so long as they think like modernists in Rome. Any change would mean for them signing the death warrant of everything they have been doing for the last 25 years.

Now they are seeking to sink us by appointing bishops who are fond of Latin but are charismatic, who are for the Council, even while being conservative. The progressives are furious, but it's only a political game. These conservatives are against us, maybe even more so than the progressives. In general these conservatives are charismatic and very pro-Council. But no ideas have changed in Rome. On the contrary, all these maneuvers are simply to put the Council into effect better than did those who went too far, too fast.

The consecrations of June 30 have brought about some extraordinary conversions. The expected rout never took place. I find that almost miraculous. Instead there was an outburst of joy and a sense of security – the Truth will continue... My health is more or less all right, but I thank God for having done the consecrations on June 30, because I am no longer capable of long ceremonies. Imagine my relief! – For 20 years I was battling more or less on my own to keep something going. Now I can see it will continue after me, because the Society has a solid structure... Everything about June 30 was miraculous. It could have been far otherwise. *Deo Gratias*!

As often, these remarks of the Archbishop will be like a breath of fresh air to some, while seeming unduly severe to others. Rome, others say, was sincere in the negotiations of the first half of last year, so the Archbishop was wrong to distrust Rome, wrong to withdraw from the Protocol of May 5 and wrong to consecrate bishops. Although these gainsayers admit that his mere disobedience did not by itself amount to schism, nevertheless they fear that his alienating the SSPX still further from the official structures of the Church gravely increases the danger of Society members eventually going into schism. Hence for the gainsayers the great hope for the Church presently lies with the newly-formed Society of St. Peter, which trusted Rome, accepted the Protocol, has chosen to stay within the official structures of the Church, and is already ordaining traditional Catholic priests, *Deo Gratias*.

Notice how this whole argument rests upon the supposed sincerity and trustworthiness of Rome in the negotiations around the Protocol of May 5. Oh, sincerity! How many crimes are committed in thy name!

Now it is perfectly true that on Rome's side Cardinal Ratzinger for instance may well have been sincere in those negotiations. God knows. It is reported that he wept a few days after they had broken down. It is certain that he sincerely believes that Vatican II is the true Tradition of the one and only Catholic Church, from which it would follow that he sincerely thought he was saving Archbishop Lefebvre from schism by striving to re-integrate him into the Conciliar Church. But however sincere or well-intentioned the Cardinal may have been subjectively, i.e., inside himself, nevertheless objectively, i.e., in reality, or outside of and away from his interior dispositions, his notion of Catholic Tradition (Vatican II is as Traditional as Trent) is way wrong. Objectively then, he was subverting the Faith when he strove to re-integrate the Archbishop into conciliar structures. Objectively then, he and all who think like him are traitors to the Church, and not to be trusted, because however good their intentions, their false ideas make them, objectively, dissolvers of the Faith. Now these conciliar prelates' subjective dispositions certainly affect the morality of their actions but in no way affect their radical inability to defend Tradition, even when they mean to be nice to Traditionalists. Hence the Archbishop, having sadly once more experienced this inability in the negotiations, was right for the sake of Tradition and the Church to break them off. And poor St. Peter's Society is no real hope, but a fond illusion fathered by subjective fraternizing of pro-Catholic liberals with pro-liberal Catholics, a fond illusion doomed to be torn apart or at least rendered sterile by the objective antagonism of Liberalism and Catholicism, as utterly antagonistic as in submission and submission to God respectively.

Why doomed? Why cannot this half-and-half house, wished for by so many, stand? Because the objective ultimately governs the subjective, and not the reverse. Because as the English proverb says, "A fact is stronger than the Lord Mayor of London." Because wishes do not make potatoes. Because wishful thinking is a delightful activity but it does not change the facts. Because the facts are that for 200 years now, since 1789 (the bursting out of Liberalism in the French Revolution), Liberalism and Catholicism have been engaged in all-out war. As the Archbishop pointed out above, the Liberal bishops are already dropping shells on the Liberolics (they want to resemble Catholics but they are still drunk on Liberalism) venturing into the No Man's land of Catho-liberalism to fraternize with the Liberal-loving Catholics. Does the Archbishop drop shells on the latter? No. If they insist on quitting the Catholic trenches, his policy is to cover their withdrawal in silence. Only let them not say he did not warn them. They will be bombed to pieces or they will effectively join the enemy, like all the Catho-liberals before them. War is war.

In similar vein, it is a pleasure to learn that for instance at St. Agnes parish in Manhattan, New York, a Latin Tridentine Mass is being celebrated in prime time, at 11 a.m. every Sunday morning. Thanks be to God for what will be a great flow of graces in the heart of New York City! No doubt much glory will go to God from the Mass. Ask New Yorkers on a spiritual starvation diet for the last 20 years if they should attend! However, when we recall that the same New York Archdiocese, a few months prior to the naughty consecrations, promised New Yorkers a Latin Tridentine Mass in the city, but on conditions such that before one was celebrated, it was taken away again, we are entitled to wonder if the Tridentine Mass at St. Agnes will last. If it does, thanks be to God! If it does not – well – maybe Archbishop Lefebvre could be persuaded to help out by being naughty again!

What times we live in! Patience! Pray that good vocations still find their way to Winona. We now have some beautiful cells to fill, but also there are extra alternatives for prospective seminarians . . . At present, we have forty-seven seminarians.

Enclosed is the latest letter from our Superior General, and the Retreats flyer for Ridgefield and Winona for the rest of this year. Here is a Winona retreatant of a few weeks ago: "When I came on the 5-day Exercises, I was sorely troubled by problems with my family, my work and career, and my faith. Through the Exercises I could feel myself being lifted above my problems. I was able to find the answers that had eluded me for months prior to coming. I left with an inner peace and direction to deal with the difficulties I faced. If you are troubled and cannot seem to come to terms with the trials of life, come to the Retreat and find yourself in your God."

May this God, the God of all consolation, bless you all, and give you a holy Season of Lent. We pray for you all at the Seminary.

NO. 70 | MARCH 1, 1989

Paul, An African Catholic

ENCLOSED ONCE MORE, after a few years' interval, is a copy of a Minimum Knowledge Requirement Sheet for Confirmation, because, God willing, Bishop Fellay and I shall in April and May be giving the Sacrament of Confirmation, according to the old and certainly valid rite, in many parts of the USA and Canada. With four bishops available, there is of course no more the hurry to have children confirmed in the Traditional rite that there was while Archbishop Lefebvre was confirming all on his own.

The Consecrations of June 30 last are bearing fruit. So if a child is too late to be prepared or registered for Confirmation this year, let him just wait until next year. Meanwhile you have another Minimum Knowledge Sheet in hand, which as a compendium of our Catholic Faith is useful for more than just confirmations. This Faith we must never forget is a gift of God, from the moment we first receive it until the moment we die. Take for example, this letter which recently came to the Seminary from an African country with which so far the SSPX has had little contact:

"Dearest in Jesus," it begins, "Your letter was received as well as the requested special issue of *The Angelus*.

Three of them arrived in a large parcel. I am very happy. I got it on October 31st. Some are criticizing it, but I know the value of the Consecrations. So do some few old Catholics who saw Catholicism in its original purity. The question is how can we in our country get your priests to minister to us since everywhere the Novus Ordo prevails here. Please if there are other people from our country who have correspondence with you, send me their names and addresses so that I can contact them in order to effectively unite with them to fight our way through for your priests and a way to support you.

"If I am the only person from this country who writes to you, please tell me also. As the new Bishop has promised to be remembering me in his Masses, I promise to pray in turn for the expansion of the Society. Error has gripped everything Catholic in our country. Long live the four new bishops, long live Archbishop Marcel Lefebvre. Thank you. Yours sincerely," and there follows the signature of certainly an African name.

Now I do not know how this letter strikes you, but what strikes me is how this Catholic, Paul by first name, is so isolated and yet sees so clearly. He does not even know if there is anyone else in his country who believes as he does – and his is a large country containing a whole Catholic sub-nation within it – yet he is absolutely clear in his mind that the Catholic Church in the whole of his country has gone wrong!

All over the world today, most wise, most learned and most prudent men are confused, and the confusion grows daily worse. Sophisticated Catholics in the West have at their disposal any amount of books, video and audiotapes, Mass centers, papers, newsletters, etc., to consult, yet despite – or because of? – this wealth of means of information, still the large majority of them miss the essential point. Our African friend, on the contrary, living maybe in the middle of nowhere, just receives a Consecrations issue of *The Angelus,* and he has the whole picture. No confusion, no hesitations, no agonizing, just: when and how can we get a true priest to give us the true Mass? Of such is the Kingdom of Heaven made, and certainly, the Traditional Catholic movement."And Jesus calling unto him a little child, set him in the midst of them and said: Amen I say to you, unless you be converted, and become as little children, you shall not enter into the kingdom of heaven. Whosoever therefore shall humble himself as this little child, he is the greater in the kingdom of heaven" (Mt. 18: 2-4).

For some 15 years now, Catholics like Paul have been calling from all over the world for priests like Archbishop Lefebvre's, and no amount of arguments, authority (misused), abuse or whatever will put down this simple uprising of the Faith, which will triumph over every obstacle. Our Lord again: "Amen I say to you, I have not found so great faith in Israel. And I say to you that many shall come from the east and the west, and shall sit down with Abraham, and Isaac and Jacob in the kingdom of heaven: but the children of the kingdom shall be cast out into the exterior darkness: there shall be weeping and gnashing of teeth" (Mt. 8: 10-12). Of course not all the sophisticated Catholics today in confusion, will tomorrow be cast into the exterior darkness, for a number of them will finally recover their sight, but for the moment they are, in comparison with Paul, blind.

Here is a great mystery of grace, reaching deep within God's divine nature: "In that same hour Jesus rejoiced in the Holy Ghost, and said: I confess to thee, O Father, Lord of heaven and earth, because thou hast hidden these things from the wise and prudent, and hast revealed them to little ones. Yea, Father, for so it hath seemed good in thy sight" (Mt. 11: 25-26). Notice Jesus' rejoicing. Does He rejoice that the wise and prudent do not see? No. He is rejoicing in the divine wisdom of His

Father's love for the little ones. But if to escape confusion depends on God's mysterious grace, a man might object, then what can he do? Answer, he must pray and strive to acquire or conserve that humility and simplicity of heart which always has access to the Sacred Heart of God, who gives His grace to the humble, but resists the proud. The unparalleled example of humility given to us by Christ in His Passion is before our minds at this time of year.

May God repay you for thinking of us when many have to think of their income tax return, and may He grant you many graces for Holy Week and Eastertide.

NO. 71 | APRIL 1, 1989

Picasso, Art, and Morality

AN INTERESTING EXCHANGE took place in the pages of an issue four months ago of the American fortnightly conservative magazine, *National Review*. It was an exchange between Roger Scruton and Arianna Stassinopoulos Huffington concerning the latter's recently appeared book on the famous 20th century artist, Pablo Picasso. The exchange is unusually interesting because it opens onto theological values which should be at the heart of National Review's conservative positions, yet which National Review generally avoids. But that is another story.

Mrs. Huffington, born in Greece in 1950, educated from 1966 in England, married and domiciled now in the United States, was overwhelmed by a visit she made to the massive retrospective Picasso exhibition held in Paris in 1980. The nearly 1,000 works on exhibition amply proved Picasso's legendary vitality and artistic creativity, such an inventiveness as enabled him from early youth to old age to hold people spellbound with his wizardry. And yet the exhibition left her with "an uneasy feeling."

In 1982 Mrs. Huffington began to write a book on the wizard, and five years later it was finished, with the title,

Picasso, Creator and Destroyer. For behind the fabulous artistic creator, she had discovered the source of her uneasiness, Picasso the destroyer. For instance much of her book is taken up with Picasso's successive relationships with seven women, of whom only the third and, finally, the seventh were ever his lawful wives, and of whom the fourth and the seventh committed suicide after Picasso's death in 1973.

However, having worked over Picasso's less than admirable private life, her book ends with a judgment on Picasso as artist:

> [H]e took to its ultimate conclusion the negative vision of the modernist world... Unlike Shakespeare and Mozart, whose prolific creativity he shared, Picasso was not a timeless genius... [but]... a seismograph for the conflicts, turmoil and anguish of his age... From the time (1908) that he shook the art-world with his Les Demoiselles d'Avignon, Picasso was out of love with the world. He saw his role as a painter as fashioning weapons of combat against every emotion of belonging in creation and celebrating life, against nature, human nature and the God who created it all... Picasso told Malraux that he had no need of style, because his rage would become a prime factor in the style of our time.
>
> And his rage did become the dominant style of our time; but there are growing signs that something beyond rage is demanded...

And so while Mrs. Huffington readily grants Picasso's "prodigious skill, complete mastery of the language of painting, inexhaustible versatility and monumental virtuosity, ingenuity and imagination," nevertheless she concludes her book on a somewhat negative question mark: "As we move toward the beginning of another world and a new century, what will Picasso, so irrevocably tied to the age that is dying, have to say to the age being born?" However, Picasso is still such a god to our own age that to call him little more than a brilliant pyrotechnician is to call down on one's head the united wrath of all liberals.

Accordingly, Mrs. Huffington's book has apparently been savaged by critics all over the world. She had hit on a raw nerve. In the exchange in the National Review, it is a well-known English critic, Roger Scruton, who takes up the cudgels. Following the proportions of her book, easily most of his article is taken up with defending more or less the artist's right to behave immorally, and with attacking Mrs. Huffington for silencing Picasso's art "by the avalanche of his misdemeanors." The last paragraph of his article at last defends Picasso's art:

> [It] should not be seen as disintegration, but rather as an attempt to re-order and re-integrate what had already disintegrated . . . Picasso sought to re-assemble the unseeable fragments of the modern world so as to make them visible and reveal their truth. The modern world may be ghastly; but the modern artist has no other world to play with. And, as Picasso showed, he can still discover in this world an order and a purity that justify his work.

Mrs. Huffington's vigorous reply begins by accusing Scruton and her multiple critics of fearing the devaluing of their cultural idol. Behind this fear she senses firstly that these critics, like Picasso, refuse to see that there is in fact another world behind the 20th century's disintegration; secondly that they share in Picasso's disordered notion of woman and of the love of woman; thirdly, that clinging to art as a substitute for religion, they do not want one of art-religion's High Priests torn down. And her article concludes: "The time has come to recognize the metaphysical lie on which Picasso's life and art were based, to re-evaluate him, and to move beyond him – in our art, in our culture, and in our lives."

In other words, the modern liberals, artists and critics firstly refuse the love of God, secondly turn to a disordered love of creatures, and thirdly suck art dry as a pacifier, or baby's dummy, to fill the void left by the God they have emptied out. Bravo, Mrs. Huffington. I do not know your religion, but your perspective is religious. The raw nerve you hit on was the panic of these liberals, that the God whom they have resolutely shut out of existence – even His, let alone theirs! – might yet come back into their lives. No doubt the profoundest thing to be said about Picasso, as about many 20th century "heroes," is that he was making war on God.

Of that war on God, Picasso's gravely disordered private life was another symptom. Faithful and believing liberal, Scruton would disconnect art and morality, and he is at least correct in saying that Picasso's immorality is not essential to the question of his art. However, in her book on the man, as in her reply to Scruton, Mrs. Huffington instinctively grasps that at the heart of Picasso was a disorder manifested in his life as in his art, and so to present the one man, her book was perfectly entitled to present the two aspects of his one disorder: who will not love God, must mislove creatures – "For my people have done two evils. They have forsaken me, the fountain of living water, and have digged to themselves cisterns, broken cisterns, that can hold no water." (Jer. 2: 13)

Contrariwise, whoever loves God will rightly love creatures, and out of such a lover will come all kinds of beauty and art. "Jesus stood and cried, saying: If any man thirst, let him come to me and drink. He that believeth in me, as the Scripture saith, out of his belly shall flow rivers of living water" (Jn. 7: 37–38). Thus whereas Protestantism as revolt against God is in all its forms iconoclastic – the posturing-Communist Picasso was riddled with the contradiction of being the supreme iconograph of iconoclasm – the Catholic Church has continually since the Incarnation brought forth the most beautiful art. For a little example, it does not show in the Seminary renovations as presented in the enclosed Verbum, but the second and third-floor chapels are now being – artistically, we hope – decorated.

May God bless you. Happy Eastertide.

NO. 72 | JUNE 1, 1989

Ecclesia Dei – Impossible Halfway House

So I DID not drop dead after all, but no doubt thanks to your prayers, arrived back here safe and sound in mid-May after an inspiring confirmations tour of over thirty Traditional Mass centers and churches in Canada and the USA (Don't tell anyone, but I thoroughly enjoyed it!).

I say inspiring, because such a tour makes it very clear that the Catholic Faith is taking hold upon a new generation. For in the large majority of these centers there is a significant proportion of young families and children, which of course guarantees a future.

Not that many of these young parents, for instance, are deeply concerned or involved in the crisis of the Church, for "I send you out like sheep amongst wolves" said Our Lord; but that, prompted by grace, they are established in the true worship of God. They have not found it in the new religion installed in their "Catholic" parish churches; they do find it in the Traditional Latin Mass and in the "old" religion that goes with that Mass, and for their reward they find therewith something solid to which they can hold their children, as opposed to the all-surrounding Liberalism which visibly makes those children disobey, disintegrate, and fall apart. So such young parents are not about to turn back to the Novus Ordo's "onions of Egypt," and once more in the history of his backsliding people, the Lord is raising up a faithful remnant. Truly, "if thy people, O Israel, shall be as the sand of the sea, a remnant of them shall be converted..." (Is. 10: 22)

Of such people's strength in the Faith, Rome had no idea when it thought one year ago that the episcopal consecrations would scatter Archbishop Lefebvre's followers, or at least that the threat of excommunication would do so. Yet on the whole of this tour, I can hardly remember the word having been mentioned. These Catholics are happily and quietly – not defiantly – practicing their faith, and to false shepherds they are paying little or no attention.

Meanwhile the false shepherds are staying on their course. You remember what Archbishop Lefebvre said back in January: Rome would grant all kinds of trifles to the Traditionalists to make them come over to the Conciliar Church, but the Conciliar bishops would object even to trifling concessions and Rome would not be able to fight the bishops. A few sample news items illustrate the accuracy of this forecast:

From a source within the *Ecclesia Dei* Commission (which you remember Rome set up just after the consecrations to welcome Traditionalists back into the Conciliar Church), I am told that they are granting permission to say the old Mass in private to all kinds of priests in order to stop people going over to the SSPX. However these grants are not having the desired effect. Firstly they are drawing few people away from the Society (which is infuriating the members of *Ecclesia Dei*, says the Archbishop): for instance in London, England, Cardinal Hume has laid on a Tridentine Latin Mass in three

London churches on Sunday morning, but attendance at the Society's London Church is only increasing! The same in Dublin, Ireland. So it looks as though people are profiting by the Indult, but not accepting its purpose (were I setting traps, such mice that ate the cheese but avoided the trap would infuriate me too!).

Secondly, these permissions are having an impact unforeseen by Rome. They are for instance creating within the official Church something like an underground Church of individual house Masses, celebrated by priests and people who are no doubt longing for the true Mass, but are still, effectively barred from its public celebration. In other words, from the standpoint of the official Church, *Ecclesia Dei* is creating a mess. Thus bishops are to be seen in many dioceses reaching for their fire-extinguishers to put out the *Ecclesia Dei* brush-fires. And so for the diocesan bishops even Rome's little concessions to Tradition are that much too much. For, insignificant as the concessions so far of *Ecclesia Dei* are in comparison with the rightful demands of Tradition, nevertheless Tradition has such a power within it, that these little concessions are seen to threaten their ongoing Conciliar Revolution ("conservative" Cardinal Law of Boston is reportedly pressing for altar-girls).

And so, as the Archbishop foresaw, the bishops are making their weight felt in Rome, and Rome is having to give way: on May 16 the Holy Father with Cardinals Ratzinger and Mayer (head of the *Ecclesia Dei* Commission) met in Rome with the heads of the Episcopal Conferences of France, Germany, Switzerland, and England, to discuss the putting into practice of *Ecclesia Dei*. Conclusion? – the Commission must in the future work in much closer collaboration with the diocesan bishops.

Now where does that leave the Society of St. Peter (whose members chose last summer to trust Rome and accept the offer turned down by the Archbishop)? They may well wonder. Probably they put their hopes in the Pope himself. Fond hopes! When the Pope returned recently from Africa, he said his travels were useful, especially in Europe, to protect Vatican II both against the progressives wishing to overtake it with Vatican III, and against the Traditionalists, symbolized by Archbishop Lefebvre, who regret its novelty: "I hope my journeys will keep the balance between the two movements, and, if they cannot make them disappear, will at least keep them out of the mainstream." From which it is clear that, for St. Peter's and whoever else will "follow" the Pope (unless and until he changes his mind, for which we pray), Archbishop Lefebvre and his whole idea of Tradition are to be left behind on the sidelines.

Clearly, the Church's official leaders are staying on their Conciliar course. Also clearly, the Conciliar course is – wittingly for some, unwittingly for others – that of the Antichrist. In Basel, Switzerland, in the third week of May was held a "Council for Peace, Justice, and the Saving of Creation," with 700 delegates, half Catholic, half Protestant, from all over Europe, including some 50 bishops, under the aegis of the World Council of Churches, and beneath the sign of the rainbow. Basel was filled for the week with rainbows, sign of the New Age. This meeting was to prepare for the world council due to take place in Seoul, South Korea, next year, which in turn is to lay the foundations of the New World Religion. The Pope sent his blessing and a message to the Basel Council. Wittingly, unwittingly? His mind is profoundly confused. His idea of Catholicism is such, that such ecumenism he thinks is Catholic.

Where does that leave the SSPX? Happily and quietly – not defiantly – we must practice our Faith, which means, carry our cross (who would ever abandon the Truth were it not for the Cross?). One of the Society's latest crosses has just come from France – many of you will have learned about it through the media – the May 24 discovery of a "Nazi collaborator" in one of the Society's priories in the south of France. Is the Society neo-Nazi? Whatever actions the now 74-year old Paul Touvier committed that may have been criminal before the French law between 1939 and 1945, the statute of limitations (which in any country reasonably stops criminal investigations going on for ever and ever) expired on them in 1967. In 1971 the French government quietly gave him what amounted to a pardon, and he ceased to be on the run. However, the vindictive Nazi-hunters, under a new French law against "crimes against humanity," subject to no statute of limitations, began to hunt Touvier all over again. Whether on May 24 he was being given refuge in the Society's house in Nice, I do not know, but if he was, it will not have been the first time the Catholic Church has harbored refugees. During the war itself, Catholics all over Europe gave refuge to unjustly persecuted Jews. Why not now to unjustly persecuted collaborators? Because it is never unjust to persecute "crimes against humanity"? Let us stop a moment and examine the idea.

No doubt the greatest "crime against humanity" of all was the Nazis' "deliberate gassing of six million Jews," notably, we are told, in the concentration camp of Auschwitz. But the supposed gas-chambers, shown as such to tourists, at Auschwitz and at two other "death camps," Birkenau and Majdanek, all in Poland, were thoroughly and technically examined between February 25 and March 3 of last year by Fred Leuchter, the American technician in charge of the Missouri State Penitentiary gas chamber. His conclusion? He found the evidence to be "overwhelming" that the alleged gas chambers at the three sites "could not have then been, or now be, utilized or seriously considered to function as execution gas chambers."

So the so-called "crimes against humanity" are definitely not what the left-wing media make them appear. Thus there is a great deal of hard evidence that the so-called "Holocaust," for instance, is largely a myth. Was then Paul Touvier being unjustly persecuted? I do not know, but I do know most of the media seize on any opportunity to associate any part of the Catholic Church with being pro-Nazi. Patience. The media do their work, and we must do ours.

Much work is now being undertaken by the SSPX at St Mary's, Kansas to set up a new college program. See the enclosed prospectus. It offers a real hope to Catholic parents of offering to their youngsters a serious Catholic college education.

Remember the Ignatian Exercises being preached through the summer for men and women at Ridgefield and Winona. Remember also the "Workshop on Modernism" for men, being given at Winona. These three days will not be a retreat, they will not even be silent. They will be based on Pope Pius X's encyclical Pascendi and on his letter on the "Sillon." They will attempt to enable thinking laymen to get a firm handle on the most perfidious heresy in all Church history, modernism, and its practical accompaniment, sillonism, arguably the most pernicious dream in all Church history. Both are totally relevant to the Conciliar Church preparing the way for the New World Religion. Non-Catholics welcome, to learn the Church's mind.

Between now and then, the seminary's great day of the year will be June 24, with the ceremony of the ordination of two deacons and four priests beginning at 9:00 a.m. It will have to be outside, so pray for good weather. I am told the Winona motels are already booked up, but there is plenty of room for campers. My dream is that one such day, there will be as many children in the meadows around the seminary as there are summer dandelions. Young parents, I have only one thing to say to you – there's lotsa dandelions! God bless you all, and may He repay one hundredfold all of you that keep faithfully supporting us. We pray in particular for your intentions.

NO. 73 | JULY 1, 1989

Tradition Miraculously Protected in Nimes

THANKS TO ONE of those machines for which the 20th century is actually useful, a FAX copier, this letter is being penned in Switzerland, where within days of ordaining four new priests (all American) for the SSPX at Winona, I have just attended the ordination of eight more Society priests at Ecône. The ordinations at Winona went off very well. God gave us beautiful weather for the Saturday of the ordinations. The seminarians worked hard, as usual, to put together the outdoor altar, the ceremonies and the banquet, guided by the seminary's stalwart friends, Emily Johnson and the Sardegna family. Some 400 friends of the Seminary attended the ordination Mass, and most stayed over to attend the four new priests' first Masses on the Sunday morning. Ask any who came if it was worth the journey, and mark in your diary next year's Ordinations Day, Saturday, June 23, 1990. The August seminary letter should bring you another souvenir edition of The Verbum in color to help those of you to visualize the ceremony who could not come this year.

The ordinations at Ecône on June 29 also went off well, as usual, although the weather was not as sunny as it had been at Winona. Each year the June ordinations bring to Ecône a large number of priests, both Society priests and friends of the Society. It is always moving to see the young priests one knew as innocent bright-faced seminarians visibly maturing in the combat conditions of today's battle for the Faith. The gleaming truck straight off the production line is beautiful, but it is only useful when it starts to get covered in mud! Not, of course, that the mud is useful, but that there is no normal sanctification without the fulfilling of one's daily duty which in this world is frequently in muddy conditions. Which hand-missal does Jesus prefer? – shiny, trim and brand-new, or battered, torn, dog-eared, greasy-thumbed, and bulging with holy cards? No prize for the right answer. It is similarly moving to meet the Society's priestly friends, some of whom come to the ordinations at Ecône year after year. One of these is Fr. Maurice Raffalli from Nimes in southern France, who told me this year a story of the famous Nimes flood in October of last year which should put heart into all of you: God is faithful to those who are faithful to Him!

The story begins with the dreadful film, *The Last Temptation of Christ*, a wholly blasphemous presentation of Our Divine Lord as some kind of impure weakling. Being introduced all over France on Wednesday evening, September 28 of last year, the film was given its very first showing on the morning of the same day in Nimes, a city of about 130,000 inhabitants, where Fr. Raffalli says Mass each Sunday in the downtown chapel of the Sorrowful and Immaculate Heart of Mary, for about 140 traditional Catholics. Of this film's first showing for Nimes, the city's authorities dared to boast in public, beforehand! – Heaven's reply did not delay.

In the night of October 2nd – 3rd, the following week, French meteorologists picked up on their instruments an extraordinary rain-cloud piling five miles high above downtown Nimes! At about 5 a.m. a rainstorm began over the city with thunder and lightning. By 8 a.m. all electricity and water mains were cut off (taking a week to be restored). By 10 a.m. the sky was as dark as night, an extraordinarily menacing copper-black color. At about 10 a.m., the streets of downtown Nimes turned into torrents several feet deep, sweeping away and destroying some 3 to 4,000 cars and causing such wreckage in the whole downtown area as will take ten years to repair, says Fr. Raffalli. By the time the rain had stopped at 11:30 a.m. (a fall of 16 inches in about 6 hours) and the flooding had subsided an hour later, the official death-count stood at 20 souls, but the popular estimate was 150 deaths (the insurance companies profit by the official estimates being kept low).

The infamous cinema of the first showing of *The Last Temptation* was totally wrecked. Amongst the people, the immediate reaction was a recognition of the hand of God, of the wrath of God. But then – sure enough – the media went to work: "Such a downpour happens every 400 years . . .it happened in Roman times . . . the communist municipality put buildings in drainage areas meant for the water to go away," etc., etc. . . . Within a few days the people had forgotten the wrath of God and were blaming just unfortunate circumstances. However, the traditional Catholics were given clearly to see the hand of God.

During the downpour itself, Fr. Raffalli had been up in one of the hills surrounding Nimes, so he was naturally worried for his church wholly exposed on a downtown street-corner. Sure enough, down the street running directly alongside the Gospel side of the church, with a door giving straight onto the street, the water had been running 2 ½ feet deep. Worse, down the left-turn street running across the bottom end of the church and past the open-footed loose iron gates of the Church's courtyard the water had been racing 4 feet deep! Imagine then Fr. Raffalli's astonishment upon entering the church to find that not one drop of water had broken in! Nor were any of his other three buildings on the same courtyard in any way damaged whatsoever! In natural terms this was inexplicable. The church door giving onto the street was by no means water-tight, and beneath the courtyard-gates, at street level, so beneath 4 feet of water, was a gap large enough for a cat to pass through. Yet during the downpour, inhabitants on the third floor of the apartment block opposite the courtyard noticed that there was no more water splashing in the courtyard itself than that of an average heavy rain!

While some 150 yards down the road, a Pentecostalist church was completely ravaged by the flood. Fr. Raffalli's own parishioners were in no doubt that their church had been supernaturally protected. On an outside wall they placed on December 8 a plaque to commemorate the Blessed Virgin's protection of their church.

This remember, is 1988! We are not speaking of the supposedly dim-witted peasants of "backward" times. Truth to tell, even the Mayor of Nimes realized his city had been punished, and asked the bishop of Nimes to celebrate a Christmas Mass of reparation in the city's Roman arena (Says Fr. Raffalli, the "Mass" was an abomination. Alas!). Still more extraordinary than the protection of Fr. Raffalli's church may have been the protection of his parishioners.

The parish organist had left his car on a street where the torrent left all cars unusable that it did not sweep away, but he found his where he had left it, so he turned the key in the ignition and it started up with no problem.

Mrs. Aucre is another parishioner. The two apartment blocks on each side of hers were wrecked by the water smashing through the windows sweeping everything out the other side, but all that her own block suffered was 8 inches of water in the basement.

Most remarkable of all, Mrs. Nourrit, a daily early morning Mass-goer, found herself taking an unusually long time to get up on the morning of the 3rd and to prepare to leave the house, and when at last she left the house, some mysterious force absolutely prevented her from climbing into her car. She could not get in. Too bad! She would have to miss Mass. Later she understood. Had she driven to church down the Ales road as usual, she and her car would have been swept away in the torrent which washed the coffins clean out of the Protestant cemetery!

Dear friends, what can one say? God exists, He has not handed in His resignation, He knows what we do, and what we do matters to Him. Even in 1989 He speaks to us, and if we have ears to hear, He speaks loud and clear. That daily Mass, or whatever be our daily duty, that day-by-day turning of the shiny Missal into a dog-eared hulk, of a shining seminarian into a war-scarred veteran, can seem to us a pointless drudgery, but that is not how it seems to God. He takes note. He rewards. He protects.

For sure and certain within the next 10 or 20 years, His wrath must come down with crushing and terrible form on great masses of mankind. Not to worry. If I have not abandoned Him, He will not abandon me. If He knows that it is best for me to be protected in this world, He has a thousand means of shielding me, and if He knows it is not best for me, then best if I go. I cannot lose, or, as King David says, "Yea though I walk through the valley of the shadow of death, I shall fear no evil."

Thank you, Fr. Raffalli, for a grand example of fidelity, and thank you, dear friends of the seminary, for another school-year's support.

NO. 74 | AUGUST 1, 1989

Ecclesia Dei Playing Softball

WHEN THE CATHOLIC Church's enemies seem to be shattering her in a thousand fragments, it is a surprising time to say that she has the structure of a rock, yet that is what is today becoming more and more clear. The sand and cement of half-truths and compromises may be able to prop up human institutions, but the Catholic Church will rest upon nothing but the granite of sheer Truth.

Ecclesia Dei and its progeny, the Society of St. Peter, are failing. *Ecclesia Dei* was the Commission formed by JP2 just after the consecrations of June 30 last year to stop Catholics from going into the "Lefebvrist schism"; the Society of St. Peter was the Society approved by *Ecclesia Dei* as a substitute for the Archbishop's SSPX from which most of St. Peter's' members broke away. It is not pleasant to document the failure of *Ecclesia Dei* and St. Peter's Society when both contain no doubt sincere and well-meaning men. Only, when hardball is being played, it is absolutely necessary to sift out those still trying to play softball.

Ecclesia Dei has met with two major setbacks. Firstly, it has failed to obtain from the Pope the much-rumored document liberating the Tridentine Mass. In 1984 you remember the Pope granted an indult for the Tridentine Mass, and in July of 1988 his Motu Proprio *Ecclesia Dei*, founding the Commission, asked bishops to make generous use of that indult. Within months of its founding, the Commission was able to document the bishops' lack of cooperation or positive hostility towards the Pope's appeals. Cardinal Mayer, head of the Commission, took this documentation to the Pope and said to him that if he was serious about *Ecclesia Dei*, he must grant a General Indult for the Tridentine Mass. "Promulgate it yourselves with my permission," replied the Pope.

Accordingly *Ecclesia Dei* drew up a document allowing four ways to say Mass: the new rite (Novus Ordo) in the vernacular, the new rite in Latin; the Tridentine rite (1962 Missal) with readings in the vernacular, and the Tridentine rite all in Latin. In mid-May of this year this document was due for triple signatures by the Pope and Cardinals Ratzinger and Mayer. Then, however, took place their meeting with the Heads of several Bishops' Conferences in Rome: "Are you worried about the extreme-left theologians?" said the bishops to the Pope (knowing full well how they worry him) – "Leave us to look after them, but in the meanwhile no more of this *Ecclesia Dei* nonsense, if you please." So the liberation of the Tridentine Mass was never signed, and the handsome document waits in some Roman drawer . . .

The thinking of the Bishops' Conferences was made known to a number of you in an article by John Travis, syndicated in American papers, and entitled "Aftershocks of Lefebvre Incident Still Reverberating." Travis quoted a bishops' spokesman as saying: "When the Pope created this Commission, it was an attempt to help in an intermediate or transition stage – not to create a new rite or a new institution. But some people now think maybe there should be a new rite. This was not the bishops' understanding." And what is not the Bishops' Conferences' understanding will not fly in today's official Church. In theory, power in the Church belongs to the Pope and to the individual bishops, but in practice, thanks to collegiality, real power lies with the Bishops' Conferences, at least until the Vicar of Christ stops believing in "collegiality." So until then *Ecclesia Dei* will conciliarize Tradition, or it will do nothing. This is hardball.

The second major setback of *Ecclesia Dei* has been over "celebrets." In the Commission's early days, since the bishops would not cooperate, it freely granted to individual priests (at any rate those not too closely associated with the SSPX) a "celebret," or permission to say the Tridentine Mass. However, since the May meeting with the bishops (briefly described in the June seminary letter), Cardinal Mayer now directs applicants for a celebret, with few exceptions, to go through their local bishop, with foreseeable results: the flow of permission has been reduced to a trickle. Moreover, where celebrets have been granted, the bishops are reining them in. In Buffalo, NY, for instance, a priest was struck off the Retirement Fund for daring to use his celebret, with the result that many priests are now too scared to use theirs. And where a priest in a Wisconsin diocese used his in defiance of the bishop, this bishop obtained a letter of support against the priest – from Cardinal Mayer who granted the celebret!

Softball player on a hardball field, Cardinal Mayer is knuckling under to the bishops, which frustrates members of the Commission, but if they insist on obeying the Pope, who obeys the Bishops' conferences, what can they do? Their Society of St. Peter is another paper tiger. The bishops give it no freedom to act in their dioceses. For instance, its most prominent American representative was recently refused entry to a North American Archdiocese, so that he was obliged to meet in private, by two's and three's, members of the sweetest Society of Softballers you could ever as a bishop hope to meet! His advice to them? No doubt welcome! – "Avoid confrontation. Be patient." But still no North American bishop will take priests of St. Peter's. This representative of St. Peter's was reportedly depressed at the turn of events. Well might he be. What man likes playing the part of a declawed pussy-cat?

So *Ecclesia Dei* and St. Peter's Society are being swept aside while the bishops speed up their hardball game of destroying the Church. In France they recommend intrinsically sinful means to protect against AIDS. In Italy they mendaciously discredit the Holy Shroud. Worldwide they sit by while blasphemous films outrage Our Lord and Our Lady. In Germany the author of a scandalous book denying that the Gospels are historical fact is appointed to the key bishopric of Stuttgart, and is congratulated on his appointment by Cardinal Ratzinger. In Rome, another wrecker of the Faith is appointed Head of the Biblical Commission, while in Denmark the Holy Father himself is again visiting the Lutherans to praise the archheretic Martin Luther (*L'Osservatore Romano*, English ed. June 19, p. 8). Whoever hoped that a pussy-cat would be able to take part in such a game of hardball? And yet we shall doubtless see more staircases of sand being proposed to us to climb out of trouble.

More than ever, dear readers, you must take your stand behind or alongside Archbishop Lefebvre, because time is proving and will ever more prove that on the side of God he is the only one who has known how to play Catholic hardball. As all mud and sand and cement get progressively washed away, the granite stands out, and with it, the rock-like structure of the Church of Truth. Have no doubt, those who scorn and spurn you today for taking your stand on Truth will thank and bless you tomorrow for having saved it for them, however few you were. Have also no doubt that if in defense of the Faith the seemingly mighty ones of this world were to falter and fail, then He would raise up, as in the early days of His Church, weak maidens to testify in their blood, with an adamantine strength, to the purity of Truth.

NO. 75 | SEPTEMBER 7, 1989

Asian Tour

THREE WEEKS AGO, I was just back from another journey around the world. This time, after a five-day stop to give a retreat in California, the journey was, at the Superior General's request, to the Far East. Asia is not the most Catholic part of the world, but it has much to rejoice and edify a Catholic heart.

The first stop was Japan. In the two biggest cities, Tokyo and Osaka, a devout and brave widow, Mrs. Shuko Nakama, small in stature but great in heart and Faith, has gathered together two small groups of Catholics with a devotion to the Tridentine Mass. These eagerly await the next occasional visit of a Society priest, and during his brief stay, they know what it is that they want of him – the sacraments! Four of the seven sacraments in one day for instance, and then sacramentals also, to be blessed by the bushel!

The Japanese are an extraordinary people. Amongst all the Far Eastern peoples St. Francis Xavier met, he is said to have liked the Japanese best. They are not a Christian people and never have been, except for a minority, but their natural virtues of discipline, work and order are such that they are presently an economic superpower, beating the West at its own game. What a shame that visitors from the West show themselves in their dress and behavior so lacking in dignity and discipline! What self-respecting people would ever wish to adopt the culture or beliefs of such unmanly men and unwomanly women as many of these Western tourists give every appearance of being? Oh, Liberalism! St. Francis Xavier was in the same upset over the poor example of Christianity given then in the Far East by the supposed Christians. Yet the Oriental peoples could of course be won for Christ.

It is an extraordinary experience to be sitting, on the floor, Japanese style, in a Japanese restaurant, amidst complete strangers of an alien culture, and hear, coming through the interpreter of their strange language, pertinent and serious questions concerning the Faith in today's world. Back one sends an answer into their wholly unknown tongue, and then the attentive faces light up with wholly known and familiar reactions – we are all children of the same Father!

After Japan, Korea. The South Koreans, saved from Communism by the United States' intervention in the Korean War in the early 50's, are another hard-working people whose natural virtues, as they come from the country into the modern city, are making of them a major industrial power. The capital, Seoul, is now an enormous city of some ten million inhabitants, and Hyundai and Daewoo cars are competing with the world-famous Japanese brands. However, Hyundai's competitiveness is being threatened by the rising demands of its workers as their country simplicity drops behind them and they require modern city wages. By the same token, that religion of materialists, Communism, is threatening South Korea even more from within than from North Korea – man cannot live by bread alone.

The Society's anchorman in Seoul, Professor Kim, teacher at Han Yang University, with two teenage sons, was dissatisfied several years ago with the direction being taken by the Korean Catholic Church. So he prayed very seriously to Our Lord to know the true way to follow. After several months of such prayer, his mind was suddenly enlightened with an overall grasp of the Redemption, which, as he explained it to me, corresponded wholly with the old catechisms, but not at all with what he found being then put forward in the Catholic churches in Seoul. This was the beginning of a prayer-group, meeting regularly in his home and attracting numbers of – youngsters! A first contact was made with the Society early last year. Before I arrived this summer, already three Korean girls from the prayer-group had ventured around the world to try their vocation with the Society Sisters in Armada, Michigan. Three more are interested. In truth, man will throw up what roadblocks he likes, but they will not stop the Lord God! Prayer is the key.

Third stop was the Philippines. This archipelago of over seven thousand islands and forty million inhabitants is the only Catholic nation in Asia (except perhaps Vietnam?), thanks to the Spaniards who discovered and colonized it back in the 1500's. The capital, Manila, has four centuries of Catholic history. Alas, this heritage of the Faith is being eroded by neo-modernism, and heavily menaced by communism. So two groups of Filipinos are interested in the Society and the Tridentine Mass: one is of prayerful parishioners, upset by the neo-modernism, the other is of devout young militants, alerted by the threat of communism. It is simply a matter of time before the Tridentine Mass puts down firm roots again in Manila.

From Manila to Hong Kong. Low taxes and its strategic location on the southern coast of China have given to this little British colony immense wealth and importance as a center of commerce. Hong Kong harbor bustles with ships and boats, and the downtown by the waterside is crowded with banks and high-rise buildings. The Catholic Church is here, but seems to gasp for breath amidst so much wealth in so little space. The Society has in Hong Kong a few good friends, centered again around a prayer-group, but outside of these, few seem even to "glimpse" the crisis of the Church. In 1997 the British lease runs out, and the Hong Kong territories are due to revert to the Chinese Communists. A mercy? Frightful to say, but from the standpoint of heaven and hell – the ETERNAL kind – probably a mercy.

Last stop, Singapore. Another bustling port and major center of trade and commerce, former British colony but now a city-nation made independent even of Malaysia since 1964, when the Malays cut it loose in order to remain masters in their own house. For in Singapore over 80% of the people are Chinese, whose – again – natural virtues under the remarkable, albeit naturalistic, leadership of Lee Kuan Yew would make of Singapore a formidable competitor in industry and commerce, were it not so limited in size. To Singapore the Society and the Tridentine Mass have been drawn in the last two years by a prayer-group, in the formation of which the action of the Holy Ghost is visible. A few years ago a retired school-teacher advertised in the Singapore press, offering to come with a statue of the Infant Jesus of Prague or Our Lady of Fatima, and with one or two friends, to pray in people's homes. Several people responded, and from the contacts a circle of friends interested in prayer arose. They bind themselves to pray 15 mysteries of the Rosary a day, to go to confession once a week and to receive Communion only kneeling. The group attracts – you guessed it – many youngsters, some of whom are now seriously considering a vocation with the Society. The group is notorious throughout the Singapore Catholic Church for kneeling for Communion, but they will not give in to pressure to do otherwise. They come together for monthly vigils requiring of each of them to pray SEVEN rosaries. Some 40 took part in the week-end Retreat I was able to give them. They loved it. They love the old Mass which most of them hardly even know, and they long for the next Society priest to bring them that Mass. As Our Lord said, "I am the good shepherd, and I know mine and mine know me."

Coming home via Europe made this the third journey around the world since I joined the Society. St Martin, it appears, was not the only Bishop of Tours!

Back in the United States, I find the number of young men enlisted to enter the seminary this year to try their vocation, is topping twenty. Of course not all will persevere, but it is still the largest number enlisting that I can remember in any one year. Several have come through retreats, so we are delighted to send you again the details of Ridgefield's retreats for the coming year.

Note also the Christmas and Easter retreats for men 17 and upwards at Winona. And as your own activity maybe picks up in the autumn, may it bring you also closer to the Good Shepherd. We are not on this earth for any other reason.

NO. 76 | OCTOBER 1, 1989

Traditional Bishops Absolutely Necessary

ENCLOSED IS A long interview with Archbishop Lefebvre. It is coming to you full length because the material in it that is already familiar to us bears repetition, and the whole of it sheds a clear light on our situation as Catholics in the Church today. Amidst all the darkness, Archbishop Lefebvre remains a beacon of Truth.

He begins with a summary of the events necessitating the episcopal consecrations of June 30, last year. The nub of his argument is that the fight for Catholic Tradition is a fight for no less than the whole of the Catholic Faith and the Catholic Church. Now the Catholic Church is made above all of bishops, because superiors make their subjects, and not the other way round. Hence today's fight for Tradition absolutely requires Traditional bishops, and the idea of defending the Faith without them is a complete illusion.

Notice in passing that the decisive power of superiors within the Catholic Church is the reason why over the last twenty years so many good laymen have – relatively speaking – lost time, and are still doing so, by trying to fight the destruction of the Church "from within," as they thought they had to do, and as so many people still urge the Society to do. For if even in a democracy the saying is true that "you cannot fight City Hall," how much more will it be difficult within the hierarchically designed Catholic Church for laymen to fight determined priests or bishops. One recent example is the poor parishioners of St. Boniface in Stewart, Minnesota, whose bishop has closed down their church because they refused to pay thousands of dollars to be group-psychoanalyzed for their rejection of anti-Catholic doctrine! Used or misused, the authority lies with the clergy.

But if God insists on giving such authority to the clergy, how does He save His Church from bad churchmen? Answer, in a variety of ways. In the 1970's He inspired an archbishop to give to the laity a fresh start of priests, and in the late 1980's fresh bishops. There is no way all these can give themselves a new Pope, but if they stay with the Truth, God will finally give them a Pope of Truth. Within the Truth is within the Church, and without the Truth is without the Church.

The steady decomposition of Truth within the official structures of today's Church is the reason why Catholics more and more each day need not, even must not, stay within those structures. Over many years Archbishop Lefebvre did all he could – just short of abandoning the Truth – to stay within those structures, but notice in his interview his realistic assessment, wise after the event, that had he "stayed within" last year, he and the Society would have been swamped.

The interview continues with an objection beloved of conservatives: Yes, but the Catholic Church is meant by God to be visible, and the visible Church today is the official Church, so to be outside the official Church is to be outside the Catholic Church.

The Archbishop's reply: what makes the true Church visible is its four marks of being one, holy, catholic (i.e., universal) and apostolic. Now the Traditional Church shows more of these marks than does the official Church (for instance, since when did holy Catholics flock to communion, by-passing the confessional?). So the true Church's visibility is more in the "Traditional" than in the "official" Church.

Yes, continues the objector, but the official Church is infallible, so Traditionalists who fight it must be wrong. Interesting reply of the Archbishop: indeed the true Church is infallible, but whereas today's official Church in effect repudiates that infallibility, Traditionalists cling and appeal to it. Hence Traditionalists are more infallibist and, again, more Catholic, than the official Church. Such arguments used against Traditionalists, concludes the Archbishop, are just words in the air, words disconnected from reality.

As for reconciliation with Rome, that is impossible so long as Rome continues to aggravate its dogmatic errors on religious liberty, ecumenism, and collegiality, because these errors mean the dissolution of any objective Truth and so the death of the Church. For Church leaders to pretend such ideas are Traditional is a plain lie. Even communists treat Catholics better than do such churchmen!

Nor are the supposedly hopeful signs of a turn for the better in Rome to be relied on, and the Archbishop says why: misunderstandings between Rome and the Communists are more apparent than real; Rome may give the right lead on basic moral issues like abortion, but it takes no strong stand to enforce that lead; Rome may be appointing conservative bishops, but these still believe in the Council and can even be our worst enemies; Rome may be indulging certain Traditionalists with an Indult Mass, but such indulgence is always the exception to their rule, which remains the New Mass and the Council.

For the time being Rome remains impenitently Conciliar, as is demonstrated by its new oath, more modernist than anti-modernist, potentially an oath of infidelity, so for Rome to become amenable to Tradition, we have to wait, alas, for more Conciliar chickens to open Catholics' eyes by coming home to roost. Only the facts, of Traditionalists continuing to build up the Traditional movement, will bring these Romans back to the negotiating table. Send for copies of this interview if you wish.

Also enclosed are these cards on which to inscribe the names of your beloved departed. These cards are placed once a month on the seminary's main altar, for a Solemn Requiem Mass for the repose of their souls. Inscribe, for no charge, you need not inscribe names inscribed in previous years. People ask if the seminary has Perpetual Masses or Mass cards for the living or dead. The answer is no, because in today's unstable world any promise of "perpetuity" might be difficult to keep, so we do not believe in taking money on such a promise. The seminary can look after normal Mass intentions sent with a stipend, but please keep such intentions separate from the enclosed cards, which are exclusively for names for the Requiem Mass which we do promise to say, month by month. All your intentions are included in the Holy Rosary recited every night of October by seminarians in front of the Blessed Sacrament exposed.

Sister Lucy of Fatima assures us that there is no problem that cannot be solved by praying the Holy Rosary. General Naaman was cured of leprosy by merely getting in and out of the River Jordan seven times (IV Kings 5) – all he needed was the humility to comply with heaven's instructions. The same applies to ourselves. Whoever wishes to slow down the evil rampant around us can do no better than start a Rosary prayer group. It only takes a few friends in the Faith. However, I suggest you not content yourselves with five Mysteries – go straight for fifteen! Our Lady needs them all, and then some! May God bless you and keep you.

Women in Arms

WITHIN THE LAST month I read in a Washington D.C. daily paper – no, not *The Washington Post*! – of a U.S. Navy ship unable to set sail because so many of the sailors were – drunk? no – drugged? no – but pregnant! Shiver my timbers! Navy in Wonderland! The fact appeared in a (woman's) review of a recently appeared book by a seven-year US infantry officer, now a *Navy Times* newspaper reporter, Brian Mitchell: *Weak Link: The Feminization of the American Military*.

The book piles up the examples to prove what no man with a grain of common sense would doubt, namely the utter and intrinsic absurdity of enlisting women anywhere near combat units. The Israelis for instance have given up draughting women into combat because they learned the hard way that each time a woman is hit, two soldiers are put out of action, for not even the most valiant redesigners of nature in creation – sorry, in evolution – can eradicate the instinct of the man alongside the wounded woman to stay and protect her.

From where then came this insanity of enlisting women for combat? That the rank and file soldiers, sailors and airmen should, at least when the bullets are not flying, raise no strong objection, is – well – understandable. But what is infinitely grave is when Mitchell says that the men's leaders and senior officers, the top brass of the US military, are, to a man, also caving in to the insanity! He says these officers all know the women cannot fight, that the forced integration, promotion and preferential treatment for the women undermine the military's combat readiness, its discipline and morale, for which they are responsible to the nation, yet not one of them will say so. Instead they impose on the military a systematic brainwashing to enforce so-called equal opportunity. Mitchell calls his book "an account of the creation of a lie." What in heaven's name is going on?

Well, the feminists are on the warpath. To achieve a gender-neutral society, they are setting out to unman the warriors, supposedly the most manly of men, and then the rest of the men can be counted on to fall into line. Yes, but what drives these denatured women to denature their men, and why do the men let them do it? The first part of the answer is that it is the men's fault, in both cases, as a young American soldier-writer, John Bruce Campbell, clearly sees in his *The New American Man, A Call to Arms*:

> The sexual revolution of the '60's and '70's took a lot of men out of the fight. Sex, drugs and rock 'n' roll are socialist tools for weakening men, [for diminishing their resistance to] . . . the Marxist fraud known as "women's liberation!" Many of these befuddled souls, attempting to demonstrate sympathy with their "sisters," became to some extent effeminate. Men began increasingly to look to women for answers...our manhood was cut slowly away...
>
> But from a woman you do not get answers... From a woman a man gets questions, all amounting to the same one: "What are you going to do?" A man must ACT and a woman can only respond to his action or

his lack of action. If a man refuses to act, or acts stupidly, a woman must and does compensate. That's where "women's Lib" came from. Men failed women.

Well said, Bruce. Men failed women. There was a great 19th century Frenchwoman, Saint Madeleine-Sophie Barat, who was aware that in founding Catholic boys'-style schools for girls, she was essentially filling the gap being left by the men as they were going soft on Liberalism. For a while the women held, but when the men continued refusing to take a stand for anything, then in the 20th century the women gave up the unnatural effort, slipped anchor also, loosed all bonds and let loose all hell.

Concerning these soft men, Cardinal Pie said, also in the last century, "There are no men today because they have no force of conviction. There is no force of conviction, because there is no Faith." Bruce, you dream of spraying Congress with an AK-47. Alas, it would not work. But pick up the Madonna's 150 round machine-gun, go with it into battle with the devil, and not one bullet will miss! Seriously – has anyone told you about the Rosary?

Thus the second part of the answer is that the men are falling prey to Liberalism because they have no Catholic Faith. An English professor at a top U.S. military academy said on a recent visit to the seminary that the real situation in the U.S. military is still worse than Mitchell portrays it. He gave us a vivid example of the collapse of nerve on the part of decent men in his own Academy. Three years ago a very fine US Marine officer, a much decorated Vietnam hero, found the Academy's English and History departments, of which he was now in charge, full of Liberal nonsense. He began an attempt to restore order by imposing a non-elected military man as Chairman of the English Department. The Department rose in revolt, and all thirty members demanded a confrontation with the would-be reformer.

Our friend describes how at this meeting the hero who could face down hordes of armed communists, could not face down a pack of unarmed Liberals. Why not? Because in his resistance there was a grain of self-doubt, which the Liberals are masters in detecting, and ruthless in exploiting. The anti-Liberal maintained his candidate, but only on condition that the nonsense in the English Department would roll on as merrily as ever. What would he have needed to be able to stand up to them? Our professor friend said, the Catholic Faith, in all its ancient strength and integrity.

Dear readers, a civilization is collapsing in ruins around our ears because the Catholic Faith on which it was built is in a terminal state of official collapse. Now if you and I and others keep that Faith despite the officials, then on the one hand the Liberals all around will do all they can to tear us down too, as they see in us the last obstacles in the way of their "triumph." On the other hand they absolutely need us to stand up to them, firstly because we know what Satan has in store for them in the next life if they do not change, secondly because they themselves suspect he is not making them happy even in this life. Deep down, the best of them are yearning for us to give them good reason not to be Liberals. Who else can do it?

Therefore, dear friends, if ever you or I feel like flinching, we must pick up our Rosary until the feeling goes away! The good Lord made man to think and lead, and deal if necessary in death. He made woman to love and follow, and necessarily nurture life. And if the feminists want to scratch your eye out when you tell them so, reply with stories like that of the young widower, heir to the French throne whose second bride might have been highly upset when she found him on their wedding night all in tears at the memory of his first wife. Instead she simply said, "Do not mind weeping, Your tears do not offend me, quite the contrary, they show me what I can expect of you if ever I succeed in deserving your love." Succeed she did. They were very happy together and had eight children, including three future kings of France.

   Remember the Spiritual Exercises of St. Ignatius are available at the Seminary here for men, age 17 and upwards, from the evening of December 26 to the afternoon of December 31. What better way of closing out the old year and opening the new? There is much seminary news in the enclosed Verbum. At this point we still have nineteen new seminarians, a good number. However, pray for their quality rather than their quantity, and receive our continuing thanks for all your prayers and indispensable support.

NO. 78 | DECEMBER 1, 1989

Indult Masses & Fatima

THE JUBILEE MASS, celebrating on Nov. 19 in Paris, France, the 60th anniversary of Archbishop Lefebvre's priestly ordination in Sept. 1929, was a great success. Celebrated in a huge steel and concrete exhibition hall near Le Bourget Airport, it was attended by some 23,000 people from all nations, races, classes and ages. The demonstration of Faith by a large and solid worldwide remnant of Catholics must have been a consolation to the Archbishop's heart.

Now 84 years old, he is in good health and in fine fettle. Judge for yourselves by his comments on the fight for the Faith: "It is inevitable that the bishops will force Rome to drop the Society of St. Peter, whose head has written to a former colleague and friend that he does not know how long Rome will continue to support them. Presently Rome is trying to combat Tradition by the Cardinals' starting Indult Masses next to our Mass Centres, but these tactics are not working. Attendance at their London centres is down to 35% of what it was at the beginning.

Nor will their "parallel Liturgies" (i.e. priestless Masses) save the Church, which in France, as everywhere else, is becoming a facade with nothing behind it. Some bishops appear Traditional by organizing seminaries with cassocks and processions, so that some say "Rome is coming round," but it is only an appearance. Their ideas and the formation they give to their priests are entirely conciliar: secularism, Liberalism, the New Mass, the new catechisms. Such bishops cannot accept St. Peter's Society in their dioceses. The bishop of the diocese in which lies the monastery of Dom Gerard, the Benedictine who left us to go over to Rome in 1988, has written in his Diocesan Bulletin that if he attended the ceremonial blessing of Dom Gerard's abbey, nobody should conclude that he (the Bishop) is departing by one inch from the Council or the renovated Liturgy. He wishes the new Abbey to make a public gesture of communion with him, and he has spoken to Dom Gerard of concelebrating the New Mass with himself and priests of the Diocese. There is no turning back from the Council, concludes the Bishop of Avignon.

In France the churchmen are supporting the invasion of their country by non-Christians whom for centuries the Popes strove to hold back. East Berliners are flinging themselves into West Berlin's immorality, World-wide forces are seeking to destroy Christendom. Our Society of St. Pius X is setting up the only solid resistance. Without ourselves, there would be nothing to effectively check the apostasy and immorality. We are small in numbers, which goes to show the power of the Catholic priesthood, the foundation stone of society.

Now the Secretariat for Christian Unity, which was the vipers' nest in the Council, is organising Gorbachev's meeting with the Pope. We are not out of the woods. The Society must build fortresses of the Faith, schools, seminaries and above all parishes as normal as possible. We are not dividing the Church but rescuing it. If God does not intervene, this situation could go on for a long time.

Richard N. Williamson

The Society's monthly magazine in the USA, *The Angelus*, is putting out a commemorative issue for the Archbishop's Jubilee. I warmly recommend the articles it will contain which are translated from the Italian fortnightly paper, *Si Si, No No*. They are a serene and profound exposition of Catholic common sense: Let me give you a sample: The writer (anonymous) compares the Society's Mass centers to oases in a desert of the Faith. There the people find everything Catholic which is being trampled underfoot elsewhere – "Is it surprising that the faithful (under the threat of excommunication in 1988) did not care to abandon these oases of living Faith? What did the promoters of the Church's new course have to offer them, other than communion in name with the Successor of Peter, for they very well know that communion in reality, i.e., in the Faith, was not being destroyed (by the 'excommunication')? All that the innovators could offer them was ruins. These faithful have not refused communion with Rome, they have simply refused to be chased back into the desert." The next best thing I could do to having written these articles was to translate them.

I also wish I had written the second volume of *The Whole Truth About Fatima* by Brother Michael of the Holy Trinity, just published in paperback in English by the courageous Fr. Gruner out of his Fatima Center in upstate New York. Entitled The Secret and the Church, 1917–1942, it documents the history of Fatima from the time of the original Apparitions through the interwar years, and upon those troubled years, deeply confused in our minds by Liberal propaganda, it throws the light of Fatima which is the light of God, a flood of light. It shows for instance how Pope Pius XI thought he could deal with Communism, and so rather than consecrate Russia to the Immaculate Heart he preferred his own backdoor negotiating with the butchers of the Kremlin.

Bitter experience of their ingrained perversity taught him what he at last taught the Church in his famous encyclical on Communism in 1937: "Communism is intrinsically perverse, and no one who wishes to save Christian civilization may collaborate with it in any undertaking whatsoever." For all those who enjoy reading and wish to understand in depth today's crisis of the Church, which did not begin only yesterday, I cannot recommend this book too highly. Listeners to the tape that I made with Bernard Janzen on Fatima will immediately recognize this book as our major source.

Pope Pius XI learned his lesson, but will Moscow-bound (in both senses) JP2 ever learn his? To help him build his utopian "better world for man" in which East and West, Communism and Catholicism, will merge, the delinquent Churchmen must smother the truth coming out of Fatima. Hence the recent purported letter of Sister Lucy, and a statement of Fatima's bishop, to the effect that Russia has been consecrated as the Blessed Virgin wished, which is certainly not the case. To see clear, subscribe to Fr. Gruner's *Fatima Crusader*, and pray for him. He must need protection.

But enough of the devil and his machinations! Let me tell you for Christmas-time one beautiful story amongst others I could tell, all recent and true: A Society priest making his way from New Zealand to France for the Archbishop's Jubilee last month, stopped over in Singapore to say Mass for the group there of friends of the Society. Visiting in hospital the dying mother of one of them, he noticed in the bed next to hers a Chinaman in his late fifties, but visibly on the brink of death. After giving to the mother the Last Sacraments, he went to the man's side and said, "I am a Catholic Priest. Would you like to become a Catholic? I am offering you life everlasting." The poor man dying of cancer could not speak, but when the priest asked, "Do you believe in Jesus Christ and the Holy Catholic Church?", he twice clutched the priest's hand affirmatively. So the priest gave him Baptism, Confirmation and the Papal Blessing in articulo mortis. Eight hours later he died.

On the following day, the priest learned that this man, a pagan, Hong Kee Koh, on entering the hospital a few weeks previously had asked the nurses to bring a Catholic priest to him, but they had not done so, maybe because his wife was opposed to him dying a Catholic. But "man proposes, God disposes." God himself led a priest to his bedside to invite him into Mother Church, Mr. Hong Kee Koh died in her arms, and in his baptismal innocence went straight to heaven, where may we all meet him!

Dear Friends, there is nothing God allows in all this tired ending of the world which, if we want to go to Him, can stop us; in fact everything He allows is designed to help us to go to meet Mr. Hong Kee Joseph Horace George Koh in Paradise! Happy Christmas. Plan your summer retreat. God bless you.

NO. 79 | JANUARY 1, 1990

Coming Decade Calls for Heroes

Happy New Year, and first and foremost, thank you for the great Christmas generosity of so many of you, which will enable the seminary to take another large chunk out of its debts. Our essential worries are not material or financial. Year by year you see to that! Thank you very much.

Interesting question, as we enter not only a new year, but also the new decade of the 1990's: What are our essential worries?

They might be economic, not on the local but on the national or international scale. Many economists foresee an imminent depression to cap the 1980's as the Depression of 1929 capped the 1920's. Certainly the escalation of public and private debt, a mountain of paper credit and a tidal wave of red ink, threaten to bring down the whole house of cards, the veritable palace of credit cards. Yet our politicians sweep gaily downhill, slaloming their way round any barriers like those of Gramm-Rudmann designed to slow them down.

So our essential worries for the decade might rather be political. For not only are our politicians financially irresponsible (in fairness, what else can one expect of men elected democratically to provide their voters with something for nothing at everyone else's expense?). Our politicians are also pretending that a change so significant is taking place within communism that the Cold War is over. The West need only share with the erstwhile communist countries in the lavish handouts – Bunnies and pornography to East Berlin, abortion made legal again in Romania – and the Big Bad Wolf will happily join in Little West Riding Hood's non-stop Friday evening party, and we shall all live globally ever after. Again, to what extent are democratic politicians to be blamed for leading the people into such a Never-Never-Land when the majority by their materialism implicitly insist on being led there?

Then our essential worries might lie above and beyond politics, in the domain of morals, the people's morals. We are getting warmer. A people of upright morals will automatically keep clean house in its economics and politics. A people hell-bent on money and pleasure will attain the hell but lose both money and pleasure. So what prospects does the New Decade hold out for people's morals?

The prospects are frightening. Now there are honorable and decent non-Christians and non-Catholics fighting the good fight on a variety of fronts, for instance, against abortion, Satanism, rock and roll, and feminism. Indeed a number of the most urgent and aware adversaries of these horrors are, in the USA, Protestants. All honor to them. However, reading even the best of their books a Catholic cannot help noticing the lack of coherency and depth which Catholic theology would give them. This ideological lameness of these honorable men, despite all their good will, is of course doubled by their practical disunity. Gallant individuals, nothing in their beliefs enables them to fuse their strength in one organization. Hence the good that these even only material heretics can do to people's morals is strictly limited.

So our essential worries must focus on the divinely instructed and structured Catholic Church. Already some 30 years ago, when a privileged soul in contact with Our Lord in Paris, France, complained to Him of the chaos in the world around her, He reportedly replied, "Yes, my child, but it is a hundred times worse in my Church." If only Mother Church would straighten out today, the world could lift its head again tomorrow; but if the Catholic Church continues to self-destruct, not all the world's wisest economists, politicians, or Protestants can lift a finger to save it, today or tomorrow.

And the state of Mother Church? Alas, to say nothing of her worst members, her best continue to resemble a computer trying to operate with two contradictory programs (Liberalism and Catholicism) jammed into it at once. A little example: the priest of Buffalo Diocese, N.Y., concerning whom I quoted a report a few months back that he had been penalized by his bishop for using his permission from Rome to celebrate the Tridentine Mass, assures me that that report is a falsehood, even a "slander" against his bishop. So be it, dear Father. The falsehood is hereby rectified and the "slander" taken back. But tell me now; if you and/or he reckon such an imputation of enmity to the True Mass to be slander, why does he, by the falsehood of conciliar obedience, enmesh you in the greatest slander of all against the True Mass, the Novus Ordo Missae, and why do you allow yourself so to be enmeshed? For if you see the imputation as slander, how can you live with the New Mass? But if as a priest you live the New Mass, how can you resent the imputation as slander? Probably, because you see no clash between the two rites. But that is sweet nonsense, like talk of dry water or hot snow. "Wahn, Wahn, ueberall Wahn"

– contradiction and confusion are everywhere within the Catholic Church.

Logical conclusion? Any events are to be wished for and prayed for in the new decade which will bring an end to the confusion in the Church; even an economic collapse – it is only money; even a World War – what is mortal blood compared with immortal souls? "But one thing is necessary," – an end to the confusion within Mother Church. That is why Garabandal's triple prophecy, of a Great Warning to forcibly remind everyone who is the real Realtor for all reality, of a Great (and permanent) Miracle to confirm the Warner's identity, and of a Great Chastisement to eventually clean house in His creation, is, whether or not authentic, at least wholly logical. Myself, I expect this to be the decade of Garabandal.

In any case the Lord God – blessed be His holy name! – is not confused! At the little village of San Damiano in northern Italy, a place of alleged apparitions of the Mother of God to a Mamma Rosa in the '60's and '70's of this century, pilgrims are so numerous from both the official Church and from Tradition that the apparition grounds have had to be divided in two. In the sector of Tradition the Swiss Traditionalists have set up a little cabin-chapel for the exclusive celebration of the Tridentine Mass. In this chapel for a week last May (1989), Archbishop Lefebvre, seeking peace and quiet, celebrated Mass each morning at 6:30 a.m., and on May 25, Feast of Corpus Christi, he exposed the Blessed Sacrament after Mass for adoration.

About mid-day the same day, four French pilgrims who had been praying in the official sector, opposite the Traditionalists, came over to the Swiss priest accompanying the Archbishop, and said to him more or less these words: "We are not with you. We do not belong in your sector. We attend the New Mass. But we are stunned. We feel bound to come and tell you what we saw this morning. We saw an immense luminous cross rising above your Chapel, up to Heaven, and bathing it in light, with an immense Host in the middle, also luminous." After hesitating for several hours, the same pilgrims repeated their vision to the Archbishop himself in the evening. His comment? – "The Cross, and the Holy Eucharist, that is our Fraternity: through many trials, serving the Mass." Surely this sign has all the more credibility and comfort for having been witnessed by no friends of Tradition. Thank you, dear Lord.

And also thank you for bringing us alive into a decade which will drive us perforce into being heroes in Thy service! Dear Friends and Benefactors, with thanks again for your own generosity we wish you happy, high, and heroic Nineteen Nineties!

Is Communism Dead?

WHAT ARE WE to make of all the turmoil over the last few months inside the Communist empire? Is Communism dead? Is the Cold War over? Are the Soviets no further threat to the western world?

The evidence is overwhelming that the Communist tiger is at the most taking one step back to spring later two or three steps forward, maybe the final spring to snatch and devour his prey. See for instance the excellent December issue of the *McAlvany Intelligence Advisor*, which shows that Gorbachev's Glasnost is the sixth Soviet Glasnost since Lenin; scripted years ago by the KGB, it calls for the appearance but not the reality of loss of Soviet control in eastern Europe; while Gorbachev purrs, the massive Soviet arms buildup continues, notably in Central America; while America stampedes to disarm, Soviet espionage inside America is exploding; while American businessmen go into feeding frenzy over the opening up of Eastern bloc markets, the Soviets calmly prepare for the moment described in 1930 by Dmitri Manuilski, professor of the Lenin school of political warfare:

> War to the death between Communism and Capitalism is inevitable. Presently it is beyond our capabilities

but in 30 to 40 years the moment will come. To overcome we will have to take them by surprise. We shall have to lull the bourgeoisie to sleep. Then we shall begin launching a spectacular and unprecedented peace movement. There will be highly publicized openings (e.g., the Berlin Wall!) and unheard of concessions. The stupid and decadent capitalist countries will be happy to cooperate in their own destruction. They will see a new chance of being friends with us. Then when they have dropped their guard we shall smash them with our clenched fist.

And McAlvany slates this final onslaught for the mid-to-late 1990's.

However, the media and our political and religious leaders present a picture rather more reassuring to our hopes and desires for peace. President Reagan: "Gorbachev is a different kind of Communist; he is a man we can trust . . . the Soviets have abandoned their plan to conquer the world . . . we are entering into a new era of peace and friendship and even association with the Soviets." President Bush: "The next ten years will mark the triumph of democracy." Pope John Paul II: "Marxist ideology is clearly exhausted." Cardinal Ratzinger: "Communism is dead." The Pope again: "The perestroika or restructuring taking place in Russia corresponds not only to the expectations of Western countries, but also to the social doctrine of the Church."

Now these voices of peace and hope might well beguile us if our discourse remained at the merely human level. Here in the USA some high class conservative commentators seem beguiled, precisely because their analysis does not rise above politics. In fact Communism has a messianic dimension, it is the messianism of materialism, a religion for the anti-religious, and only in a religious frame of reference can it be seen for what it is. Let us then briefly cast the light of three truly Catholic minds firstly on Communism's latest front, then on Communism itself, and lastly on what lies behind Communism.

Firstly, its latest front, or "socialism with a human face." In October of last year Archbishop Lefebvre was asked by a German journalist how the democratic socialism based on human rights, being promoted in the East, corresponded to the Catholic Church's social teaching. He replied:

> Such a socialism is indeed being promoted, in Poland one might even say it is the Pope's own handiwork. He has created the impression there that a Christian Communism might be possible, which would uphold sufficiently acceptable social principles. I think this is a grave error. It is unthinkable for Communism to become what it is not – unless it ceases to be Communism. If Pius XI was right about Communism, namely that it is intrinsically perverse, I do not see how it can suddenly be accepted, so long as there are only a few outward changes involving praxis and not doctrine. Yet that is Pope John Paul's thinking, I do believe. He calls himself anti-marxist but not anti-communist. That is an unbelievable distinction.
>
> The Pope is certainly still in contact with international Freemasonry, which stands for similar principles, an agreement with Communism is possible on the basis of human rights, and I know not what else. But say what you will, those are just empty words, because Communism will never accept any version of human rights corresponding to the Church's social teaching. I think the Russians are playing games, which are deceiving the West and could lead the West into a kind of Communist-like socialism. We would end up somewhat in Poland's present situation, perhaps soon the situation of East Germany and other countries . . .

Question: Is all this moving in the direction of the Antichrist and of a global political and religious union? Archbishop's reply:

> One can in any case say that a political union close to Communism is being prepared; probably it will not be called Communism, but it will be socialistic and will glorify the same principles as Communism does. In the ecumenical field, property would be in the hands of international corporations. In the religious field we would have a kind of global religious society. We shall soon see what the ecumenical meeting in Seoul will bring forth. We may fear that the foundation will be laid there for an international religious society based on wholly Freemasonic principles: solidarity and equality of all religions, and pacifism. Religion would in effect become a means of promoting a world-wide communistic socialism.

The basis of Archbishop Lefebvre's analysis here was the intrinsic perversity of Communism in itself, as laid out by Pope Pius XI in his encyclical of 1937, *Divini Redemptoris*. Secondly then, let us get behind Communism's most recent front, to Communism itself. Why does Pius XI castigate it as "intrinsically perverse?"

Enclosed you will find a one-sheet two-side summary of the encyclical's 82 paragraphs as numbered in the edition of the Daughters of St. Paul. In Sections I and II Pius XI lays out the diametrically opposed teaching of Communism (#9–13) and the Church (#26–33), on God, man, family, society and the state. If they clash on these, what can they agree on? From Communism's implacable hatred of God and of everything, supernatural or natural, instituted by God, flows one horror after another for Christian civilization (#19–22). When it comes in Section III to putting Church doctrine into practice, notice the Pope's conclusion, #57 and #58 above all. Keeping

Richard N. Williamson

Gorbachev in mind we must quote both paragraphs almost in full:

> In the beginning Communism showed itself for what it was in all its perversity but very soon it realized that it was thus alienating the people. It has therefore changed its tactics and strives to entice the multitudes by trickery of various forms, hiding its real designs behind ideas that in themselves are good and attractive. Thus, aware of the universal desire for peace, the leaders of Communism pretend to be the most zealous promoters and propagandists in the movement for world amity. Yet at the same time they stir up a class-warfare which causes rivers of blood to flow, and, realizing that their system offers no internal guarantee of peace, they have recourse to unlimited armaments. Under various names which do not suggest Communism, they establish organizations and periodicals with the sole purpose of carrying their ideas into quarters otherwise inaccessible. They try perfidiously to worm their way even into professedly Catholic and religious organizations. Again, without receding an inch from their subversive principles, they invite Catholics to collaborate with them in the realm of so-called humanitarianism and charity; and at times even make proposals that are in perfect harmony with the Christian spirit and the doctrine of the Church. Elsewhere they carry their hypocrisy so far as to encourage the belief that Communism, in countries where faith and culture are more strongly entrenched, will assume another and much milder form. It will respect liberty of conscience. There are some even who refer to certain changes recently introduced into Soviet legislation as a proof that Communism is about to abandon its program of war against God.
>
> See to it, Venerable Brethren, that the Faithful do not allow themselves to be deceived! Communism is intrinsically perverse, and no one who would save Christian civilization may collaborate with it in any under-

taking whatsoever. Those who permit themselves to be deceived into lending their aid towards the triumph of Communism in their own country, will be the first to fall victims of their error.

For the accuracy of Pius XI's analysis of what changes (#57) and what does not change (#9–13) in Communism, listen to the great Communists themselves, and think again of Gorbachev: Marx: "We call 'Communism' the movement which will overthrow the present state of affairs." Stalin: "Communist strategy changes every time the Revolution moves from one stage to the next. At any given stage of the Revolution the tactics can continuously vary, according to the ebb and flow, the rise and fall of the Revolution." Lenin: "The duty of a truly revolutionary party is not to proclaim its refusal of all and any compromise, but through all the compromises to succeed in remaining faithful to the principles and purpose of the Revolution . . . to use zig-zags, conciliatory maneuvers and withdrawals, in brief all the shifts necessary to take power." Gorbachev is a faithful pupil of Marx, Lenin and Stalin, as numerous quotes of his own go to show.

But let us leave him behind, for with these Communists' talk of the Revolution, we come to our third and most profound quote, unveiling what is behind Communism. Listen to a French bishop, Msgr. Gaume, speaking over 100 years ago, of the spirit behind all modern revolutions. Some of his examples from the 18th and 19th centuries may be unfamiliar to us, but it is easy to find 20th century equivalents to place in brackets alongside them:

> If you snatch off the mask of Revolution, and ask her, "Who are you?", she will reply:
>
> "I am not who you think I am. Many speak about me, but few know me. I am neither carbonarism (Council on Foreign Relations) conspiring in the shadows, nor the

riot raging in the street, nor the change from monarchy to republic, nor the switching from one ruling family to another (Trilateral to Kremlin), nor the momentary disturbing of the public order. I am neither the howling of the Jacobins (radicals) nor the wrath of the populace, nor the fighting on the barricades, nor the pillaging nor the burning, nor the agrarian law (anti-farm legislation), nor the guillotine (firing squad), nor the massacres. I am neither Harat (Trotzky) nor Robespierre (Lenin), nor Babeuf (Daniel Ortega), nor Mazzini (Gorbachev), nor Kossuth (Janos Kadar). These men are my sons; they are not me. These things are my works; they are not me. These men and these things are creatures of time, whereas I am a permanent state.

"I am hatred of all order not set up by man and in which man is not both king and God at the same time. I am the proclamation of the rights of man with no regard for the rights of God. I am the founding of the religious and social state upon the will of man in place of the will of God. I am God dethroned and man put in his place (man becoming his own end). That is why my name is Revolution, that is to say, turning upside down."

With these words, penned or spoken long before the Russian Revolution broke out in 1917, the timeless essence of Communism is laid bare – war on God. That is why Communism has a religious dimension, and why only religious people, like Alexander Solzhenitsyn, can understand it. That is why Pope Pius XI says (#78) that merely political or economic remedies are futile. That is why our liberal West is not only powerless to resist Communism, but is continually favoring and promoting it, because liberalism also is convinced that it has a mission to abolish God's order, to dethrone God and to enthrone the rights of man. That is finally why at Fatima Our Lady called for entirely supernatural countermeasures – the five first Saturdays, and the Consecration of Russia by

Pope and bishops to her Immaculate Heart. That is why liberal churchmen are now seeking to smother Fatima by pretending that the consecration as requested by Our Lady has already been done, which it certainly has not. But what a well-timed pretence! Communism has no more powerful allies than liberal churchmen.

All of which being so, dear readers, you might well be tempted to wish you and your children had been born in some other age than ours, but you would be wrong. For instance 200 years ago you might have believed in a Constitution to guarantee life, liberty and the pursuit of happiness – since 1973 you have seen it made to protect abortion; 100 years ago you might have believed in universal education to enlighten the world – now you see the public schools to be the scourge of youth; 50, 30 years ago you might have believed in a governmental New Deal or New Frontiers to solve the nation's problems – today all you see is bureaucratic red tape and red ink running out of control.

As more and more of these devices by which liberal man tries to hold together his existence are being shown up for what they are, namely without God wholly inadequate to the task, so do you and your children have more and more chance to discern where true salvation lies – in the revolution by which a man turns over, but turns himself over to God, through Our Lord's unchanging Catholic Church, outside of which – yes – there is no salvation. For especially since Vatican II your children can be taught to see that Protestantism is the grandfather of Communism.

Then lift up your Catholic hearts and rejoice, and whenever the devil's sulphurous breath presses too close upon your nearest and dearest, throw him back with a famous prayer taught for protection in our times by the Mother of God to a holy priest in the middle of the last century, just when hordes of demons were by man's fault and God's permission being unleashed upon earth from the depths of Hell:

> August Queen of Heaven and Sovereign Mistress of the Angels, who didst from the beginning receive from God the power and mission to crush the head of Satan: Send forth, we humbly beseech thee, the legions of Heaven, that, under thy command and by thy power, they may seek out all evil spirits, engage them everywhere in battle, curb their insolence and hurl them back into the pit of hell. "Who is like God?" O good and tender Mother, thou shalt ever be our hope and our love. O Mother of God, send forth the holy Angels to defend me and drive from me the cruel foe. Holy Angels and Archangels, defend us and keep us.

NO. 81 | MARCH 1, 1990

Our Lady of Akita

IT IS NOT going to be necessary month after month to come back on the question of Communism, but in a Liberal age, it is always necessary to come back upon the primacy of God and upon the dependence of all things, including politics, upon Him.

In the year 590 B.C., the people of Juda with their king, Sedecias, were being besieged in the city of Jerusalem by the mighty Assyrians (or Chaldeans) from the East, when from the Southwest came up the army of Pharao out of Egypt, long-standing enemy of the Chaldeans. Thereupon the Chaldeans withdrew from around Jerusalem, giving the Jews hope of escape from the Chaldeans' clutches. Fond hope, said the Prophet of God, lifting the discourse way above mere politics or military logistics:

> And the Chaldeans shall come again, and fight against this city, and take it, and burn it with fire. Thus saith the Lord: Deceive not your souls, saying: The Chaldeans shall surely depart and go away from us: for they shall not go away. But if you should even beat all the army of the Chaldeans that fight against you, and there should be left of them some wounded men: they shall rise up, every man from his tent, and burn this city with fire.

Richard N. Williamson

(Jer. 37: 7–9)

Which is of course what happened in 587 B.C. From which it is clear for our own time that even if Russia were economically bankrupt, ideologically exhausted and, let us imagine, militarily crippled, still a handful of Russians would inflict whatever chastisement God had appointed they should inflict upon the sins of the apostate West. The problem is, first, last and foremost, religious.

In our own century God's representative who, just as Communism was about to seize hold of Russia, highlighted that apparently military or political problems are in fact religious, was of course Our Lady of Fatima. In the First Secret, on July 13, 1917, she showed to three little children the fires of hell, "where sinners go if nobody prays for them." In the Second Secret, to prevent Russia from "spreading her errors throughout the world, causing wars and persecutions of the Church," she called for two entirely supernatural and religious countermeasures: the Consecration of Russia by the Pope to her Immaculate Heart, and the Communion of Reparation by Catholics on five successive first Saturdays of the month, with confession, meditation, and rosary. (A rosary, to stop tanks? – Yes, a rosary to stop tanks!)

In the Third Secret, there is good reason to think that she highlighted the religious problem even more, especially within the Catholic Church, but the churchmen locked the secret away in 1960, preferring in 1962 their own political way of handling Communism: the infamous Vatican-Moscow agreement.

In her two Messages of 1961 and 1965, straddling Vatican II, the Council which kept a disgraceful silence on Communism, the Lady of Garabandal again warned that our problems were primarily the offending of God, especially within the Catholic Church, e.g., "Many cardinals, bishops, and priests are on the road to perdition, and are taking many souls with them," but some churchmen smothered her voice, saying she was not Our Lady.

But no matter. In 1973 Our Lady said the same thing again, and this time it certainly was herself. For in 1984, just before retiring at a venerable age, in one of his last official acts as Diocesan Bishop of Niigata, Bishop John Shojiro Ito, the competent authority, in contact and in consultation with the Church's highest authorities in Rome – they did the right thing this time – wrote a pastoral letter in which he recognized as being authentically of the Mother of God, the extraordinary series of events that had taken place from 1973 to 1981 in a little lay convent within his diocese, at Akita. Hence in Akita we are dealing with a Church-approved intervention of Mary, as sure in this respect as Lourdes or La Salette or Fatima.

The events at Akita, authenticated then by Bishop Ito, began with miraculous occurrences clearly preparing the 42-year old Sister Agnes and the community around her for her role as messenger of Heaven. Then, all in 1973, there were three Messages. Finally to corroborate the Messages, the wooden statue of the Madonna in the convent wept human tears, literally and physically, 101 times, between April 1, 1975 and September 15, 1981, each time before numerous witnesses. Find a copy of the 202 page book Akita, The Tears and Messages of Mary, by Fr. Teiji Asuda, in order to find the eyewitness account, testimonies, and documents. Suffice it here to quote the third and no doubt most important of the three Messages:

> My beloved daughter, listen closely to what I now tell you and then inform your Superior. Just as I have said earlier, if Humanity does not repent and amend its ways, the Father will allow a supreme punishment to fall on the human race. The Father will inflict an unprecedented chastisement, more crushing than the

Deluge. Without the slightest doubt it will be a punishment such as has never yet been seen. Fire will plunge from the sky. By such calamity most of humanity will be annihilated. The clergy will perish, no less than the laity. Any who are spared will know such suffering and desolation that they will envy the dead. The only defenses remaining then will be the Rosary and the Sign given by the Son.

Every day pray the Rosary on behalf of the Bishops and Priests. The wiles of the devil invade even the Church, which is torn by internal strife. Cardinals will rise against cardinals and bishops will confront bishops. Priests who venerate me will be despised, combated and vilified. The altars and churches will be vandalized. The Church will abound with agents of compromise. Numerous priests and religious, seduced by the temptations of the devil, will betray their vows and desert their sacred call to serve the Lord. The devil will most specifically target those souls which are dedicated to God the Father.

The perdition of so many souls is the root of my Sorrow. If sins persist, and even intensify beyond the current level, then even the forgiveness of sins will finally vanish.

What sign "of the Son" is being referred to halfway through this Message is still unclear: maybe the Cross, maybe the Holy Eucharist. The last sentence is at first puzzling, insofar as we all know that as long as one priest is still alive, the availability of confession is still there, but who can deny that the actuality of confession is virtually disappearing in the mainstream Church? I am told the American National Conference of Catholic Bishops issued about one week ago a White Paper on the disappearance of confession in the USA, which in effect merely compounded the problem by bracketing out the sacramental life! No, the Third Message of Akita is right on target.

"But it is depressing." Personally I find such a return to reality in today's miasma of all-round blasphemy, lies and fantasy like a breath of oxygen in a putrid atmosphere. What matters, obviously, is not when or how we die, but whether or not we die with the grace of God in our souls. Such a Message is a forcible reminder to be prepared. Said American patriot, Patrick Henry: "For my part, whatever anguish of spirit it may cost, I am willing to know the whole truth, to know the worst, and to prepare for it."

"But no Catholic is obliged to believe in private revelations." True, but through Lourdes, a private revelation, tens or hundreds of thousands of souls must have been saved. If the Mother of God intervenes, and if a serious Catholic bishop officially authenticates her intervention, and if it is grave, how can we say it is unimportant?

"But there is nothing we can do about it anyway." Untrue. Nobody better than Catholics can react religiously. The salvation of the world is in the hands of Catholics. Especially in Lent Catholics can apply themselves with a renewed zeal to doing their duty in whatsoever state of life it has pleased God to place them. "Do your duty, and all will be well," said Pius X. "Your daily duty is your penance," said Our Lady of Fatima to the three children (How true today!). "Pray, hope and do not worry," said Padre Pio.

NO. 82 | APRIL 1, 1990

Sedevacantism Not Obligatory

A**N INTERESTING BOOK** is just becoming available to Catholics in the English-speaking world, thanks to our friends who publish the monthly *Catholic* in Australia.

The book is called *Peter, Lovest Thou Me?*, and it was written in French two years ago by an Ecône seminarian, Abbe Daniel le Roux. Its subtitle is, *John Paul II, Pope of Tradition or Pope of Revolution?* The book sets out to answer this question, relying on literally hundreds of textual quotations from John Paul II's own speeches and writings, so connected and grouped together as to bring out the steady line of thought underlying them.

Now any one of these quotations or even a whole speech, taken on its own, might by a devout Catholic be given a benign interpretation, because one of the two faces of a Liberal Catholic is Catholic, and so his words can often be given a Catholic sense. But when, as in this book, the quotations are all put together, one after another, so that a coherent pattern emerges, and when this pattern is confirmed by a series of photographs of the man acting in accordance with that thought pattern, then something emerges with devastating clarity: this man does not have a Catholic mind.

Of course Abbe le Roux is not the first writer to have noticed this, but he may be the first to have laid out the evidence in quite such a devastating fashion. That is why a friend wrote to me recently: "Though 'PLTM' is an excellent book, I do fear that it can lead substantial credence to the 'Pope is not Pope' faction, if we neglect to defend the Society's position."

The position of the Society to which our friend is referring is that despite many hereticising words and deeds of Popes Paul VI and JP2 in particular, nevertheless the Society holds them to have been or to be Popes unless and until clear proof emerges to the contrary. On the other hand those who consider that their heresies have disqualified them from being Pope are called "sedevacantists," a word taken from the Latin expression "sedes vacans," meaning that the Apostolic See is vacant.

The SSPX has from the beginning rejected sedevacantism and continues to do so. Catholics are told that if they find any Society priest taking that position, he is out of line with the Society, and in fact numbers of Society priests have left the Society, or forced their own dismissal, because of their aggressive sedevacantism.

Like the SSPX, many Traditional Catholics instinctively reject sedevacantism. Their arguments may be simple but they are not false for all that: how could the Catholic Church, designed by Our Lord to be a visible structure, long survive without a visible head? For instance, if the Popes since 1958 or 1963 have been invalid Popes, how can they have appointed valid Cardinals? And if there are few valid Cardinals, how can another valid Pope ever be elected? Apparently inextricable difficulties for the survival of the structure and so of the very Church. Again, if there is no Pope, who will consecrate

Russia to the Immaculate Heart? It will be done, said Our Lord in 1931, but it has not yet been done. One may also think that it is only by the divine promise to Peter that the liberalism of these recent Popes has been held back from completely wrecking the Church, as when the democratising Paul VI defused collegiality with the famous Note added to *Lumen Gentium,* or when after looking like liberalizing contraception, he finally condemned it with *Humanae Vitae.* Not to be forgotten is that these Popes are still Catholic enough to be hated by ultra-liberals.

Yet good Catholics do fall into sedevacantism. Many, because of a false dilemma. They say: if he is Pope he must be obeyed; if he need not be obeyed then he cannot be Pope. The error here is an error on obedience. The truth is that absolute obedience in everything is owed to no superior except to God (a tape and a flyer are always available from the Seminary on the question of true and false obedience). I am perfectly entitled to "disobey" the Pope when he gives me an unlawful order, but that does not entitle me to disobey his lawful orders.

Others fall into sedevacantism because they are afraid that to hold these liberal Popes to be true Popes is somehow to minimize the damage these Popes are doing to the Church, just as some fear that to say that the Novus Ordo Mass can be valid is to affirm its harmlessness. But the contrary is true: to say that the Novus Ordo Mass can be valid is to explain how its poison avoids being rejected outright by Catholics and so how it succeeds in doing so much harm; similarly to say that these liberal Popes are still Popes is to explain precisely how they retain so much power to damage the Church. Archbishop Lefebvre says there is nothing worse than a liberal on the See of Peter.

However, what traps a number of Catholics in sedevacantism is an apparently logical argument –

- Step One: the recent occupants of the See of Peter hereticize, i.e., they say and do things which are heretical.

- Step Two: He who hereticizes is a heretic.

- Step Three: Every heretic is cut off from the Mystical Body of Christ, or the Church.

- Step Four: Whoever is cut off from the Body cannot possibly be its head.

- Conclusion: These hereticizing "Popes" cannot still be Popes.

On this argument there are many things to be said, but there is not much space left this month to say them, so we may have to come back to the question next month, or another time. Meanwhile, let me be brief.

Step One of the argument is incontestable. The great value of Abbe le Roux' book is that it places squarely before us the evidence. Woe unto those poor Catholics who think there is no problem for the Catholic Faith in what these recent Popes say and do! Such Catholics are at least losing their grip on their Faith.

It is between Step Two and Step Three that the major weakness of the argument arises. True, whoever hereticizes is at least a material heretic, i.e., one who speaks or acts against Catholic truth without realizing it or without meaning to do so; but he is not yet a formal heretic, i.e., one who consciously and pertinaciously denies what he knows to be revealed Catholic truth. However, to be cut off by heresy from the Mystical Body, or excommunicated, one has to be at least a formal heretic. From which it follows that by no means everyone who hereticizes is thereby excommunicated. So both Paul VI and

JP2 may well hereticize, but that does not as such suffice to cut them out of the Church.

That is not the only weak link in the essential chain by which the sedevacantists who argue bind themselves and seek to bind others. For instance, because of Christ's words to Peter, "I have prayed for thee, that thy faith fail not: and thou being once converted, confirm thy brethren" (Lk. 22: 32), the Church has great theologians who question even the possibility of the Pope's falling into formal heresy, let alone the fact, and indeed Abbe le Roux's book should be read with these words of Our Lord always in mind. But read the book!

May Passiontide remind us that Our Lord's way of overcoming the evil all around is by good, and may Eastertide be as joyful supernaturally as the springtime is naturally!

NO. 83 | MAY 4, 1990

Rome Puts Out Feelers

THE END OF last month saw another of those beautiful Society occasions when, after celebrating last November in Paris Archbishop Lefebvre's 60th Priestly Jubilee, it celebrated on April 29 in Friedrichshafen in South Germany its own twentieth anniversary.

Twenty years! Exactly speaking, a little less than 20 years from the SSPX's official founding an November 1, 1970, when His Excellency Bishop Charriere, the then Bishop of Fribourg, Geneva and Lausanne, gave his entirely official approval as Diocesan Bishop to the founding Statutes of the fledgling International Priestly Fraternity of St. Pius X, but still, a little more than 20 years from the time when the ecclesiastically much-decorated Archbishop Lefebvre renounced his well-earned retirement in Rome, and began gathering around him in Fribourg, Switzerland, the few Church students who would be the first in a line of, later, hundreds upon hundreds of Society seminarians and priests.

It is an astonishing story when one looks back on it. From tiny beginnings, against all odds, against in particular the mighty opposition of Rome which is normally – and rightly, but not this time – decisive within the Catholic Church, to a position of worldwide prominence, as stable as is possible without the Pope's continued backing; and all this over these twenty years when something like an ever more violent tidal wave of evil has washed across the face of the earth – it is an astonishing story and well worth celebrating.

The Archbishop himself, now 84, came from Switzerland for the occasion, and celebrated the Pontifical Solemn High Mass, lasting between three and four hours, and including a substantial sermon, delivered as usual without notes. Imagine a beautiful late April Sunday morning in one of those picture-postcard southern German towns situated on the northern shore of Lake Constance, amidst rolling hills and well-tended fields so thick at this time of year with dandelions massing to glorify the month of Mary, that from a distance the pasture-land looks yellow instead of green – such was the setting.

In one of those large modern exhibition halls, the Society's German brothers and seminarians from Zaitzkofen had erected an altar beneath a 20-foot tall image of the Mother of God, surrounded with banks of thousands of white and yellow flowers – but not dandelions!

The entry procession, lasting itself a full 25 minutes and including all four new bishops, wended its way towards the altar through a crowd best estimated at about 8,000 people, but that may not include the numerous children, so numerous as to be specially mentioned by the Archbishop in his sermon. The mood of the people throughout the Mass, which was impeccably executed by the Society's German priests and seminarians, was quiet, attentive, devout. The Archbishop noticed the difference from 1976 when, in the autumn following the "hot summer" of his own "suspension" by Pope Paul VI, in the thick of controversy, the Society held its first major public celebration in Germany, also a Pontifical Solemn

High Mass in Friedrichshafen. The crowd had then been larger, maybe 10,000 people, but many had come out of curiosity, even antagonism. In 1976 the Archbishop had sent out like a clarion call to rally the broken ranks of Catholics bewildered in the wake of the Council; in 1990 he was like consoling and confirming the ranks he had done so much to reform. Friedrichshafen 1976 may have been as much an end of the pre-Council as a beginning of the post-Council; Friedrichshafen 1990 had nothing about it of a breakup or end. With so many young people, it was essentially a future.

Accordingly the Archbishop who a few weeks before the ceremony had wondered if he would have the strength to be the celebrant, after the ceremony gave little sign of tiredness. Returning afterwards to his German hosts, in no hurry to rest, he who speaks no German happily chatted for a while with them, who speak little French! "I have meat to eat which you know not . . . my meat is to do the will of him that sent me." (Jn. 4: 32, 34)

The occasion then seemed to have given heart to the Archbishop. What a dream it would be if orderly and powerful Germany would reunite in the Catholic spirit shown in Friedrichshafen on April 29! Today, men will not have it so, neither the forward-pushing liberal materialists of the West, nor the backtracking communist materialists of the East. However, "Der Mensch denkt, Gott lenkt," man proposes, God disposes. Tomorrow, God may have it so, notwithstanding.

And Rome today? The Archbishop said in his sermon at Friedrichshafen that there was no hope of any Roman turnaround for the moment. If Rome is now allowing in certain cases the old Mass, that is in contradiction with their profession of faith in the Council, and in the spirit of the Council, expressed in the new Mass which is the destruction of the old. Catholics accepting compromises with this Rome will soon find themselves obliged to accept the new Mass, he said.

In private the Archbishop added that the rumor had recently gone around Rome that he wanted to be reconciled with Rome. Cardinal Oddi immediately telephoned Ecône to offer to act as intermediary, all the Archbishop need do is write a little letter of apologies, he said. "But," replied the Ecône priest picking up the call, "it is not as simple as that. The problem is one of the Faith, not just of discipline." "Oh, no, no," protested the Cardinal. But when asked if he had read Cardinal Ratzinger's profoundly uncatholic book on principles of theology which appeared a few years ago, Cardinal Oddi admitted he had not. In truth, however well-intentioned and benevolent towards the Society Cardinal Oddi may be, he clearly has no idea, but no idea, of what the whole dispute is about! The same holds for the "best" of his colleagues.

Archbishop Lefebvre said he had also received an affectionate letter from his old pupil and friend, Cardinal Thiandoum, expressing the desire to meet him and to do anything he could to help towards a reconciliation. The Archbishop said he had replied that after 25 years of battle between the Council and Catholicism, there was no question of reopening the dialogue so long as the Council's errors held sway in Rome. Since then he has not heard again from Cardinal Thiandoum, no doubt a dear man. "For they are all honorable men," as Mark Anthony said – speaking of Julius Caesar's assassins!

A third feeler from Rome reached the Archbishop through none other than Dom Gerard, head of the French Benedictine monastery, famous among Traditionalists until it compromised with Rome immediately after the episcopal consecrations two years ago. The feeler gave the Archbishop to understand that Rome would be ready to receive him.

It is a thorn in Rome's flesh, commented the Archbishop, to have to admit the almost complete failure of its efforts to break Tradition by means of the Fraternity of St. Peter, "*Ecclesia Dei*," and so on. That Fraternity's head, said the Archbishop, came recently to the USA to visit out West a retired American bishop, more than sympathetic with St. Peter's Fraternity. The Fraternity's head had hoped that this bishop would be able to help in gathering together in the USA the American seminarians of St. Peter's who have run into great difficulties over in Europe (One of them wrote to me two months ago that the main difficulty causing him to leave was that St. Peter's did not seem to know where it was going – copy of the letter on request, I am sure the author would not mind). The bishop out West duly contacted the two most likely colleagues of his in the USA, but both refused . . .

It is painful for Rome to run up against this opposition of the bishops, said the Archbishop, for Rome is looking for a way to do away with us, and they would prefer to do it by dialogue, because that is their way. However, Cardinal Ratzinger now recognizes that as long as there is no Tradition in Rome, there will be no dialogue. Alas, concluded the Archbishop, they and we just do not have the same notion of what Catholic Tradition is.

As the Archbishop recognizes but some Romans do not, what we have here is what the French call a dialogue of the deaf, for as the Latin axiom has it, when you disagree on basics, what is there to discuss? Interesting meanwhile to note that whereas the Archbishop used to go to Rome, since the "excommunications" it is Rome which is coming to the Archbishop. As another French proverb has it, "caress him and he will bite you, bite him and he will caress you."

Now, dear Americans, I have a bite that the Society needs you to take. The Society's own Sisters are urgently in need of a new home for their Novitiate, presently housed in Armada, Michigan. Their efforts to find somewhere have till now proved so vain that they are sorely tempted to build. But that is absurd when one thinks on the one hand of today's building costs, on the other hand that convents today are falling empty all over this wide land, and many must be being sold at knockdown prices. Remember what you did for us? A palace for less than $400,000! Can you not do the same for the Sisters? They are looking for a building with anywhere around 35 to 50 rooms, with a measure of isolation, in about 10 to 20 acres if possible, with refectory and chapel in particular, with preferably not too long a winter. Surely some such convent building can be found by one of you? These handmaids of Christ deserve a home of their own.

Enclosed you will find a flyer for the Seminary's booklet and tape on Gregorian Chant, and another flyer for the Ordination and first Masses of the new American priests two of whom are due to be ordained in Winona on Saturday, June 23, by Bishop Bernard Fellay. Pray for good weather, and come in large numbers. How about a crowd of 8,000 on this side of the Atlantic? If you have never attended the ordination of a priest, it is a unique experience to see before your eyes a man who is not a priest become one with all the awesome powers of the Catholic priesthood: one of those men without whom everything is doomed to ruin.

May Our Lady obtain for your priestly candidates graces proportional to their needs, and may she obtain for yourselves consolation to match her lovely month of May.

NO. 84 | JUNE 4, 1990

The Modernist Church Self-Destructing

A FRIEND OF ours in New York has interesting things to say about the situation evolving within the Catholic Church. Here he is:

> In the United States the Church is not drifting, it is moving arrow-straight in a certain direction – the destruction of the priesthood. More and more people are becoming aware that the aim of those in control is to eliminate the sacramental priesthood, and level it down with the people.
> Amongst the U.S. bishops there is a strong body of opinion for doing away with priestly celibacy. The U.S. bishops have been holding private meetings with representatives of two organizations of ex-priests, "Corpus" and the "Fellowship of Christian Ministry." One-hundred and fifty-two U.S. bishops have already signed in private a common agreement that they will incorporate married clergy in their dioceses, provided they overcome Rome's objections. Some of the Roman authorities involved have shown themselves willing listeners, based on an argument derived from the Pope's admission of Anglican clergymen with families to ordination and to pastoral activities.

Richard N. Williamson

In July of this year, these U.S. bishops will meet in San Jose, California, to discuss in particular the acceptance of ex-priests back into the active priesthood. Representatives of "Corpus" and "F.C.M." will be there.

Over the crisis of homosexuality showing itself in the ranks of the U.S. clergy, the U.S. bishops will do nothing. This year they paid out over $100 million in out of court settlements. The homosexuals have established a powerful networking within the clergy.

The Maryknoll priests, working with the Fellowship of Christian Ministry and in concert with the bishops, will launch a campaign of petitions and studies for deaconesses and married priests, to be discussed at the bishops' meeting in November, along with the ordination of women.

Here in New York, Cardinal O'Connor and Bishop Daly are prevaricating on the issue. The sense is being lost of what the priesthood is. Recently the U.S. Bishops' Liturgy Committee was asked whether the "Body of Christ," said by the priest to a Catholic on giving him Communion, means "This is the Body of Christ." No, came back the answer, it means the Community of Christ, and the Committee moreover forbade priests to say "This is the Body of Christ." Soon Catholics will find it hard to go to Communion.

The bishop of Tallahassee refers to the old-fashioned priests as 'slaughter-house priests,' presumably because they celebrate Mass as a sacrifice. However, grace is at work in the young priests who never knew the Tridentine Mass but are beginning now to celebrate it. One of them said to me recently, 'it is a complete disorder to celebrate Mass facing the people'.

In Rome, a few things are now clear to most people. The official Commission for Tradition, "*Ecclesia Dei*," has become a bad joke, ineffectual. There are no celebrets issued unless the recipient is also willing to celebrate the Novus Ordo Mass or to adulterate the Tridentine Mass. Cardinals Gagnon and Mayer have their heads on the block. The Fraternity of St. Peter will be used and abused. Individual priests who follow Tradition on their own are good but uncoordinated. That leaves the Society of St. Pius X, whose continuing success despite all Rome's efforts is stuck like a bone in Rome's gullet – Rome cannot swallow the Society down, nor cough it up!

Concerning Fatima there is a complete collapse in Rome. They would like to suppress it totally. Last August the entire Apostolic Delegation in Lisbon was changed. The previous Apostolic Delegate was favorable to Fatima. His replacement hates Fatima. A watchdog has been set on Sister Lucia.

As for Pope John Paul II, his position in the Church is more precarious than ever. More and more members of the Curia are against him. He wanted to sign into existence a Traditional Ordinariat, but there was a fight, and he let himself be overwhelmed. He will not wield his authority.

Similarly, Cardinal Ratzinger did not dare to write the preface, as he wished, to the American edition of an excellent book called "Celibacy in East and West" which demonstrates that priestly celibacy as a historical fact goes right back to the Apostles. Ratzinger is behaving as though he is impotent. He so lacks courage in defending the Faith as to place in question his own faith.

When all is said and done, it is a crisis of authority. The Pope will not wield it. Ratzinger cannot. The disarray in the Curia is something awful. We have mental disequilibrium in the highest places. The word has gone out to kill off Tradition, by fair means or foul.

However, more and more people are realizing that Archbishop Lefebvre was right when he said, there are antichrists in Rome. As people see the Church and the priesthood being destroyed, so they are changing their minds about the episcopal consecrations and the entire Society of St. Pius X. This is a great opportunity for the Society. Its stance is everything. But please, no arrogance, no fanaticism, no blindness. The Society may have two to five years to capitalize on this situation.

Richard N. Williamson

How? The direct confrontation of June, 1988, is, in a certain way, a thing of the past. The Society has kept all its principles and all the strength of its belief. People believe a believer. And, given the failing condition of the Church structure, people are getting desperate. The rising hunger for truth and spirituality amongst the laity, priests and a small quota of bishops is an opening for the Society. Without the Society diluting its Faith or principles, let it only be a little conciliatory in its manner, and there is a rich harvest awaiting it.

The two-week Confirmation tour of the United States which I completed a few days ago confirms that there is a harvest awaiting, but not yet being gathered in. The Society's priests in the USA are working hard, and the Society's churches and centers are holding firm, *Deo Gratias*, but these centers are few and far between, and no doubt large numbers of Catholics in distress are still hanging back from the Society, afraid of moving "outside" the Church. The harvest is surely ripening but not yet ripe. Patience.

Most encouraging on this tour was to meet four non-Society priests who were in the Novus Ordo but are now working with or alongside the Society. For a variety of reasons such priests can prefer to gallop alongside rather that jump on board the Society's freight-train, "going so fast!" That does not prevent them from recovering, had they lost it, the true sense of their priesthood in ministering to real faithful with the true Sacraments. One of them, 25 years a priest, said to me he had never been so happy in his priesthood as these last two years when he has returned to the Tridentine Mass and picked up a demanding Society Mass circuit! A tiring, luminous, happy life.

As for the Society's own workers for the harvest, three seminarians were ordained subdeacons here on Whitsun Eve. Quality will have to make up for the lack of quantity. It seems clear that to bring in the harvest mentioned above, many non-Society priests will be needed. How God will provide will be a wondrous spectacle.

Meanwhile the seminary draws to the end of another school year. We thank all of you that have faithfully supported us through the year. This letter does not each month express our gratitude, but if it comes to you each month, it is to give you some return on your support. May the Sacred Heart repay you.

In His happy, tiring and luminous service.

NO. 85 | JULY 1, 1990

Sedevacantism Fails to Grasp Modern Mind-Rot

THREE MONTHS AGO I wrote in this letter that I might come back to the question of sedevacantism. Since then one lady wrote to discourage me from doing so on the grounds that it raises unnecessary and hurtful questions in many people's minds. It would be more loyal to the Holy Father simply to ask for prayers for him, she said.

However, the problem set by the recent Popes is already very much there in many Catholics' minds, and so is the hurt – witness the variety of more or less wild explanations to which they are liable to have recourse: the drugged Pope, the prisoner Pope, or dummy Pope, the KGB Pope, the Freemason Pope, etc. Notice that each of these explanations, seen from the correct angle, has a grain of truth; for instance, these Popes are like drugged with their utopian dreams, and they are impregnated with freemasonic ideals. Nevertheless, these explanations do not leave the Catholic mind at peace because they raise more problems than they solve.

There are then two reasons to lay out in a longer letter than usual what is surely the true solution: the main reason is to give in general an explanation as satisfying as possible of the mystery of these occupants of the See of Peter doing so much damage to the Church, and this explanation not out of disloyalty to the Holy Father, but on the contrary out of loyalty, namely in the hope of helping Catholic minds to ride out in peace the present storm and to stay by the Pope's side without falling into his errors; the accessory reason is to resolve in particular the main argument or objection of the sedevacantists.

Let us begin by recalling that argument: "The recent Popes say and do heretical things (such as would have earned instant excommunication had any Catholic bishop said or done them 50 years ago). Now heretics are outside the Church. Therefore these Popes are not even members of the Church, let alone true Popes." Recall also the solution very briefly given three months ago: a Catholic who says and does heretical things is a material heretic, or has in him all the material of a heretic, but that material does not form into a proper or formal heretic, such as is excluded from the Church, until he is "pertinacious" (Old Code, c. 1325 c2), i.e., fully aware that he is denying revealed Catholic dogma.

The question we want to go into here and now is how a number of these intelligent and capable Church leaders, apparently of good will and despite being trained before Vatican II, can still be unaware that they are flouting eternal Catholic truth. In one word, the answer is – Liberalism.

Proceeding from the craze for Liberty to the refusal of reality, Liberalism in its ultimate form is a mind-rot whereby a mind becomes capable of thinking and saying and doing totally contradictory things. Starting out from Nominalism and Protestantism, building up over centuries of intellectual corruption, this mind-rot achieved its greatest victory for Satan when it penetrated the Church 100 years ago in the form of modernism.

Pope Pius X did his best to root it out, but it so grew back that now his successors are destroying the Church while convinced they are saving it! Let us look at the case of JP2.

Biographical data, as given for instance in *Peter Lovest Thou Me?*, show that Karol Wojtyla, born in 1920, was one in a long line of Catholics seeking to come to an understanding or compromise with that world which, insofar as it is "seated in wickedness" (I Jn. 5: 19), is always opposed to the Church. Such Catholics are especially numerous in our own generation, because the Church has now for nigh on 500 years been fighting the Great Apostasy building up through Protestantism, Liberalism and Communism especially, and it has been a tiring fight, and apparently it has been a fight in vain, because the Apostasy just seems to go on winning. So when the Devil makes the world look reasonable and attractive, the temptation to make a deal with him and with it can become overpowering.

However, if one was, like the Polish Karol Wojtyla, born in a country and culture steeped in the benefits of Mother Church, there is no question of simply abandoning her. On the contrary, one believes in her, one even believes profoundly in the goodness of what she does. Hence what one believes in most profoundly of all is a mixture of the world and of the Church; a combination of everything admirable in the modern world with everything admirable in Mother Church, for one is profoundly convinced that since both are so admirable, they cannot be irreconcilable; on the contrary, all that is needed is a new synthesis of the two, a synthesis that everyone is waiting for.

Alas, the last five centuries are littered with the wreckage of such syntheses, for the very simple reason that in our age the essence of what is modern, as modern, is independence from God, diametrically opposed to Catholicism's dependence upon God. Hence all such syntheses break down, as so many efforts to mix oil and water. Nevertheless, for as long as men will let themselves be mothered by the Church and seduced by the world, such efforts will continue. Thus from the time that the young intellectual Karol Wojtyla entered the clergy as a seminarian in his early 20's, he was attempting to put together a philosophy which would blend Catholic with modern thinking, Thomism with existentialism and personalism.

Here we must pause for a moment to explain what we mean by "philosophy" in men's minds. Generally speaking what passes for philosophy today is such arrant nonsense that philosophy is discredited as a whole, and people think that all philosophy is nonsense. But if one takes a man's philosophy to be the mental framework of his grasp of reality, then obviously every man does have some "philosophy," and that "philosophy" is central to his way of thinking and so of living.

Now the philosophy in this real sense (mental grip on reality), which is natural to all men, is to subordinate their minds to reality outside of them. If I see one tree outside the window, I do not pretend I see three. That is common sense, magnificently protected and developed in depth by Catholic thinkers, especially St. Thomas Aquinas from whom the Church's favorite philosophy, Thomism, takes its name. However, modern man likes no kind of subordination. With Protestantism he began by liberating himself from subordination to the Catholic Church, but even when he had gone on to liberate himself from Jesus Christ and from God, he still had to liberate his mind from the ultimate outside domination, from any outside reality imposing itself on his mind. From here arose modern philosophy whereby reality is no longer what is, but what I feel, what I like, or what I want. I thus make the ultimate declaration of independence: I declare myself henceforth independent of any reality I do not like. This is the ultimate Liberation philosophy, or Liberalism.

Now you may object that such detachment from reality is madness. You are right. Modern philosophy is ideologically insane. But not clinically – at least not straightaway! Whereas a clinically mad man has become involuntarily mad and can no longer choose what he takes for reality, your modern philosopher is voluntarily and selectively mad, that is to say, he readily admits that his cup of coffee is real coffee, because if he felt it was poison, he might become rather thirsty! So amongst all the realities around him, he readily admits to be real those that serve his purpose, but he carefully denies to be real anything that diminishes his own rights, independence, or dignity. Thus he has made himself the master of reality, reality is no longer the master of him. From which logically follows the lunacy, to each man his own reality, as it suits him.

It is not difficult to see how such a philosophy completely unhinges the Catholic Faith. By that Faith, a series of supernatural truths, in perfect synchronization with all natural truths, are presented to my mind, in just the same way that those natural truths are presented, from outside my mind. Now, I may refuse to submit my mind to Jesus Christ being God just like I may refuse to submit my mind to there being one tree and not three outside the window, but the Catholic knows that even if everyone (including himself!) denied it, Jesus would still be God, just as common sense knows that even if the emperor and all his men denied it, there would still be only one tree and not three outside the window. Things supernatural and natural are what they are, independently of our minds.

But imagine now these supernatural truths presenting themselves before the bar of the mind of a Liberal

Catholic whose frame of thinking, or philosophy, is modern: "Eternal hell exists" – now, do I feel that? Definitely not! How could God be so cruel, etc? And so I plunge into heresy, for in Greek heresy means choosing, and with my modern philosophy of feeling truth, I am well into choosing what of the Catholic "Faith" is true for me and what is not. Moreover, "Jesus Christ is God" – now do I feel that? Yes? Then it is true. But do you not feel it? No? Then for you it is not true. From which logically follows the lunacy of ecumenism, to each man his own religion, as it suits him – any religion is good for any man who feels it.

The Catholic Faith is of course devastated in such a mind. However, the devastation goes much further than just the denial of certain dogmatic truths. When a Protestant refuses certain Catholic truths, he admits it, he is even proud of it, he puts himself outside the Catholic Church and if he attacks the Catholic Faith, he can only attack from outside. On the contrary your Liberal Catholic with a modern philosophy, or your modernist, logically does not admit there are Catholic Truths out there that he is refusing, so he does not admit that he is outside the Church, rather he is convinced he is an improved (updated) Catholic and that he has a mission, from inside the Church which he has not left, to "improve" the rest of the Church.

No wonder then that when Pope St. Pius X denounced modernism at the beginning of this century, he did so in the strongest possible terms – what could be more deadly for the Church than having within the gates such a deceptive and self-deceiving enemy as modernism?

Alas, that question has an answer: more deadly still is the renovated modernism, or neo-modernism, of the 1960's! For of course when the original modernists of the 1900's came under the Pope's hammer, consistently with their system, they did not "feel" the condemnation was true, so finding the condemnation had nevertheless made it difficult for them to "improve" the Church, they went underground to wait for better times, when the imperatives of being modern would have made enough Catholics sympathetic to having their Faith "improved."

Sure enough, this time came, in the 1960's. Pope John XXIII launched the Second Vatican Council, determined to "update" the Church, and Paul VI, profound believer in the modern world, enabled the neo-modernists, 1960's version, to gain virtually complete control of the Church. However, there was this crucial difference with the modernists of the 1900's; whereas the modernists of 1907 had had the Pope absolutely against them, the neo-modernists now had the Pope largely with them, as well as the whole modern world inside and outside the Church. So whereas a modernist after Pius X's condemnation could not have, at least in public, a good conscience, your neo-modernist after Vatican II could only in private have a bad conscience! The collective folly of the Church now bolstered him in his errors. (Of course the Lord God would not let Truth be silenced, but how could two old bishops be taken seriously against two thousand?).

Thus by the time Karol Wojtyla emerges from the Second Conclave of 1978 as the Conclave's elected choice and is acclaimed as Pope by the Universal Church, he finds neo-modernism firmly established in the upper ranks of the Church. And so what can he know "Catholicism" to be but this "improved" version which he himself strove with conviction to promote at Vatican II; which was shared with him by all the choice and master spirits of the Council; which duly prevailed in the Council and in its aftermath, and which he now finds accepted by virtually all Catholics except a numerically insignificant minority (that's us)?

In which case from 1978 on, whom does he find that can get through to him that his "Catholicism" is way off track? Nobody above him who could do it with authority, because he now is the supreme (albeit tiara-less) authority. Nor is there anybody alongside him or beneath him to protest that his thinking is heretical, because his predecessor Paul VI has deliberately cowed or crushed within the Church all opposition to the "improved" Catholicism. Then who or what remains to tell him his thinking is not Catholic? Only a scattered handful of universally discredited "followers of Lefebvre" (that's us). While a mass of "conservative" Catholics by their support, and a mass of radicals by their revolt, give him to think that his stand is not Liberal but altogether Catholic!

In which case how can he still know for instance that his ecumenism is flouting Catholic dogma? It takes mind-rot to believe all he teaches and to believe it is Catholic, but that mind-rot is in him and all round him, so one may well believe he is basically unaware of how he is wholly undermining Catholic dogma. But just as a man who unawares tells an untruth is not properly a liar, so a man who unawares flouts Catholic dogma is not properly (formally) a heretic. So JP2 may well be destroying the Church with his ecumenism, but until he wakes out of his Liberal dream and becomes aware of the fact, he is not by formal heresy out of the Church (and one may well think that if he did become aware of what he is doing, he would change course). Hence the main sedevacantist argument falls to the ground.

But Mother Church's crucifying problem remains – assuming that mind-rot has so engulfed the Catholic hierarchy ("Satan reaching to the very summits of the Church"), what is the way out? How can it all end?

Humanly, the situation is irredeemable. Man has dug himself into a pit he can no longer get himself out of. When he will admit as much, and beg for God's saving help, God will step in and save him from his folly. As for the Catholic Church, no question but that salvation will come through the Pope. "Satan hath desired to have you (plural – Apostles) that he may sift you as wheat: but I have prayed for thee (singular – Peter), that thy faith fail not: and thou, being once converted, confirm they brethren."(Lk. 22: 31,32)

When Peter ran away in the Garden of Gethsemane and then thrice denied his Master, his faith failed massively but not totally; he converted, and built his Master's Church. JP2's faith, one may argue, has massively but not totally failed; he (or his successor) will convert, and at that moment the Pope will need a support system to rebuild the Church in the true Faith. At that moment when he converts, a totally new rainbow coalition of until then scattered sheep, many Traditionalists, some Fatimists, some anti-abortionists, some sedevacantists, some Novus Ordo Catholics, some Papists, etc., will rally around him (and many that are last will be first and first will be last), but the kernel of this support system must be the Traditionalists who, with all their faults, have never betrayed the true Mass and the true priesthood which are the uranium in the reactor of the Church, and to which the Church cannot not come back. Therefore our function in the Mystical Body of Christ is to not let go one jot or tittle of Catholic Tradition until the rest of the Church sweeps back to reclaim it, and to fulfill this sacred function we must, as Our Lord said to Peter in the same Garden, in the same hour of Satan and power of darkness, watch and pray. "Every day pray the Rosary for bishops and priests," especially the Bishop of Rome. Lady, you are right: readers, pray for our poor Pope.

And those of you with children of school age, think hard of sending them to St. Mary's Academy in Kansas – flyer enclosed. The new Rector sent away many children last year, and no doubt each child sent away was an unfortunate case, but with each child sent away there could be more clearly seen the emerging outline of a proper Catholic school capable of attracting the parents worth attracting.

Take courage. The storm is still rising, but it will make some first-class sailors for Heaven!

Archbishop Lefebvre Charged with Racism

A NUMBER OF you know that on June 21 Archbishop Lefebvre was tried in front of a French civil court on a charge of "racism" for remarks he had made last November concerning the flow of Mohammedans into France. Judgment was given on July 12: the Archbishop was acquitted of "racism," but was condemned to pay a 5,000 franc fine (about $850), and to publish the court's judgment in two newspapers, because he had "defamed" the Muslim community. (Probably his sharpest remark referred to the Mohammedans' practice of kidnapping European girls for their harems in cities which they dominate).

This judgment, apparently a compromise, may or may not satisfy the parties to the lawsuit. On the one hand the plaintiff, Licra (International League Against Racism and Antisemitism), may appeal in an attempt to make its accusation of racism stick; on the other hand Archbishop Lefebvre could counter-appeal by proving that what he said about the Mohammedans was not defamatory but factual.

Now, given that Archbishop Lefebvre spent over thirty of the best years of his life in service of the Catholic

Church in black Africa, why should Licra, whose President is a Jew of the same venerable age as the Archbishop, wish to prove him a "racist"? Cardinal Thiandoum, Archbishop Lefebvre's French African colleague and successor as Archbishop of Dakar, wrote a public letter before the June 21 trial to a well-known French editor, Jean Madiran, to encourage him in his defense of the Archbishop's cause:

> Dear Mr. Madiran,
> Let me firstly greet you in Jesus Christ and express my fraternal communion with you in his. I was truly "disgusted" to learn of the decision taken by Licra to haul Msgr. Marcel Lefebvre, Archbishop, in front of the law-courts on a trumped-up charge of racism! I wish you to activate your talents as a man of letters, writer and Catholic to bring to naught such a perverse enterprise. I hope that the lawyer chosen by Msgr. Lefebvre will nullify the action being undertaken by Licra.
> I rejoiced profoundly at the way in which you refuted the charge of so-called racial discrimination leveled at Msgr. Lefebvre. If such a suit were filed in Africa, its authors would have been made to suffer for it! . . . In truth, as you have so well written, this trial is being directed, through Msgr. Lefebvre, at your country's Catholicism.
> I shall be grateful if you will keep me informed on this question. Meanwhile, since we are at the end of Holy Week, I wish you a Joyful Easter, thanking you in advance for all you will do to stop Licra's suit against a bishop.
> +Hyacinth Cardinal Thiandoum, Archbishop of Dakar

So in black Africa, says the African Cardinal, it is the "anti-racist" Licra which would have got into trouble for attacking the Archbishop, whereas in white France Licra gets a hearing and half a victory! What is going on?

A gigantic religious war is being waged for the hearts and souls of Frenchmen between two radically opposed

Richard N. Williamson

views of life and of the world, both religious but one pretending not to be: Catholicism and Secular Humanism. On this side of the Atlantic, columnist Patrick Buchanan admirably brings into focus the same clash behind many events in the USA; but in France, "eldest daughter of the Catholic Church," the clash is still sharper than here.

On the one side is the Catholic worldview: God exists, and He created a world of varied creatures, with order and inequality in their variety. That inequality in all creatures, as issuing from God's hand, is not punishment of any sins of theirs, but the variety in order and order in variety are designed to show forth the infinitely varied goodness of God Himself a little less inadequately than would a creation without any such inequality or variety (imagine a garden with only roses, an aviary with only eagles, a zoo with only lions, etc.). Wisdom therefore consists in working with this order of God and not against it; in acknowledging the differences and not denying them; in synchronizing the variety and not in leveling down the inequality.

On the other side is the Secular Humanist worldview: all inequality is injustice, so if any God exists who created such inequality, he or she deserves to be kicked out of his (or her) creation, and mankind must correct God's handiwork by leveling down all inequality and by denying all differences, for instance, of age, sex, class or race. Hence from ages 15 to 75, all will pretend to be 25; between man and woman all will pretend there is no difference; all social classes will be abolished; all racial differences will be ignored.

Now a minimum of common sense tells us that this latter worldview will be continually flying in the face of facts, but such common sense forgets that that is just what this worldview wishes to do; it wishes to rewrite the charter of the universe, and it would turn everything of God's upside down if it could – universal Revolution.

Hence behind the beautiful ideal of universal "equality," as preached today, stalks Luciferian revolt (not even in heaven will all men be equal, but all of us will be graded according to the degree of our charity). Similarly, behind the media's preaching of "anti-racism" stalks the diabolical desire to discredit and dissolve those nations which have in the past best served the Church, so making way for the world-triumph of those racists (sic) who have most fought the Church!

Hence the moment a Catholic prelate sets out to rally his fellow countrymen against the dissolution of their race or nation and the dilution of their Faith by the poisonous falsehoods of their politicians and their media, he must for the purposes of the Antichrist be immediately struck down, regardless of the facts. Hence Licra's accusations against Archbishop Lefebvre. Cardinal Thiandoum is right, but it took an African to see it, or at least to say it: Licra's real target is France's Catholicism. Again, that the poor secular humanists should be blind is normal, so to speak. What is grave is when Catholics every day ingurgitate their poison, for instance from the media. Readers, if you regularly frequent the media, do not be surprised if "anti-racism" seems to you the next best thing to patriotism – Televisio ejicienda est! Throw out that television set!

Then the SSPX is racist, you will say? Tele-idiot! Go back to Cardinal Thiandoum's remarks about Archbishop Lefebvre! Just two months ago the Archbishop flew down to his old stomping-ground in Gabon, the heart of French Equatorial Africa, to bless the Society's newly-built church in Libreville where the Society has a thriving mission. The ceremony was attended by 1,200 Africans. It takes a tele-idiot, or a maker of tele-idiots, to accuse anyone or anything Catholic of "racism"!

And may God bless you and give you and your families sane time of vacation.

NO. 87 | OCTOBER 1, 1990

Principles with Wolves' Teeth

ENCLOSED IS ANOTHER landmark conference of Archbishop Lefebvre. He is always, when one understands him, saying the same thing, but like a rock continually reappearing beneath the crash of the waves, he is, in today's riptide of sentimentality, steadily offering to the Catholic mind and soul a stable footing.

Addressing his priests just a few weeks ago in the motherhouse of the SSPX, he clearly sensed the danger coming to them once more from the left – the tug of Rome, the hurt of the continuing separation from the authorities in Rome, and now, since the summer of 1988, the additional hurt of division within Catholic Tradition's own ranks, and separation from close friends who left us then to rejoin Rome: can we not get together again, if not with Rome, at least with our friends? Why these divisions? Why all this divisiveness? Look at what Cardinal Ratzinger is doing for Tradition! Why do we need to shun those who are so close to us? Charity! Unity!

The Archbishop's answer is as clear as it is unsentimental: the Liberal Revolution of the last 200 years is directly opposed to Our Lord Jesus Christ. Rome is now in the hands of that Revolution. However well-meaning Cardinal Ratzinger may be, his principles are still those of the Liberal (freedom from God) Revolution. Hence to go over to him as did our former friends in 1988, is in fact to betray Our Lord Jesus Christ. We have a clear choice between Christ and the Revolution, and no friendships on earth entitle us to abandon Our Lord. Shaking hands with liberals is what has destroyed Christian civilization.

The great service rendered to us by the Archbishop is that he keeps discerning and uncovering the wolfish principles of liberalism beneath the layers and layers of sheepskin that are laid over those principles to disguise them. "We are reforming the Church," said the Protestants, as they tore the Church in half. "We are tightening up the Church," said the Jansenists, as they mixed Protestantism with Catholicism. "We are reaching out to the modern world," said the liberals, as they mixed the Post-Jansenist Revolution with Catholicism. "We are updating the Church," said the modernists at the beginning of this century, as they smuggled liberalism into the Church. "We are renewing the Church," said the bishops of Vatican II, as they double-talked modernism back into the Church. "And we are regularizing Catholic Tradition," say the Catholics who went off to put their Catholicism back under the officials of Vatican II.

As each successive sheepskin wore out and showed through, another was laid on. The same old wolves' teeth were always there to see, but is it not much nicer, sweeter, kinder, gentler, more loving and more caring to fondle sheepskin than to yell "Wolf!"? Well, when wolves are around, someone has to do some yelling, or there will soon be no more sheep around, nor even any sheepskins!

In his address of September 8th the Archbishop denounces for example the dear, good, kind, sincere and conservative Cardinal Ratzinger, not because he is dear, good, kind, sincere and conservative, but on the contrary because despite being dear, good, kind, sincere and conservative, he is also a flaming Revolutionary! (How are the two combinable? See last July's letter – by the each day deeper universality of liberal mind-rot.)

He is a flaming Revolutionary because despite his desire, evident throughout the "Instruction on the Ecclesial Vocation of the Theologian" (the document to which the Archbishop refers), to rein in the wild theologians who are causing the conservative Cardinal so much grief, still he turns round and gives them all they need by way of a stick with which to beat him to death! For – read carefully on page 5 the Cardinal's own words quoted from the *L'Osservatore Romano* by the Archbishop – the Cardinal takes immensely weighty decisions of Pope Pius IX and St. Pius X – it is easy to argue that Quanta Cura belongs to the Extraordinary Magisteriun which is infallible! – and reduces them to "provisional dispositions," "expressions of pastoral prudence," "substantial anchorages" whose "core is valid" but whose "individual details influenced by the circumstances at the time may need further rectification."

No marks for imagining the reaction of one of the "wild" theologians that the Cardinal is trying to get under control: "Dear Cardinal, no doubt the core of your Instruction is valid, and it is a fine expression of your pastoral prudence, a substantial anchorage in the problem of the Congregation of the Doctrine of the Faith for 1990. So as a provisional disposition, it is admirable but, you see, we theologians are looking to the future of the Church, and so we cannot take all those individual details of your Instruction seriously which we know have been influenced by the circumstances of 1990 and, therefore, need further rectification. Get lost."

And the Cardinal having taken upon himself to rectify out-of-date Popes, how can he resist the theologians rectifying himself, a mere Cardinal? The poor man has not left himself a leg to stand on! Poor man, because the conservative values which in most of the "Instruction" he valiantly tries to build up with his right hand, with one sweep of his left hand he knocks to pieces in this section quoted from his own presentation of the "Instruction." His right hand knows not what his left hand is doing. And he is – can you believe it? – the Prefect or Head of the Congregation for the Doctrine of the Faith, in other words the man in charge of guarding the Church's Catholic Faith! And here he is, absolutely undermining some of the most solemn declarations of that Faith! In vain Pope Pius IX raised his "Apostolic Voice" to "reprobate, denounce and condemn" all the errors laid out in *Quanta Cura*; here comes the good Cardinal to declare *Quanta Cura* to be a "provisional disposition" needing "further rectification!"

Poor man. More to the point, poor Church! The Faith being the basis of that by which a Catholic is a Catholic, and by which the Church is the Church, what is Mother Church going to do so long as such a man is entrusted with guarding her Faith? – go on being torn basically to pieces. Dear readers, you may not care for horror tales of wolves' odontology, but if in the coming storm our Faith rests upon the sands of sentimentality, it is going to be washed away, and our souls with it. We must build on rock, and keep before our minds what rock is.

Good news? Archbishop Lefebvre continues to be well. As you will read, he thinks all he has left to do is to die, but we shall see. He may even come on a brief visit to the USA in the spring. He will find at the seminary most of 36 old seminarians and the remainder of 15 now incoming seminarians. Pray if you like that these become lambs of God, but kindly pray also that they tear the sheepskins out of their minds! They and we will be praying the Rosary for you each day through the month of October.

NO. 88 | NOVEMBER 1, 1990

SSPX Celebrates 20 years

NOVEMBER 1 – this is the day on which 20 years ago the International Priestly Society of St. Pius X officially came into being, because it was on All Saints Day, 1970, that Bishop Charriere of the Swiss diocese of Geneva, Lausanne and Fribourg gave his canonical approval to the erection within his diocese of the Society as an institute of the Catholic Church.

What an extraordinary 20 years! About a one-hundredth part of the time elapsed since our Redemption by Our Lord Jesus Christ. Nearly 100 years ago his enemies were bragging: "We have long past taken care to discredit the priesthood of the goyim, and thereby to ruin their mission on earth, which in these days might still be a great hindrance to us. Day by day its influence on the peoples of the world is falling lower. Freedom of conscience has been declared everywhere, so that now only years divide us from the moment of the complete wrecking of that Christian religion . . .We shall set clericalism and clericals into such narrow frames as to make their influence move in retrogressive proportion to its former progress."

No doubt, by God's mercy, the great Pope from 1903 to 1914, St. Pius X, and the Popes who followed in the line he had traced out, Pius XI and Pius XII, slowed down the timetable of Our Lord's enemies, but there is equally no doubt that by God's justice, with the Second Vatican Council running from 1962 to 1965, these enemies took another giant step forward towards their goal, Satan's goal, the destruction of the Catholic Church.

Some Catholics reveled in the sea-change wrought within the Church by that Council – the new religion was "up to date." Other Catholics slowly grew used to it – after all, the new religion was rather easier than the old one. Others were uneasy with the new religion and remained uneasy, but they clung to the familiar surroundings of the Catholic institutions they had known, and which Our Lord's enemies had been cunning enough to leave standing at least as shells, it was merely the substance that had been emptied out.

These Catholics were – and are – like dock-workers in a seaside port which once was busy but now by a shift of the sea's currents is being left high and dry, miles inland. Busily they continue to operate the familiar cranes, and they run in and out of the warehouses they have known all their lives, but there is less and less water, there are fewer and fewer ships – the Faith is all the time ebbing away. But with these poor souls, operating yesterday's structures comes before locating where the Faith is to be found today. Here they are described by a friend of ours:

> One thing I have done this summer (1990) is to look critically at all the Catholic magazines and organizational statements that have come my way. They are all bankrupt, and they are all bankrupt for the same reason: they cannot see, or they refuse to see, the life-and-death struggle going on in the Church between the champions of Vatican II and the Traditionalists.

For of course from 1965 onwards, there was another group of Catholics who, as they saw the Faith ebbing out of subsidiary Church structures, instead of quitting the Faith, quit those structures, then made for the sea, and began rebuilding as best they could, but at any rate by the edge of the living waters of the Traditional Faith. There was no lack of sea, and no lack of seaside, yet there was – and is – a heap of abuse and mistreatment from the dock-workers who insisted on remaining stranded inland.

Such is the story of the SSPX, founded within the Church five years after the Council, "dissolved" by churchmen five years later, yet still very much alive and active after another fifteen years, making twenty years of life so far. Happy Birthday, dear Society!

Immensely dear to a remnant of souls, for which it has been the only sustenance of their faith, hope and charity. Dear also to many other souls presently trapped inland, but who long for the living waters, and who watch from afar – not all is lost as long as the Society holds aloft the integral banner of Christ the King.

Yes, but can the Society survive for another 20 years? Answer, God knows. Humanly no, no more than it could have survived so far with merely human resources; but if God wills, yes, and if God does not so will, certainly He will raise someone or something to take its place, because the souls who wish not to abandon Him cannot be abandoned by Him. For that to happen, the Good Shepherd would have to cease being the Good Shepherd – impossible. So let us thank God for the immense graces that have come to us through 20 years of the Society, and let me also on behalf of you all express our ongoing thanks to the Society's Founder, Archbishop Lefebvre, 85 years old at the end of this month, November 29. Happy Birthday, your Grace!

The Death of Malcolm Muggeridge

So Malcolm Muggeridge has died, at the venerable age of 87. He was a famous journalist and broadcaster in the English-speaking world, but especially in his own country, England, and in his later years he converted to Catholicism. Countless souls seeking God owe him a great deal. I was one of them. Dear Malcolm!— "God rest him all road ever he offended."

When I returned to England in 1965 after two years in Africa, and, school-mastering in London, found the schoolboys, like their country, ravaged by, notably, four unworthy mopheads known as the Beatles, I looked around for a voice of sanity, or respresentive of worth, and standing out in his articulate, amusing but relentless condemnation of our worthless twentieth century, leaving it no chance of appeal, was Malcolm Muggeridge.

With crafted clauses and crafty glee, his articles that I would read went for the tin gods of Liberalism, and without mercy or malice tore them to pieces. Poor Liberals accused Malcolm of being "negative," of being "destructive" – you know the whole silly line! – but for anyone with eyes to see or ears to hear there was more to him than that. Firstly, someone who has nothing to say does not usually bother with style or craftsmanship to say it, but Malcolm always had style and he was a craftsman with the English language.

And then secondly, behind all the impish mockery and iconoclasm there ran a coherent sense of there being some real values by which all the posturing poltroons who betrayed them stood condemned. Accordingly, although he was not a Catholic at the time, nor even, as I recall, professed himself to be a Christian, he attracted a large number of implicit and explicit believers who had nobody else to defend their minds and souls against the great lie of Liberalism with which their official leaders were, to a man, more or less going along.

So one day I got on a bicycle and rode over to his cottage in Robertsbridge, Sussex, to see him. I cannot remember whether I had announced my (completely unimportant) visit beforehand or not. In any case he and his wife Kitty received me very kindly, sat me down to lunch, and we talked, and he listened, and he essentially understood everything that "my dear boy" had to say about the woes of teaching abandoned youth in mid-20th century London.

I have fond memories of maybe half a dozen such visits to Malcolm and Kitty over the next few years. I am in no way boasting that I was a special friend of theirs, only that Malcolm was a good friend to me, a friend in need as I have no doubt he was to hundreds, maybe thousands, of spiritual derelicts of the 20th century who made as I did the pilgrimage to the Sage of Park Cottage.

How good God is! I think had Malcolm been a fully-fledged Roman Catholic at the time, I might not have gone near him. As it was, with his sharp and independent mind which had gone right into left-wingery and come out the other side, with his total refusal to buy into 20th century illusions, and with his wisdom and goodness of heart manifested in his ready ear and warm hospitality, he greatly helped me towards the time when I left London and went ahead of him into the Catholic Church.

"Ah, my dear boy, so now you are a full card-carrying member," was his greeting to me as I next visited him in the South of France, as though I had done something like joining the Communist Party! But I can remember how I went with them to a local Mass, something he told me that he and Kitty did every day, and how they sat at the back . . . Malcolm said the mere idea of receiving Communion was something still alien to him . . . yet the reverence with which he attended the Mass, how describe it? This white-haired man withdrawn to the rear of the dark church, with his life's companion beside him and with years of life and of life's battles behind him, several decades of striving and questioning, all dropped into silent homage before the great Mystery in which he sensed, but could not yet discern, the Answer . . . And we would emerge into the daylight, and the 20th century would pick up again with coffee and breakfast and banter.

So it was no surprise when maybe some ten years later he and Kitty entered the Church. *Deo Gratias.* However, Catholic readers of his several autobiographical books might be surprised for instance by his un-Catholic choice of heroes, with exceptions like of course of the great St. Augustine whom he loved. Alas, I never met Malcolm again after he became a Catholic, so I cannot be sure of how he evolved, but I suspect that he came into the Church by his heart, drawn especially by the example of, and contact with, Mother Theresa of Calcutta, while a certain part of his head remained outside, with the existentialists and their progenitors. But let such readers be reassured that a large part of Malcolm's head was Catholic – how many Catholic rectors of a prestigious university would step down, as he did, years before he became a Catholic, in protest at contraceptives being made available on the campus? He believed with complete sincerity in so much of what many "Catholics" had quite simply abandoned. In any case, he was a beacon in the darkness to many of the spiritual waifs of our time like myself. Dear Malcolm, thank you, and good bye!

> Earth, press not hard upon these bones
> Of Malcolm, humbug-hater –
> To rise, they are too weary now
> And nothing will stop them later.

Readers, say a prayer for Malcolm's soul and for Kitty whom he has left behind him.

Meanwhile our beloved 20th century is dragging one more year to its close. 1990 has seen the putting in place of a major Third World War trigger in the Middle East – will 1991 see the pulling of the trigger? God knows, and He knows what He is doing – He has better things to do than to make the world safe for swimming-pools!

Back here at the seminary you friends and benefactors have looked after us well through the year, and we thank you warmly for all your generosity. We do not have that many seminarians, their number is back below fifty, but if they are faithful to the graces Our Lord is giving them here, they have all that is needed to give back light, warmth, hope and youth to a dark, cold, desperate and aging world. Thank you for relieving them of material worries.

Enclosed is another copy of the latest "Crisis in Faith" tapes flyer, in case you failed to order the first time or need to order more. Modesty forbids me to recommend these tapes, but they may be a winner in the race for Christmas presents which risks otherwise ending in a tie.

I shall be in Latin America for all of December, so if you are thinking of sending me a Christmas card, do not hesitate not to do so! I will take it for granted that you wish all of us at the Seminary a Happy Christmas and New Year – your generosity is proof of that – and to all of yourselves I wish all the blessings of the Advent and Christmas Season. Fear not. Does not the defenseless Baby remind us with what humanly insignificant means God overturns all the schemings of the mighty? 1991 can hold for us nothing that is stronger than the Love of God.

NO. 90 | FEBRUARY 1, 1991

Gulf War I

So we are into 1991 and into the Gulf War. There is much to fear. Now matters military and political are not the Church's immediate domain, and events can take unexpected turns, but there are underlying factors which do not change. Let us take a few supernatural sightlines.

Most naturally, one may fear bloodshed, especially of kith and kin. Now as the attack on Iraq began, pilots could be heard on our radios describing the dropping of bombs like the scoring of goals in a football game, but the bombardment has caused no immediate surrender and in at least one institution of the American military the mood is turning from euphoric to serious as they realize the war will not be over in a week. So without predicting the course of such an unpredictable as war, one may fear the battlefield turning from football field into killing field.

As World War II raged, a privileged soul in Italy who could converse with Our Lord, complained to him of the number of young men being cut off in the prime of life. Yes, replied Our Lord, but think how many of them will save their souls this way who living on in a sinful peace would certainly have lost them. Good news from Saudi

Arabia is that the chaplains are working hard. Catholics must pray that the war be the occasion for many souls to be saved, and that does not exclude one's enemies.

Secondly, behind the Gulf War one may fear Russia. Russia's military help to Iraq is well-known; not only a mass of tanks, radar-transmitters and rockets, etc., but also thousands of "technical assistants" to operate them, and, for instance, an outstanding tank warfare general to guide and ensure the swift success of the original invasion of Kuwait. What is less well-known is Russia's military help to the United States: for instance, the reported lending of two heavy transport ships to help get US war material across the Atlantic, and the revealing to Secretary of State James Baker in Moscow in October of key information concerning that same Russian war material supplied to the Iraqis.

It becomes easy to imagine Russia playing at balancing the war which way she likes by supplying further equipment to the Iraqis or further information to the Americans. Certainly it is in Russia's interest not only to see Iraq destroyed as an obstacle between herself and the Oil Gulf, but also to see destroyed as much as possible of the American forces that stand between Russia and the invasion of Europe, and also to have world attention diverted from her own brutality in her Baltic front-yard. "If my requests are heeded (for the Consecration of Russia to the Immaculate Heart and the five first Saturdays' Communion of Reparation), Russia will be converted and there will be peace. If not, she will spread her errors throughout the world, causing wars and persecutions of the Church . . . " (Second Secret of Fatima).

May we not fear then that as World War II pretended to be making the world safe for democracy but in fact was making it safe for Communism (e.g., the take-over of Eastern Europe), so the Gulf War pretends to be in defense of Kuwait (since when did democracy there get a fair sheikh?) but is in fact designed to kill with one stone two – or three – obstacles to the advance of International Socialism?

Supernaturally, one must reply that the Western nations have only themselves to blame for their suicidal blindness if Russia marches through the now unguarded gateway to Europe. This blindness comes from their apostasy and their materialism whereby they are gravely offending God. Communism is no more nor less than a divine scourge permitted by God to embody His justice. While then nobody in his right mind may rejoice in the suffering as such which it causes, one may well rejoice in any salutary shock administered to the once Christian nations such as may awaken them from their sinful slumber. Such an awakening is the necessary prelude to the triumph of the Immaculate Heart, also promised by Our Lady at Fatima.

However, behind the Gulf War and even behind Russia, may one not, thirdly, fear the looming figure of the Antichrist? Before hostilities are over in the Gulf, expect Israel to be looking to "solve" the Palestinian problem by removing King Hussein of Jordan, by turning Jordan into a client Palestinian state and by forcibly moving there all Palestinians from Gaza and the West Bank, to "make room" for the Jewish immigrants from Russia (cf. *Washington Post*, August 26, 1990). Imagine how such an idea appeals to the Arabs! In which case one understands why so many friends of Israel in the USA were and are whooping for the United States to break the Arab strongman.

Supernaturally seen, such a scenario, capable of many adaptations, represents one more in many steps of the Jewish people towards their appointment with God at the end of the world, when, maybe converted by the heroism and endurance of the Catholics undergoing persecution by their Antichrist, they will at last convert

(Romans 11) and discover their own true Messiah, Jesus Christ, who has never ceased to love them as His own people. However, until they rediscover their true Messianic vocation, they may be expected to continue fanatically agitating, in accordance with their false messianic vocation of Jewish world dominion, to prepare the Antichrist's throne in Jerusalem. So we may fear their continuing to play their major part in the agitation of the East and in the corruption of the West. Here the wise Catholic will remember that, again, the ex-Christian nations have only their own Liberalism to blame for allowing free circulation within Christendom to the enemies of Christ. As these make society more and more oppressively anti-Christian, he will profit to raise his sights above this world and look to the things of heaven – "When these things begin to come to pass, look up, and lift up your heads, for your redemption is at hand" (Lk. 21: 28). Remembering also that Annas and Caiphas induced but never obligated Judas to betray Jesus, and that the Apostle's betrayal was a crime far worse than the Jews' deicide, He will look at the state of the Catholic Church today, and see why the enemies of Christendom are being given so much power . . .

The mainstream Novus Ordo Church is falling apart. There are recent signs in Canada of current priestly difficulties reaching up to a higher level, which fits Novus Ordo doctrine. When I teach that all sin is social, what individual behavior is still sinful? In at least one American seminary, crucifixes are having to be replaced with "resurrexifixes," and seminarians' spiritual direction is by women. In New York, besides spiritual direction, women are also taking over visiting of the sick and diocesan administration – when they are sufficiently in control, they plan to declare that they can say Mass.

The conservative Novus Ordo is little better. Opus Dei attracts decent Catholics in distress, pushes a pacifier of conservative appearances into their spiritual mouths, and then feeds them a pro-capitalist, pro-banks, pro-One-World doctrine of worldliness that is the same Revolution, only better disguised.

As for the "traditional" branch of the Novus Ordo, it is paralyzed by internal contradiction. As head of *Ecclesia Dei*, Cardinal Mayer wrote recently to an American layman that Mass said facing the people, or with the 1970 Lectionary, is not an unlawful intermingling of rites; whereupon Novus Ordo priests obviously feel free to import into the Indult Mass little doses of the Novus Ordo; which makes the true Mass as attractive as a barrel of whisky with a little gasoline poured into it; which chases away souls thirsty for Tridentine whisky; which enables "obedient" bishops to close down the Indult distillery they never wanted open in the first place. Rename it – the Indulterated Mass.

Similarly, a St. Peter's Fraternity priest tried last March to use his *Ecclesia Dei* Tridentine permit in St. Peter's Basilica, Rome, to say the Tridentine Mass. Permission refused. The priest – reasonably – complains to *Ecclesia Dei*. *Ecclesia Dei* in April consults the Vatican Secretary of State. May 1990 the Holy Office comes back to *Ecclesia Dei* with the answer: in St. Peter's Basilica, what the Basilica authorities say, goes. *Ecclesia Dei* is at the 24-hour mercy of the local bishops.

As for St. Peter's Fraternity, I am told that its seminary in Wigratzbad recently lost thirty-one seminarians including thirteen Americans (I cannot vouch for these figures), whether by its choice or theirs. Those who chose to leave gave apparently a variety of reasons, for instance the introduction of subtle little items of the Novus Ordo. Poor St. Peter's! As the product of a cross between the noble steed of Tradition and the asinine Novus Ordo, they should have known that mules cannot produce little ones, but then they would not listen to Archbishop Lefebvre's horse sense!

In brief, conditions are worsening, the rape of the official Church continues at speed, the individual Catholic within it has no institutional pickup or backup. Of the official Church one may come to say: in the framework is death.

For refreshment, take a few long draughts of another interview given recently by Archbishop Lefebvre, enclosed. It comes to you without divisions or subheadings, but there are a few highlightings. What is not Catholic whisky is horse sense, and what is not horse sense is Catholic whisky!

Alas, it is not certain he will be able to visit Winona in the spring, but it is certain that four present deacons are scheduled for ordination to the priesthood this year.

And last but not least – for that is what this letter is primarily about – many thanks to all of you for your great support of the seminary over the Christmas and New Year season. We are praying for all of your intentions, each day. Keep us in your prayers also, for we are in the thick of a spiritual desert storm, and we could more easily do without your pocketbooks than we can do without your prayers.

God bless you, and give you many graces in Lent. It is by our fidelity and example that we will resist the enemies of Christ and finally overcome evil with good. Our Faith is our victory over the world.

Visit to Latin America

IN LATIN AMERICA the faithful remnant is faithful but it is only a remnant. Such was the conclusion from the journey I made there from late November to early January.

The first stop was Columbia. This was the third time I had visited Latin America. Each time I visit I get a sense of the extraordinary accomplishment of Spain in setting up a rosary of Catholic nations from Mexico in the North to the foot of Chile and the Argentine in the South. Today Catholicism and colonialism are heavily devalued, so that in Latin America they are regretting that the continent was opened up by the Spaniards. It is the exact opposite of matter for regret. From the standpoint of the Faith, how many millions of souls must have gone to heaven from these countries, thanks to the Spanish "Conquistadores" having brought with them the Faith, and missionaries and priests, to plant it firmly amongst the local peoples.

This sense came over me again soon after landing in Columbia. True, this country which at the turn of the century had a highly Catholic Constitution, was in November just about to elect a majority of Communists to rewrite that Constitution; true, Columbia is presently preyed upon by the drug trade which is also protected from on high by the Revolution; nevertheless, not far beneath the surface of Columbia, the values, history and mentality are Catholic. What a blessing for a country to have been founded in the Faith! The practice may be corrupt, but deep down lie good principles which shed light even when they are abandoned. The hallmark of Protestant countries is that even with the best will in the world men believe in principles that will tear any society apart.

Pray for the Society's two young priests in Columbia, both in their mid-twenties, Fr. Martinez ordained one year ago, Fr. Zendejas (the Superior!) ordained two years ago, neither of them Columbians, both several hours by airplane from the next closest Society priest, between them carrying two priories on their shoulders and the defense of the Faith in a whole country collapsing under the Revolution! Ordinarily speaking, it makes no sense at all, but there they are, and that is the Society. May Our Lady protect them and reward them!

Next stop was Chile, where the Society has a priory with three priests in the capital, Santiago. Chile is very different from Columbia. Well led by General Pinochet – yes, well led by General Pinochet – Chileans had worked themselves into such a favorable economic situation as even the Liberals were obliged to admire, but that of course did not stop them using their vile media to get him out of office in a vote genuinely free such as only a non-Communist will allow. Now Chile is no doubt getting back into the bankers' debt, into the communists' clutches and into the media's favor, unless the people rise up to restore Pinochet. I was taken to the spot where he was waylaid in a highly professional ambush on a country road some 40 minutes out of Santiago in 1985. Five men of his escort were killed, and gunfire rained down accurately on the back window of the car in which he was riding. The protective glass was battered but did not give way. The Chilean people were indignant at the vile assassination attempt, and the figure of the Madonna and Child seemingly punched out on the glass by the bullets – copies of the picture on demand – suggest that she at least is not afraid of mixing politics and religion!

Then why did Pinochet fall from power a few years later? Maybe, just maybe, because although three Society priests separately urged him to consecrate Chile to the Sacred Heart, he failed to do so. "O ye of little faith . . . " It is heartbreaking to visit in Santiago a great and handsome convent building occupied by a handful of nuns only holding on because of a Mother Superior heroically resisting the diocesan authorities who are doing all they can to fill the whole convent, like its church, with dust . . . When Mother Veronica ten years ago opened the church to Society priests arriving in Chile, they and she must have hoped in a popular reaction, in an upswing of the Faith, in the refilling of the dusty pews. It was not to be. "My thoughts are not your thoughts," saith the Lord.

From Chile to the Argentine, circumstances enabled me to make the passage by road over the majestic Andes, the same pass taken by the much impressed St. Frances Cabrini on her missionary travels years ago. What labor for men to cut a pass by road or rail over such heights, but, for the mountains themselves, what insignificant and fragile surface scratching such a pass represents. "O Lord, how great are thy works! Thy thoughts are exceeding deep... Thou hast multiplied thy wonderful works, O Lord my God; and in thy thoughts there is no one like to thee. I have declared and I have spoken, they are multiplied above number." (Ps. 39: 6)

The Argentine is the Society's base of operations in South America. It is the most European of the Hispano-American countries, having received for instance many post-colonial immigrants from Italy, and it boasts a depth of Christian civilization and Catholic culture which the financial manipulators and engineers of corruption have not yet succeeded in destroying. The inland city of Cordova had a magnificent Jesuit baroque church and university long before Harvard University was even a gleam in a heretical preacher's eye.

Today, I was told, the uncrowned king of the Argentine is the American Ambassador, and the present Argentinian President is a theatrical puppet. Just before I arrived a failed military putsch had, one may think, been laid on to persuade the visiting President Bush what good democrats the Argentinians are, yet when the financiers will have passed away with all their pomps and all their works, the baroque church, one suspects, will still be standing.

Meanwhile the Society profited by the Argentine's Catholic leadership of the continent to launch there in the late seventies its mission to South America. Now the Society has a thriving parish in the capital, Buenos Aires, another parish in Cordova, and a sisters' novitiate and a priestly seminary a little way outside the capital. Alas, a rigorist putsch within the seminary in 1989 emptied it of half its seminarians. Of the two dozen left, I was privileged to ordain in mid-December an Argentinian for Mexico and a Mexican for Columbia. Youngsters, to minister virtually unaided to an aging and ailing world . . . Sheep sent out amongst wolves . . . "Eppure si muove."

The next stop was Brazil, where I was to spend three days as the working guest of the Traditional Catholic priests of the Diocese of Campos, a city lying a few hours by car to the northeast of Rio de Janeiro, city little in size but great in faith, having given to the world over the last thirty years the living proof that no diocesan bishop or diocese was obliged to follow Vatican II in its soft apostasy. It is well-known that Dom Antonio de Castro Mayer, bishop of Campos from 1949 for over thirty years, is the only bishop in the world to have stood in public beside Archbishop Lefebvre in his resistance to the neo-modernists' destruction of the Church; it is also known that Dom Antonio's diocesan priests stood behind him and maintained the Tridentine Mass when the rest of the Church was dropping it; what is less well-known is how after Dom Antonio's resignation the large majority of those priests, driven out of their parish churches by Dom Antonio's modernist successor, have since hung together and, with the vigorous support of their people, are rebuilding eleven new churches, from ground zero, to continue keeping the Faith!

I was able to meet a good number of these priests. Humanly speaking they are ordinary enough men, humble and solid workers in the Lord's vineyard, but divinely speaking, the example of Catholic fidelity which they are giving to the world is an extraordinary accomplishment. As always, the disproportion between the humility of the instrument and the sublimity of the achievement demonstrates the finger of God. May He richly bless and long preserve these faithful priests!

They are the fruit of Dom Antonio's episcopacy. Dom Antonio, now in his 87th year, is mostly confined to bed where his priests will let no one else look after him and where I was able to visit him. His mind is completely alert and with his twinkling good spirits he continues to be the supernatural inspiration of his priests. They are seriously considering consecrating one of their number to succeed him, and that is another thing that might divert Archbishop Lefebvre from North America this spring. But successor or no successor, the story of Catholic resistance in the Diocese of Campos is no less than an epic.

Last stop on the way back to USA was Mexico, maybe the most privileged of all the Catholic nations in Latin America. Our Lady of Guadalupe is Patroness of the Americas. However, in God's Providence Mexico has also been severely tried by the proximity of its immediate non-Catholic neighbor to the North, from where Freemasons have repeatedly interfered in Mexican history, for example in 1929 when they helped to frustrate the Cristeros of their imminent victory in their bloody three-year struggle for the Faith. But the Faith is still alive in the Mexican people, so that hundreds of Catholics attend Mass in each of the Society's two largest and most recently purchased buildings in Mexico City and Guadalajara. The Society landed in Mexico like by parachute, but it is putting down roots, thanks especially to our retreat house near Colima, and to the Spiritual Exercises of St. Ignatius.

For these Exercises for men in Easter Week in Winona, see the enclosed yellow flyer, giving also the dates for the Exercises for the rest of the year in Winona, and in Ridgefield, Connecticut. Sign up. There is also a flyer for the summer camps being held by the Society of the United States this year for boys and (separately) for girls: Next on blue paper is a Profession of Faith for the 1990's by our Superior General, Fr. Schmidberger, most usefully addressing itself to the errors attacking the Faith today. This Profession of Faith should be valuable to put into the hands of Catholics asking what "Tradition" is all about. Lastly, the twice-yearly SCSF or Seminary Continous Support Fund card is enclosed for those of you wishing to pledge regular support to the seminary with the help of a return envelope reaching you each month by first class mail. By all means return the card if you wish to make an address correction but then kindly make it clear you are not making a pledge.

We are full into Lent and Passiontide begins soon. Profit by the graces of the season. There is nothing like the Passion to help understand this crisis of the Church, and nothing like this crisis to help understand the Passion. It is through weakness, humiliation and defeat that love emerges triumphant. Divine mystery!

Death of Archbishop Lefebvre

As THE GREAT majority of you surely know already, Archbishop Lefebvre died in the early hours of Monday morning, March 25, Western European time. He was in his 86th year and he felt he had fulfilled his mission on earth, so for his part he was quite ready to depart this life. Yet for us his death was still a shock.

For many years he had seemed in such good health that few if any of us took seriously his own repeated references to his coming death. We readily imagined his living for another ten years to continue guiding the SSPX with his irreplaceable experience and wisdom, especially through the next few years. Truth to tell, whenever he were to have died, it would have seemed too soon. But now he is gone from amongst us here on earth.

He was hospitalized in Martigny in the Canton of the Valais near Ecône in Switzerland on March 9, as a result of violent pains in the abdomen. The doctors having discovered an alarming lump, they decided on an operation which took place on Monday, March 18. A large cancerous tumor was removed. For several days he seemed to be slowly recovering until on Sunday morning March 24 he fell into a high fever. Antibiotics reduced the fever but also overwhelmed the organism – at 11 p.m. on Sunday night he lapsed into a coma. Reanimation could not save him. At 3:30 a.m. in the early hours of Monday morning on the day which is normally the Feast of the Annunciation he breathed his last, and gave back to God his heroic and pure soul –

> Here cracks a noble heart. Good night, sweet prince,
> And flights of angels sing thee to thy rest.

(*Hamlet*, Act V)

No doubt they did. Imagine, whenever it took place, the Archbishop's triumphal entry into heaven! Was it coincidental that a specially bright Aurora Borealis lit up the Northern sky in Europe and in parts of the US on the night of his death? It was a suitable omen for a worldwide event, because the whole world has lost in him one of those great pontiffs whose intercessory prayer shields us from the wrath of God. In 1968 Padre Pio died, in 1969 arrived the *Novus Ordo Missae* ... What new peril draws near this time?

The Catholic Church also enters into a new era without him. Since for the last twenty years he has stood for the Truth as no other bishop has done and as none other than a Catholic bishop can do, and since the Catholic Church revolves around the Way, the Truth, and the Life as no other institution on earth does, then willy nilly, these last twenty years of the Catholic Church have been, as history will show, the era of Archbishop Lefebvre.

For during this time even his enemies within the Church have depended upon him. For instance, had he not consecrated bishops in the summer of 1988, *Ecclesia Dei* and St. Peter's Society would not even exist, and all those conservative Catholics who condemn his disobedience or hubris would have no Indult Mass from the comfort of which to spurn those consecrations. Similarly had he not braced the whole Traditional wing of the Church in the 1970's, the left-wingers would have swept the middle-of-the-roaders and themselves to destruction years ago, they would all by now be One World social workers, and there would have been, had it depended upon them, no official Church left standing from the platform of which to suspend or excommunicate him.

He sustained his enemies even as he nourished his friends, for he sustained the Truth, and even liars need a half of truth to market their wares. He passed for being the greatest enemy of recent Popes – certainly he was the only one they excommunicated – yet by resisting their corrosive Liberalism, he alone will have saved their Papacy which, left to themselves, they would have destroyed. Thus friend and foe in the Church leant on him. Now he is gone. Mother Church moves into the post-Lefebvre era.

As for his own foundation, the Priestly Society of St. Pius X, of course the enemies of Tradition have long been waiting for the Archbishop's death to ensure its disintegration, and humanly speaking, given the value of Archbishop Lefebvre's presence and advice right up to the end, they will normally be right. However, before he died Archbishop Lefebvre provided his Society with all that it needed by way of structure and successors to carry on his work.

Firstly, as Superior General to run the Society, he had himself replaced as far back as 1982 by Fr. Franz Schmidberger for a 12-year term running until 1994, for the first two thirds of which term the Archbishop was always available to help and advise him. Now Fr. Schmidberger is on his own. We must pray for him in earnest, especially as Rome is bound to start up the carrot and stick routine all over again.

Secondly, in his functions as bishop the Archbishop consecrated four successors to ordain and confirm, on that famous June 30 of 1988. How wisely he provided! Imagine where Tradition would now be without those four. Yet it was a truly agonizing decision at the time, and a stupendous achievement. Single-handed, for such decisions are absolutely lonely, the Archbishop created out of his faith and courage and thin air a viable future for Catholic Tradition, and for the Catholic Church.

So by this historic action the Society was equipped with all that it needs to continue operating as the Church's emergency lighting system, until such time as the main lights get turned on again. If it too fails, it will not have been the Archbishop's fault.

Will it fail? If it depends on human weakness, yes; if it depends on God's grace, no. And what does the Lord God have in mind? Only He knows. We had fondly thought he would conserve the Archbishop to guide us for many years yet, but the Archbishop was right, it was not to be. We may now fondly think that the Society is meant by God to be His light-bearer until the Church's crisis is over, but the Lord God is not short of alternatives, and He may have in mind still more darkness. It would not be undeserved.

However, it is never to be forgotten that, as St. Augustine said, He abandons nobody who has not first abandoned Him. With or without the great Archbishop, with or without his little Society, no sheep that seeks the Good Shepherd will be forced to lose Him. That is an intrinsic impossibility. "Fear not, little flock, for it hath pleased your Father to give you a kingdom." (Lk. 12: 32) Then while grieving for the loss of the Society's founder and father, let us thank God that we had such a leader for so long, and let us rely on God's grace to carry on where he left off.

The Catholic Church cannot fail, so for the machinery of its continuance God will provide, even as He provided us with the Archbishop. When we see how God has steered us through the last twenty years, it is not difficult to put our trust in Him for the next twenty.

Concerning the Archbishop personally, a journalist asked recently what was my outstanding memory of the man. I gave maybe a surprising answer: his objectivity. He had of course a uniquely attractive personality because he was a saint – gentle, simple, kind, humble, humorous and so on without a trace of sentimentality, but that was not the point. Underneath all that lay a great intelligence and faith and firmness of character, but that was still not the point. Essentially he was a man empty of self and full of God. To meet him, to talk to him, was to see, through him, the Truth, Our Lord Jesus Christ, the Catholic Church. He was like a window on the interests of God. Not he, but Christ, lived within him, and yet he was Marcel Lefebvre and nobody else. And what a marvellous man he was! Shakespeare again –

> His life was gentle and the elements
> So mixed in him that Nature might stand up
> And say to all the world, "This was a man."

(*Julius Caesar*, Act V)

However, even these noble lines on the stoic hero fall a long way beneath doing justice to the supernatural hero, the saint who has left us . . .

. . . left us in a darker world without him? Yes and no. Sanctity is infectious, saints breed saints. We are the legacy that the Archbishop bequeaths to the world. Oh no, we are not saints, but we of the SSPX have had a marvellous saint amongst us, we should have caught the infection, and if we have, then we need only spread it for what was marvellous in him to continue. Archbishop Lefebvre lives!

When I accompanied him once on a journey to Ireland, our plane, waiting to take off from London Airport, was being shaken by the thunderous roar of the supersonic Concorde leaving just in front of us. What a marvellous piece of work is man, I commented, to have invented the Concorde. The Archbishop quietly replied, how much more marvellous the God who invented the inventor. Similarly, if it has been so marvellous to know one of Jesus' great saints and master-creations here on earth, how much more marvelous to know Jesus himself in heaven!

With much serenity I shall attend the Archbishop's funeral on April 2. Count on me to lay by his casket all that I can imagine of your gratitude, affection, and prayers.

NO. 93 | MAY 9, 1991

Death of Bishop de Castro Mayer

A NUMBER OF you will have been wondering what happened to the seminary's May mailing. Some of you may have guessed it would consist in a Commemorative Issue of *The Angelus* for the death on March 25 of the founder of the SSPX, Archbishop Marcel Lefebvre. The seminary has had to shake out its piggy-bank to be sending it to you, but one's founder dies only once! And then the better we appreciate God's gifts, such as a great Catholic bishop, the more inclined will God be to send us more like him: "If thou didst know the gift of God . . ." says Our Lord.

And now the bishop who had the honor and glory of being the only bishop in the world to stand by Archbishop Lefebvre in the Church's hour of need, Bishop Antonio de Castro Mayer, retired bishop of the Diocese of Campos in Brazil, has also died, one month to the day after the Archbishop, in a hospital in Brazil, on April 25. Thus God has seen to it that the companions in arms on earth are also companions in heaven.

Bishop de Castro Mayer was born one year before Archbishop Lefebvre, and became bishop of the Diocese of Campos, small city some 200 miles northeast of Rio de Janeiro, in 1948, when he was in his mid-forties. He was strong in canon law and theology, and a Pastoral Letter on "Problems of the Modern Apostolate," which he wrote for his diocese in 1953, and which contained a "Catechism of Opportune Truths to Oppose Today's Errors," spread far beyond his own diocese, inside and outside of Brazil.

His strength in doctrine was the reason why, when the tornado of Vatican II struck the Church, neither he nor his diocese were blown off course, a feat achieved by no other bishop with his diocese in the whole Church! Many a bishop during and after the Council must have felt extremely uncomfortable with the new religion being introduced, but unless he had a very clear mind he will have said to himself, "Well, I don't like it and I don't feel it's Catholic, but the Faith doesn't go by likes or by feelings, so if that's what the Pope says, I must obey." Only if he knew with a clear mind that the doctrine of the Faith itself was gravely endangered by the changes, could he quietly and steadily resist them, as did Bishop de Castro Mayer.

What is more – what is much more – his priests stayed with him. When the New Mass came in, they followed him in keeping to the Tridentine Mass, and when he reached the age of 75 and was obliged by the new Church's rules to step down, still the great majority of his two dozen priests kept the Tridentine Mass. No doubt thanks to him, they had understood.

He was replaced by a modernist bishop who proceeded to drive all Bishop de Castro Mayer's priests out of their parishes. A few of them gave up the fight, but it was again the great majority of them who literally took to the streets, and when they decided to build new churches from nothing, then – further testimonial to the former bishop and his priests – they were followed by the great mass of the people, so that there are now 11 brand new churches being built. I saw three of them when I was in Brazil last December. They are not small, and the one that I saw finished was very fine – and already too small! What one good bishop can do!

No doubt Dom Antonio's last great moment was when he stood by Archbishop Lefebvre's side to co-consecrate in the Consecrations of June, 1988. In the course of the ceremony he gave a brief sermon stating why he had come. He said he had been under much pressure to stay away, but for him it was such a duty that he considered he would have committed a mortal sin had he not come.

Archbishop Lefebvre was immensely appreciative of his assistance. Bishop de Castro Mayer was in all respects so completely independent of Archbishop Lefebvre, that when he stood with him against all the world, it was the clear demonstration that the Archbishop was not just inventing everything out of his own head. Quite uninfluenced by the Archbishop, one other Catholic bishop facing the same confusion had arrived at the same dramatic decision: better incur "excommunication" than remain inactive. Thenceforward nobody could dismiss the Archbishop as a lone eccentric.

Just how much the Archbishop appreciated his companion in arms, let this extract tell, the beginning of a letter written by the Archbishop from Switzerland on December 4 of last year to Dom Antonio, bed-ridden in Brazil:

> Very dear Monsignor Antonio de Castro Mayer,
>
> Rumors reach me from Brazil concerning your health which they say is declining! Is the call of God drawing nigh? The mere thought fills me with deep grief. How lonely I shall be without my elder brother in the episcopate, without the model fighter for the honor

of Jesus Christ, without my one faithful friend in the appalling wasteland of the Conciliar Church!

On the other hand there rings in my ears all the chant of the Traditional liturgy of the Office of Confessor Pontiffs! . . . heaven's welcome for the good and faithful servant! if such be the good Lord's will.

Little apparently did Archbishop Lefebvre guess that he would be the first one home, but from there he clearly did not wait long to draw his companion after him. "Lovely and comely in their life, even in death they were not divided: they were swifter than eagles, stronger than lions." (II Sam. 1: 23)

The Archbishop's funeral which I attended in Ecône on April 2 was solemn, but consoling rather than sad. There are several pictures in the enclosed *Angelus*, and a little of the scene at the graveside is evoked in the piece entitled, "What he stood for could not die." The time for sadness will be when, if ever, his work dies.

This announcement is late because there was no place for it in the letter for April. Worry not, there will be Confirmations next year, God willing. What matters is that the youngsters know and love their Faith. Better – hungry souls, take note – love the Sacraments and not have them than have them and not love them, insofar as God is drawing close to the first state but drawing away from the second.

May Our Lady bless you for what remains of her own month. She will triumph, as we shall see.

NO. 94 | JUNE 10, 1991

Unity and Perseverance in Tradition

MANY OF YOU have had to wait for the arrival of our May mailing from the offices of *The Angelus* in Dickinson, Texas, but I doubt if many of you were disappointed after the long wait. *The Angelus* team did magnificent work to get out the commemorative issue on Archbishop Lefebvre. It is a keepsake which will no doubt be treasured in many a Catholic home for years to come.

The Angelus team also did tremendous extra work to collate and get into the mail copies for the entire seminary mailing list (currently about 12,500 names). Well done, ladies, and thank you very much. You did the Archbishop proud! Extra copies, as many as you like, can be ordered either from the seminary or from *The Angelus* at $10 each, with 10% discount for bulk orders. *The Angelus* will also have 8" x 10" or 11" x 14" color reproductions available of the picture of the Archbishop on the cover of the commemorative *Angelus*.

It is the same picture as the card enclosed, of which you can also order from the seminary here as many as you like. We have had tens of thousands of them made up. No fixed price. Donations not refused!

Also enclosed is the complete letter of Archbishop Lefebvre to Bishop de Castro Mayer from which you read the first two paragraphs in last month's seminary letter. The complete letter shows the Archbishop's concern for the future of Catholic Tradition in the Diocese of Campos in Brazil, together with his complete respect for the independence of the Catholics of Campos. At no time since the founding of the SSPX did Archbishop Lefebvre seek to pull into or under the Society, priests from outside the Society, unless they asked of their own free will to join the Society, and even then he was reticent.

This was, and I think remains, despite what many of the Traditional laity think, doubly or triply wise. The laity, bless them, long to see Traditional priests all getting together, because their Catholic instinct is that priests who share the same true Faith should all be united, and what they see amongst their various Traditional priests is – I do not wish to exaggerate – a certain amount of division. Now the largest single body of such priests that they can see is the SSPX, so friends especially of the Society are liable to wish that all independent priests would join the Society. Under normal circumstances such a wish is entirely correct, but it surely mistakes the will of God in today's particular circumstances, firstly as to the Church, secondly as to the Society, thirdly as to the priests concerned.

First and foremost, there is one man and one man alone who has from God the mission and the faculties to pull the Catholic Church together in unity, in fact to make the unity of the Church, and that is the Pope. If the Pope does not or will not unify the Church, nobody else can, because that is how Our Lord Jesus Christ designed His Church, and there is no other way upon earth in which it can be built, unless one wants to build some other "Church," which for Catholics God forbid. Now the present Pope has such uncatholic notions in half of his head (like the curate's egg, it is good in parts) that he has no idea how to pull the Church together in the Faith, even if he wished to, so that for the moment the Church cannot be united. Hence the lack of unity amongst priests cannot for the moment be cured, so it must be endured. Instead of lamenting this lack of unity by hierarchy, Traditionalists might be wise to thank God for the remarkable degree of unity by Faith amongst their priests. They will be wise also to keep praying for the Pope who is so bitterly attacked by the radicals that he must be doing something right.

Secondly, those who wish independent priests would join the Society surely mistake the mission of the Society which is to preserve the Faith, the priesthood and the Mass for better times, but not to replace Rome. To be Roman Catholics, all Catholic priests must be somehow attached to Rome, but they need not be attached to the Society which has a particular origin and a particular character making particular demands, capable of wide but not of universal extension. True, a Catholic priest should normally be under a bishop and the Society has bishops, but these bishops are expressly not hierarchical, and if a priest is without bishops through no fault of his own, God clearly can give emergency graces of guidance to leaderless priests. Of course priests must be attached to the Faith to which the Society is attached, but that is a different matter. While it brings many a faithful priest alongside the Society, it does not put him into or under it. Again, rather than lament how few priests jump on board the Society train, Traditionalists might well thank God for each of those galloping alongside, and pray for more – there are many priestly Nicodemuses.

Thirdly, it is, humanly speaking, expecting a great deal of priests with maybe long diocesan or religious experience to put themselves, within the Society, under the orders of relatively young superiors. Of course inexperience is, as they say, a disease which is cured each day with another 24 hours' worth of experience, and many an old man's responsibilities resting on young men's shoulders is making the youngsters of the Society learn fast (how swiftly some lose the youthful expression and waistline they had as seminarians!). Nevertheless, with all the good will in the world an older man can hardly unlearn what he reckons it has cost him hard knocks to learn. As old Father Barrielle used to say at Ecône, there are as many standing miracles in the Society as it has houses still standing, for there is not one mistake the youngsters miss! "Eppur si muove," as Galileo is meant to have said: and yet it moves. Despite all, the Society works, a major reason again to thank God. For we face trials. Listen to this forecast –

> Rome will make full use of the occasion of the Archbishop's death to try to entice the sheep out of the fold. They will do it so kindly and so deviously that they will pull some of the shepherds away also . . . However, we must not be dismayed in the least, regardless of the defections. It is the hand of the Good Shepherd separating more intensely the sheep from the goats. There are yet many half-breeds in the flock, neither sheep nor goat (and consequently goat!) . . . they will not be allowed to remain.
>
> The "troops" who reach the final stages of "battle-readiness" must be totally committed, fully trained and firmly convinced, body, mind, heart and soul, of the cause for which they fight. Anything less is a danger to the forces of Good.
>
> The Superiors must warn of the dangers from Rome, and from within, but they must not anxiously try to hold back those who would leave, nor be disheartened at the numbers lost. Our strength is not in numbers,

but in each soul's full surrender to God. Many who are with us now will not be soon; and many that are scorned and looked down upon by the Traditionalists now, will be the strongest members in the future. Any who have sought out the Tridentine Mass and Sacraments and then lay back, smug in their "Catholicity," will not come through the test.

Truly, these are glorious days, and a person burns to prepare for battle – more prayer, penance and careful attention to daily duty, thus ever closer union with God and more battle-readiness . . . May she who prepared Christ for His sacrifice, prepare us also for ours.

Foreboding words, but plausible. A first-class means of prayer, penance and preparation for spiritual warfare is always the Spiritual Exercises of St. Ignatius. Sign up on the yellow flyers. Time is certainly running out. May Jesus bless each of you persevering.

NO. 95 | JULY 1, 1991

Should Abortionists be Assassinated?

So another school year at the seminary has drawn to a peaceful close with the Society's bishop from the Argentine, Bishop Alfonso de Galarreta, ordaining four seminarians to the priesthood and eight to the diaconate here at Winona on June 22.

Everything went off perfectly except for the surprisingly cool weather on the morning itself of the ordinations, starting in the low 40's! O, Minnesota! Notwithstanding, God's grace was poured out in abundance. Of some 400 visitors including many stalwart friends of the Society, not one can have regretted making the journey to see the beginnings of some of their future priests. Of the Society priests they already know, a number were in attendance to draw strength and inspiration from the family atmosphere and the solemn ceremony.

Think seriously of coming next year – Saturday, June 20, 1992 – when eight priests should be ordained, if God wills, easily the largest ordination yet from the Society's American seminary, and all of them Americans. Especially if you have never before come to an ordination, come, and stay of course for the Sunday when the new priests celebrate their first masses, another outpouring of grace.

This year on the evening after those first Masses two young men from the Wild West came into my office, to ask me a serious question – given that the abortionists are waging war on the unborn, and given that the present peaceful methods of fighting them are being rendered somewhat ineffective by wicked decisions in the law courts for instance, and by apathy of the general public, are pro-lifers entitled to think of taking out (assassinating) "doctors" notorious for baby-killing?

The question is not as wild as it may seem when one considers that this unchecked slaughter of the innocents is screaming for vengeance from Heaven, and that it looks like the vengeance is descending upon our society as a whole. The fight against abortion is, for all of us, self-defense. But the answer to the question was still, no.

In my opinion, the killing of the killers might be justified if it would be effective in stopping the abortions, as unquestionably it would be if it was the government that took out the killers by capital punishment in accordance with sane laws of the country. But what use will it be for young braves to take the law into their own hands when the foreseeable result is that a corrupt public opinion, misled by the vile media, will turn the executed abortionists into martyrs? Then the executions would be directly counter-productive.

I told the two young braves that they were up against an insoluble problem, as set at present. Abortion can only get worse, because it flows, believe it or not, from principles which many decent people hold sacred. For instance, if the American Constitution stands for democracy, liberty and equality, then abortion is not happening despite the Constitution, as many decent citizens wish to think, but because of it:

- Liberty – the liberty of each individual citizen to lead his life as he or she see fit, so the liberty of woman to do as she likes with her own body . . .

- Equality – the sexes are equal, so why should woman not be as free as man from any unwanted after-effects of exercising one's right to pleasure?

- Democracy – we, the people, are sovereign, so if our laws have approved of abortion, then what can be wrong with it?

Abortion flourishes in Western democracies because the principles of liberalism which these hold sacred open the door wide to it, as to a host of other horrors. Those principles have to be reversed.

For supposing the people believed in the sovereignty of God, and in His inalienable rights, starting with His absolute right to be obeyed in all Ten Commandments, notably "Thou shalt not kill" and "Thou shalt not commit adultery?"

Supposing the people understood that all souls are equal before God who will judge them all alike, when they appear before Him at the end of their lives, on the good or evil they have done, but that in all other respects, observably, almost no two souls are equal in any way, least of all men with women? And supposing the people came to understand that real liberty is freedom from sin and from Satan? Where then would abortion be? Back in the dark corner out of which it crawled into public acceptance, when the principles of Christianity were steadily eroded by those of liberalism.

Therefore the Truth of Our Lord Jesus Christ must be re-established in people's hearts and minds, and who has the authority and grace to do that, if not his Catholic priests?

Richard N. Williamson

"My dear young braves," was the conclusion, "this may not have been what you were expecting by way of reply to your original question about baby-killers, but it is the real answer: if neither of you are married, go away and think seriously about coming back here as seminarians to become Catholic priests like those you saw ordained yesterday. Whereas the two of you – as you well know by bitter experience – are walking into nothing but insoluble problems, the four of them are nothing but walking solutions. Let them only be faithful to their priesthood of Our Lord Jesus Christ, and they carry with them the answers to all of men's real problems. See you in September?"

It is a wonderful thing that the world has four new old-fashioned priests this summer from Winona, nine from Ecône and three from Zaitzkofen. Make sure to thank God, pray for them, and He will give us more. Winona's enrollment for September looks promising at present.

Also promising is the prospect of another Traditional bishop, in Campos, Brazil, to replace the recently deceased Bishop de Castro Mayer. The Catholic priests and faithful of the Diocese of Campos who under the leadership of that great bishop from 1948 through to this year have never allowed their religion to be changed, as it has been changed in every diocese in the world, including now the official Diocese of Campos, have made public their decision to request the bishops of the SSPX to consecrate for them a successor to Bishop de Castro Mayer who can continue to shield their Catholic Faith and give them the sacraments of Confirmation and Holy Orders. And the Society's four bishops have made public their decision to accede to that request.

We shall no doubt be accused again of fomenting schism, but just how far we are from any thought of founding a counter-Church – or even a counter-Diocese!

– should be clear from the two documents of Archbishop Lefebvre, one enclosed with last month's letter, the other with this letter, which express the sense and meaning of the consecration due to take place on July 28.

Refusing neither the Pope nor his normal authority, in this case to appoint bishops, we are not schismatic. Acting in an abnormal emergency neither invented nor created by ourselves, but created only by Rome's apparent incapacity to give to the Catholics of Campos a bishop who will look after their Faith, we shall be, according to both old and new Code of Church Law, neither excommunicated nor excommunicable. However, I am confident that the Catholics of Tradition will take this new consecration in their stride as easily as they did the consecrations of June, 1988. Like the previous four bishops, the fifth will certainly be ready to put back in the Pope's hands all his episcopal powers, as soon as the Pope returns to his Catholic senses. For which consummation, devoutly to be wished, let us unceasingly pray, and may God bless you.

NO. 96 | AUGUST 1, 1991

Consecration of Monsignor Rangel

NO DOUBT ANOTHER great blow was struck for the liberty and exaltation of Holy Mother Church with the episcopal consecration in Brazil on Sunday, July 28, of Msgr. Licinio Rangel.

From amongst the two dozen priests formerly constituting under Bishop de Castro Mayer the diocesan clergy of the Diocese of Campos which lies some three hours by road northeast of Rio de Janeiro, Msgr. Rangel was the choice of Bishop de Castro Mayer himself before the bishop died last April, and he was also elected by his fellow priests. He can be seen on the front cover of the 1991 *Angelus* Calendar looking over the right shoulder of Bishop Fellay, the bishop farthest to the right in the picture. Now 55 years old, he was under Pope John Paul II in 1981 made a domestic prelate with the title of Monsignor, a reward for years of quiet and faithful labor in a series of diocesan posts which he occupied under the guidance of Bishop de Castro Mayer while the latter was still the official Bishop of Campos.

Today of course the Campos priests who remained faithful to Tradition are no longer the official priests of the diocese (because by being obedient they became "disobedient" so that without being schismatic they fell into "schism" – do you not love our 20th century?), so the question can be raised, why did they need a bishop of their own in addition to the Society's four bishops who could on regular visits provide them with the sacraments of Holy Orders and Confirmation?

The answer is that the Campos priests are, because their dismissal by the modernist successor of Bishop de Castro Mayer was extremely unjust, continuing with their diocesan work. Now diocesan priests need a local bishop like a family needs a father. They need, to guide them, to hold them together and look after them, much more than just a provider of those sacraments which require the fullness of the priesthood to be administered. If no Traditional bishop succeeded Bishop de Castro Mayer, those priests he held together could not stay together, they would be broken up and his work would come to an end.

But his work was important not only to tens of thousands of souls in and around the city of Campos. It was, in the darkness following Vatican II, a beacon of light and hope for the whole Church, proving on the diocesan level – as Archbishop Lefebvre proved on a missionary level – that the true Faith was alive and as efficacious as ever. Hence for the souls of Campos and for the good of the whole Church, the Society's bishops decided to consecrate a Catholic bishop for Campos, as Archbishop Lefebvre had recommended before he died.

This does not mean that the Campos priests or Bishop Rangel (or the SSPX) do not recognize the official Bishop of Campos. They recognize him in the same way that they recognize the Pope, in other words they acknowledge his authority but refuse to follow him in his grave errors. Bishop Rangel makes no pretence of having that official authority over the Traditional priests and faithful of Campos, but his moral authority will come from his being the guardian of their Faith and the guarantor of their sacraments.

Bishop Rangel is not a Society bishop, nor does he come under the Society, but he profoundly agrees with the Society's positions, just as Bishop de Castro Mayer profoundly agreed with Archbishop Lefebvre. All are aligned on the same objective truth. Twenty-five Society priests from Europe and Latin America attended Bishop Rangel's consecration, and the harmony between the Campos priests and the Society priests was complete, because objective. However, since Bishop de Castro Mayer was the only bishop to stand by Archbishop Lefebvre, the Campos priests are unique in the world, and so there is no prospect at present of the Society bishops undertaking any further consecrations.

Not that such consecrations still so need to be explained as they until recently did. Thus on Saturday morning, July 27, the day before the consecration of Msgr. Rangel, the spokesman of the Campos priests, Fr. Fernando Rifan, organized a Press conference to explain the consecration. Now just a few years previously, anyone attempting to prove such a consecration to be Catholic would have been covered in ridicule. Yet here, anyone of good will listening to the arguments had to be convinced. The "new" truth was in possession. An astonishing reversal, which will continue to reverse and to astonish.

In fairness, most of the dozen journalists from all of Brazil responded very fairly to the presentation of the truth. The consecration itself received front page articles and pictures in all four major newspapers of the Campos area, and entire page articles in newspapers of Rio de Janeiro.

Outside of Brazil, however, silence. Signs are that the puppet-masters of Rome are in the process of putting some more juicy cheese on the Indult mouse-trap in order to catch us foolish Traditionalists, so it probably sent out instructions that no one should know of courageous mice looking after the production of their own cheese!

As for the mice of Campos, you should have seen and heard their reaction to the consecration! The people had long been fervently praying to have a bishop, so they saw in the event of July 28 the answer to their prayers. As they waited for the ceremony to begin and the three bishops, one consecrator and two co-consecrators, came in view, many women openly cried and the men held back their tears – the Church lives!

For a detailed description of the ceremony, see the September *Angelus*. During the ceremony the people were quiet, attentive and pious. They frequently wanted to applaud, but obeyed the ceremony commentator, Fr. Possidente, asking them from the microphone to hold their applause in check. At the Offertory he explained how the new bishop "out of his gratitude and great generosity" presents his consecrator "with gifts of bread and two barrels of wine" – the people waited to see normal-sized barrels and on came two tiny tubs the size of soda siphons – general amusement of the people! I recalled how in 1988 Archbishop Lefebvre was cheated with the same two mini-barrels being presented to him by each of the four new bishops! However, the formalized beauty of this gesture brought a radiant smile to the face of the consecrator of 1991.

At the end of the four-hour ceremony – and the people were not tired but expected more – now four bishops stood in line to be photographed and the people's exultation could be checked no longer: led by the dynamic young parish priest of Sao Fidelis, Fr. Jonas, their joy exploded in one "Vivat" after another: Fr. Jonas: "Long live the bishops!" – explosion: "VIVAT!" Fr. Jonas: "Long live the new bishop!" – explosion: "VIVAT!" – "Long live

Dom Tissier!" – explosion: "VIVAT!" "Long live Dom Lefebvre!" (He is dead) – "VIVAT!" "Long live Dom de Castro Mayer!" (He is dead) – "VIVAT!" – a good two dozen explosions running through all of Fr. Jonas' heroes, like a series of firecrackers. At this point the Society's District Superior of France, beaming all over, stepped forward to get a better view of Fr. Jonas on the sanctuary stage above – I can see the Society's French District being instructed to take a leaf out of the book of the effervescent Brazilians!

Dear friends, let us get missionising, let us rebuild another Catholic diocese, and to the consecration of its bishop I promise to invite Fr. Jonas! We may die, but if we keep our Catholic Faith we shall not die of grief! God bless you.

NO. 97 | SEPTEMBER 1, 1991

Slacks I

SUMMER'S END MAY not seem to be the cleverest moment to choose to write about women's dress. Surely the arrival rather than the departure of the warm weather would be the time to inveigh against immodest clothing. However, several ladies happen to have raised with me this summer the question of women wearing trousers or shorts (pants), and the problem is broader and deeper than just immodesty, grave though immodesty is.

For instance Bishop de Castro Mayer used to say that trousers on a woman are worse than a miniskirt, because while the miniskirt is sensual and attacks the senses, the trousers are ideological and attack the mind. For indeed women's trousers, as worn today, short or long, modest or immodest, tight or loose, open or disguised (like the "culottes"), are an assault upon woman's womanhood and so they represent a deep-lying revolt against the order willed by God. This may be least true of the long "culottes," trousers most closely resembling a skirt, and at best mistakable for a skirt, but insofar as "culottes" establish the principle of dividing woman's outward apparel from the waist down, they merely disguise the grave disorder.

Richard N. Williamson

What disorder? ("Excellency, this time really you have flipped your lid!")

In the beginning, God created man and woman, both human but quite different, firstly man, secondly woman (Genesis 1: 27; 2: 22); woman to be man's helpmate like unto himself (Gen. II, 18), woman for man, not man for woman (I Cor. 11: 9), for "the man is not of the woman but the woman is of the man" (I Cor. 11: 8). Thus even before original sin happened, God ordered between man and woman distinction, inequality, and the headship of man over woman for purposes of living in society and in the family upon this earth.

Original sin, whereby Eve made Adam sin and not the other way round (I Tim 2: 14), entailed Eve's being punished, amongst other things, by the turning of her natural and painless subordination to Adam into a punishing domination of his over her, for she had shown by seducing him that she needed to be controlled . . . "thou shalt be under thy husband's power, and he shall have dominion over thee" (Genesis 3: 16). Thenceforth with the transmission of original sin to all children of Adam passes to all daughters of Adam (except, of course, the Blessed Virgin Mary) this punitive subordination.

As with all problems of sin, the only true solution is the grace of Our Lord Jesus Christ. For instance in a Catholic marriage the painful control of man over woman, evident in all non-Christian cultures and reemerging in our own anti-Christian culture, becomes by supernatural grace more and more that subordination of woman to man which is in accordance with their nature and which is profitable to both, which Eve had before she and Adam fell.

But away with Eden by grace! The modern world will have none of Jesus Christ's solutions to Adam's and Eve's problems. Making idols of liberty and equality, to refuse any inequality or subordination of woman to man, it will deny any distinction between them, it denies of course any order of God in His creation, any need for Redemption, and it will deny if necessary God's very existence. Today's feminism is intimately connected to witchcraft and satanism.

These considerations have taken us a long way from the question of women's trousers, and of course not every woman putting on a pair of shorts is consciously thinking of defying God or of defying her menfolk. She is, however, conscious of something. She is clearly aware that divided shorts are not like an undivided skirt, and the difference is that abandoning the skirt gives her a vague feeling – surely of unease, or emancipation, or both . . . What is that feeling based on?

Clothing divided for the legs obviously liberates the mobile lower half of the body for a number of activities for which clothing undivided like a skirt is relatively cumbersome. Adam then having to earn his family's bread by the sweat of all kinds of activities outside the home, it is entirely normal for the man to wear trousers, and if a girl gets it into her head to join him in these activities, obviously trousers likewise emancipate her to do so. Shorts are the outward and visible sign of her liberation from the restricted range of homemaking activities.

However, she is uneasy because trousers are not the natural wear of a woman. Howsoever it be with other species, in the human species the female is designed to attract the eye of the male much more than the reverse – compare the number of male and of female beauty magazines on the market. Now original sin wounds human nature with concupiscence (unlawful desire) particularly in the senses of sight, touch and imagination. It follows for questions of clothing that what might rouse concupiscence needs more to be disguised in woman from man's eye than in man from woman's eye. Hence as trousers benefit the activity of the man, so skirts disguisingly loose befit the dignity and honor of the woman. Hence while donning his emancipatory trousers, she feels uneasy – at least until her conscience is dulled – as she is moving away from her identity and role and dignity as a woman. In her conscience is resounding the voice of the Lord her God pronouncing in the Mosaic Law: "A woman shall not be clothed with man's apparel, neither shall a man use woman's apparel: for he that doeth these things is abominable before God" (Deut. 22: 5). And trousers are normally man's apparel, for reasons given above.

Of course if one denies the original sin which inflamed man's concupiscence (Gen. 3: 7) and sharpened woman's subordination (Gen. 3: 16), women's trousers are not so unreasonable, but see all around you the absurd consequences of denying original sin ! – sweet Polyanna goes to the office dressed fit to inflame a stone, but woe unto the poor male colleague in the office who fails to react like a stone, because with recent laws (in the USA) she will attack him in court! Insanity! Places of work will soon have to extract in advance from women sworn declarations whether they do, or do not, want to have advances made to them! But what was to be expected when women were pulled out of their home? It all serves the liberal men right for so misleading their women.

Contrast the reflective good sense of an American grandmother who said to me this summer when she was on retreat here in Winona that, looking back on her Californian youth, she could see she had often been induced to wear trousers, and now she regretted it – she could see now that each time her womanliness had been diminished. As G.K. Chesterton said, there is nothing so unfeminine as feminism. Women's trousers are a vital part, maybe the crucial breakthrough, of feminism.

As for the true womanliness of woman, its importance cannot be exaggerated. It all turns on women being essentially designed by God for motherhood; for the bringing of children into this world, and for their rearing; for the giving of life, warmth, love, nursing, and nourishment, everything represented by mother's milk. For this, men are not designed, of it they are intrinsically incapable yet upon it they are wholly dependent if they are to become human, as opposed to inhuman, beings. In a valuable book, *The Flight from Woman*, a cultivated Jewish psychiatrist, Karl Stern, tells how he could discern in countless ills of the big city patients coming through his Toronto practice after World War II a pattern of womanlessness with which he was familiar from the works of famous modern writers such as Goethe, Descartes, Tolstoy, Ibsen – not a lack of women, but a lack of truly womanly women, because modern men and women alike are trampling upon the womanly qualities and virtues. Shakespeare distilled this spirit in Lady Macbeth, proto-feminist and satanist:

> Come you spirits
> That tend on mortal thoughts, unsex me here,
> And fill me from the crown to the toe top-full
> Of direst cruelty . . . Come to my woman's breast
> And take my milk for gall, you murdering ministers . . .

(*Macbeth*, Act I, Sc. V).

Heaven help us! The womanliness of our women is being rooted out and the result is a way of life doomed to self-destruction, doomed to abort.

Girls, be mothers, and in order to be mothers, let not wild horses drag you into shorts or trousers. When activities are proposed to you requiring trousers, if it is something your great-grandmother did, then find a way of doing it, like her, in a skirt. And if your great-grandmother did not do it, then forget it! Her generation created your country, your generation is destroying it. Of course not all women who wear trousers abort the fruit of their womb, but all help to create the abortive society. Old-fashioned is good, modern is suicidal. You wish to stop abortion? Do it by example. Never wear trousers or shorts. Bishop de Castro Mayer was right.

Enclosed is a flyer of tapes made by Bernard Janzen, a Canadian friend of the seminary with whom I have made a dozen tapes myself. The seminary would surely not endorse every statement on each of the tapes. For instance, Malachi Martin's latest book, The Keys of This Blood, showed him to be deeply divided between the conservative and the Traditional analyses of the crisis of the Church, two analyses which one might love to reconcile but which are irreconcilable. This reconciling of irreconcilables makes his tapes very popular, and they might greatly help someone struggling out of the Novus Ordo, but they might equally confuse someone making the last part of the climb up to Tradition. Be careful to whom you might give them. Similarly Michael Davies is conservative rather than Traditional, he is certainly not 100% behind the SSPX, but like Malachi Martin he can reach many a listener closed to the Society, at least for now. With that proviso, these tapes can surely be recommended. Please order direct from Canada and not from the seminary.

A new school-year opens in a few days' time. Pray for seminarian Michael Rios from Texas who on August 22, returning home from Mass, had a terrible accident which killed his mother and a friend in his car, crushed beneath a truck and which has left him paralyzed at least from the waist down. God's way are mysterious, but in Michael's place He does seem to be sending us some more fine young men to try their vocations at the end of this month. On their behalf, thank you always for your support, which please maintain, and for which may Our Lord continue to repay you.

NO. 97 | SEPTEMBER 1, 1991

The SSPX as Pilot-Light

AND ANOTHER SCHOOL year has quietly started, with 39 old seminarians coming back from their summer vacation, and 18 new seminarians stepping into the ranks. Of these 18, eight are from the United States. The remaining ten will, for as long as they persevere over the next six years, enjoy the hospitality of the United States, but they come from all four corners of the – pardon me the expression! – Empire – two from England, one from Scotland, two from Canada, one from Nigeria, one from New Zealand, one from Australia, two from South Africa. It is certainly this seminary's most international in-take ever. Thank you, American benefactors, it is mostly on your backs that these young men from all over the world will work their way towards the priesthood.

Eighteen young men out of today's world! Archbishop Lefebvre would have said, eighteen miracles. Some of them have had in mind for years to give the seminary a try, others make up their minds at the last moment. Obviously not all will reach the priesthood, but it is interesting that one can never tell in advance who will persevere and who will not. Of 1989's entry of 22, only 9 were still there after one year, whereas of 1990's entry of 15, fourteen lasted their first year. A vocation is something altogether mysterious.

Of course between eighteen young men, and the needs of hundreds of millions of souls in danger of eternal damnation throughout the English-speaking world, there is no proportion, except in God's eyes. Why is it that He is not calling many more young men to the true priesthood, or to the Society's seminaries? Firstly, of course it is not He who is to be blamed. The tales told for instance of young men's true vocations being deflected or destroyed in the training grounds of today's mainstream "Church" are nothing less than horrific. A true vocation is exactly what that "Church" does not want.

Yet still one may ask, given the worldwide emergency, why does the Lord God, whose grace is all-powerful, not reach through to more young men to lead them to where they can become true priests? A consoling thought which is hardly consoling: the young women reaching for the religious life seem, at any rate in the English-speaking world, to be even rarer than the young men. Maidens! Look around you at all those children of young families at the Tridentine Mass! Who is going to be their spiritual mother to put them on the path to Heaven? Of course we have some wonderful laywomen to teach them, but you do realize how much farther into their little souls a Sister in habit can reach? Physical mother of eight, or spiritual mother of eight hundred? The Sacred Heart needs you! You do realize how much more of a man He is to spend your life with and give your heart to than even the most wonderful Prince Charming that Hollywood could make you dream of? As the chief steward says at the marriage feast of Cana (Jn. 2: 10), every other man puts out his best wine first, and it gets worse as one goes on, but with Our Lord the best wine is reserved for the last. Blessed the faithful Sister! What a happy life!

What a happy death! But few seem to seek that happiness today.

Alright, but maidens apart, why such a mere handful of male vocations to that priesthood on which the Church's survival depends? A more consoling consolation: on Saturday, June 20 of 1992, if everything goes to plan, the fourth of the society's four new bishops to come to Winona, Bishop Bernard Tissier de Mallerais from France, will ordain eight seminarians to the priesthood, the largest ordination yet in any one year from the Society's American Seminary, and all eight from the United States. Mark the day down in next year's calendar and plan to come to the family occasion, both to receive great graces and to show God how grateful you are for the immense gift of each new priest.

For indeed, if the Lord God seems to be calling relatively few to the Traditional priesthood, it is surely because relatively few faithful are calling for Traditional priests. Let us not deceive ourselves. We are living through, if not the Great Apostasy itself told of in Scripture (II Thess. 2), at least the dress rehearsal for it. Either, way, these days are such that unless they be shortened, no flesh shall be saved (Mt. 24: 22). The great mass of men are turning away from God, they do not want Him, they do not want His Church, they do not want His kind of priests, so God will not impose these by force, but as a punishment He withdraws them from among mankind, as He withdraws Himself.

He is chastising, sifting, and purifying mankind, especially His Church. It has gone into a tunnel, it looks like going through a good deal more darkness before it comes out into the light again on the other side. This tunnel is the logical conclusion of centuries of Catholics' infidelity, and it is the prophesied harbinger, by God's mercy, of an unprecedented Catholic triumph. Meanwhile He is guaranteeing that His Church does not altogether perish, so the order of the day is survival, and to the fulfilling of that purpose our eighteen young men are proportionate.

I have compared the SSPX to the pilot light on a gas stove. When the gas is turned off, the gas-rings go dead, no cooking can be done and very little heat comes off the pilot light, but so long as one can see the pilot light still lit, one knows that the action will resume as soon as the gas is turned on again. But turning on the gas is not within the power of the pilot light itself.

The stove is the Catholic Church, the gas is the grace of God which has been turned off by the fault of men, so that one gas-ring after another has gone out, and the Catholic priesthood and the Catholic Mass have been almost extinguished. However, the SSPX like a little pilot light is still lit, and its function is to stay lit until such time as God sees fit to turn on His grace once more, at which point the clergy and faithful of the Society and its valiant companions in arms, still lit and warmed by the true Mass, however few they be, will be on hand with the true practice of the Faith to reignite the multitudes of men then returning to God. It is not a question of numbers. It is a question of fidelity, or faithfulness. Pray these new seminarians keep the Faith, and we will pray the same for you, especially each evening of October at Rosary and Benediction.

I am asked what I think of events in Russia. I think the "coup" of August 19 was a fraud (Since when do only four people get killed in real tussles for power?). The leading Communists have changed little more than the name of Communism. They have lost no real power. Their ability to deceive the suicidal West foreshadows the Antichrist's future deceiving of the world. The Red Army is more dangerous than ever, continually arming, arming, arming. God is not mocked (Gal. 6: 7). War is the punishment of sin (James 4: 1).

Do, in time, an Ignatian Retreat. As you see from the inside (not from the pre-printed outside) of the enclosed yellow Retreats flyer, the Society has opened up a new Retreat House in California, in Los Gatos near San Jose. There are now these powerful retreats year round in the East and in the West. Do not turn down the call of grace to go through these gateways to Heaven. As for the enclosed violet sheet, it reproduces two texts concerning the meeting in 1967 of Padre Pio and Archbishop Lefebvre. The first text is a pack of lies currently circulating in the USA and disturbing some souls. In the second text the Archbishop sets the record straight. Of course, responsible for the lies is not Padre Pio, but the author of the book about him.

NO. 99 | NOVEMBER 3, 1991

Slacks II

FEW OF YOU will be surprised to learn that the September letter appealing to the women not to wear trousers caused a strong reaction, comparable only to the reaction to the seminary letter which referred to scientific evidence that certain famous "Holocaust gas-chambers" in Poland cannot have served as gas-chambers at all.

Truly, "I believe in the Holy Ghost and the Communion of Saints" has been replaced by "I believe in the Holo Caust and the Emancipation of Women!" So when with Bible in hand one calls in question these dogmas of the new media religion, it is surprising at how old-fashioned a stake many people wish one to be burned! Or, it is not surprising. As far as this media religion goes, one is a heretic!

So dozens of readers asked to be taken off the seminary's mailing list – done – and a number of you wrote letters. These were about evenly divided, half for women's trousers and half against. Of the letters in defense of women's trousers, most confined themselves to saying, some politely, some less politely, that his Excellency had indeed "flipped his lid." However, a few letters reasonably argued that surely women should not be barred from these and those activities which surely require trousers. The question is worth examining again, even at the risk of alienating dozens more readers (fortunately we are not in a popularity contest), because in the West today, man-woman relations are in profound disarray, and where can Christ's grace come to rest if nature is in upheaval?

Witness in the USA the widely publicized recent Senate hearings in Washington, D.C., on Judge Clarence Thomas' suitability for nomination to the US Supreme Court. The consensus of serious opinion is that he was innocent of supposedly "sexually harassing" several years ago the lawyeress who was brought in by the Judge's enemies at the last moment to torpedo his nomination. Yet before the hearings there was like a hysterical uprising amongst women across the land to insist her phantasizing be heard, during the hearings it received an inordinate amount of attention, and after the hearings there has been a spate of lawsuits being filed by her imitators who feel themselves similarly victims.

Now the vile media played no doubt a large part in inflating the issue out of all proportion, in order amongst other things, whichever side won, to bring the Supreme Court into disrepute: "[I]t is indispensable to stir up the people's relations with their governments in all countries so as utterly to exhaust humanity with dissension, hatred, struggle, envy ... so that the goyim see no other course open to them than to take refuge in our complete sovereignty in money and all else" (Pr. 10).

Nevertheless even our media require some raw material to work with, or to inflate, and that raw material was in this case, whether the harassment be real or unreal, a deep sense of grievance on the part of many women – like a feeling they have been betrayed. Something is going profoundly wrong in man-woman relations.

Richard N. Williamson

Take another example of this grave disruption of nature in the USA today: the invasion of public life by gays and lesbians, men and women being "delivered up to shameful affections... changing the natural use into that which is against nature" (Rom. 1: 26), then flaunting their unnatural vice in public and being rewarded by the vile media with a blaze of publicity. And decent citizens seem unable to do much about it, partly no doubt because "in countries known as progressive and enlightened, we have created a senseless, filthy, abominable literature" (Pr. 14), which literature such citizens allow to prevent them from seeing the so-called "alternative lifestyle" for what it really is, namely one of four sins, as the Catholic Church teaches, so horrible as to cry to Heaven for vengeance.

Again, something is going profoundly wrong when men in large numbers turn from women to men, and women from men to women. Might not women wearing trousers be contributing to this blurring and confusion of the sexes? In any case this upheaval, this earthquake in the realm of morals, is the correct backdrop against which to view the arguments for women's trousers, only this time the appeal will be to the men.

Men, let us suppose that your womenfolk need to go skiing, sailing, mountaineering, Operation Rescuing, engineering, home repairing, parachuting, etc., etc., and that for these activities they absolutely – or for modesty – require trousers. Nevertheless, if with trousers they gain the activity but lose their femininity, is not the price too great? Today, you want to go mountaineering. Tomorrow, she wants to go with you. The day after she loses her womanliness. The day after that, your son turns to his own kind. Obviously, that is to fast forward the process involved, but the fact remains that when women are allowed, encouraged or pushed into activities in any way diminishing their womanliness or their modesty, they are being betrayed.

"But, Excellency, you are talking as though we men still have some control over what they do!" Reply:— if men have lost control, it is only because they have wanted to lose control. Even disobedient modern woman is still, believe it or not, only following her disobedient revolutionary man. If he would obey his God, she would much more easily obey her man. If he is liberal and lawless, why should she not be? "The head of every man is Christ; and the head of the woman is the man" (I Cor. 11: 3). The responsibility is man's, coming from God. Modern women have, in general, been betrayed, by the liberalism of their men.

"But, Excellency, the logic of what you are saying is that the men must no longer go mountaineering, skiing, etc., etc.!" The objection is grave, resting as it does upon, for instance, the modern city-dweller's serious need of recreational exercise, and so on. Reply:— if modern life necessitates for the man a measure of activities requiring for the woman to accompany him that she forfeit her womanliness or her modesty, then modern life is not viable, and will destroy itself, as, arguably, it has already gone a long way to doing. Turn the question which way you will, that woman be womanly and that her womanliness be protected by her man, is not an optional extra, it is an absolute necessity for human survival.

Menfolk! Here are seven practical suggestions:

- First and foremost, yourselves obey God, submit to His Law and give that example to your womenfolk who will find it that much easier to obey you when they see you are not a law unto yourselves. Kneel down, in front, to recite the family Rosary.

- Secondly, throw out, without mercy, that television set as being the prime poisoner of your mind and the minds of those around you. And waste little time on newspapers. The media are vile.

- Thirdly, stop wallowing in Hollywood slush and video mush, of which that which is pornographic bestialises you, while that which is romantic unmans you by exalting feeling over reason. No amount of "macho" sports will make you a man when your entertainments make you mentally a beast or a woman.

- Fourthly, give your womenfolk all the affection they need, even a bit more, but do not wrap yourselves around them. The bean-plant wraps around the pole and not the pole around the plant!

- Fifthly, absolutely yourselves abstain from, and discourage (or forbid!) your womenfolk's participation in, any activities necessitating immodest dress on their part, e.g. tennis parties or athletics meetings, especially when these also set women in graceless competition with one another. Fighting may build manliness, but it destroys womanliness.

- Sixthly, do not abstain yourselves from manly activities, on the contrary, but rather than have your womenfolk accompany you on them even in modest trousers, e.g. skiing or sailing, remember that they need your company ("thou shalt be under thy husband's power" – Gen. 3: 16) and devote enough of your time to activities where they can accompany you if need be without forfeiting anything in womanliness or modesty.

- Seventhly, never admire your womenfolk when they are unfeminine or immodest, readily admire them when they are feminine and modest. The granting or withholding of your admiration may well succeed where your commands and prohibitions fail.

The rest is easy enough to work out along the same lines of old-fashioned common sense. Along such lines you may spare yourself the punitive shock of having a son or daughter come home one day and announce they have taken up living with one of their own kind! – Heaven help us! What more shall the times force us to address of which Saint Paul might have preferred "it not so much as be named amongst you"? (Eph. 5: 3)

Why Rome Must Take Out the SSPX

JIMINY CRICKET! IF ever the writer of this letter were to fear its readers going to sleep, all he need do would be to write "Slacks III"! From "Slacks I" and "Slacks II" the mail is still coming in, continuing about evenly divided for and against women's trousers. No, this letter will not be "Slacks III," the writing of which will be held over as a threat to keep some of you in line! (Yes, Madam, I heard you – nothing will keep you in line!) However, we will be printing (anonymously) some of the very fine letters received here in praise of skirts for women. Be warned, these will be printed on brown paper, so when they arrive, whosoever wishes may direct them straight into the circular file! For indeed the writing of this letter is a tyranny, but its reading is a democracy!

Meanwhile on the Superior General's blue paper is coming to you this month an interview given last summer by the SSPX's Superior General, Rev. Fr. Franz Schmidberger, to the international magazine *30 Days*. Fr. Schmidberger was asked principally about ongoing relations between the Society and Rome. In his replies one can see the SSPX continuing along the lines laid down by Archbishop Lefebvre: openness to Rome, respect for Rome, the classical attachment of any Roman Catholic to Rome, but a firm refusal to follow today's Rome in its modernist errors.

Fr. Schmidberger tells that since Archbishop Lefebvre's death last March, there has not been much contact between Rome and the Society. Elsewhere Cardinal Oddi was quoted last autumn as saying that henceforth Rome is disregarding the Society. All honor to his Eminence and to his colleagues, but I for one do not believe him. The Pharisees pretended to disregard Our Lord, but they spied on his every step!

After all, Rome cannot help keeping watch on the Society, or on any coherent group with large numbers of Catholics keeping the Faith. The reason is not hard to find – such groups are the main obstacle to the advance of the Antichrist.

In our time towards the end of the world, the infinite Wisdom and Justice of God have allowed His enemies a great deal of control over world affairs. These enemies consider they are today on the brink of achieving their One World Government, towards which an economic crash, or threat thereof, is about to give a powerful push. However, religion has even more power than economics over men's minds and hearts. So, Roman Catholicism being amongst world religions the one with an incomparable prestige and worldwide levers of spiritual power, the One Worlders owed it to themselves to infiltrate Rome and harness it to the purposes of the Antichrist. This with Vatican II they largely succeeded in doing, as the fruits of its aftermath continually demonstrate. Another recent example in the USA, quite independent of the SSPX, is the dealings since 1988 between Rome and Queen of the Holy Rosary Chapel in Vienna, Ohio. One may hope the complete documentation of these dealings will be published which demonstrate once more that Rome is clearly out not to defend but to destroy the Catholic Faith and Catholic Church of all time.

However, to sweep all Catholics into the clutches of the One World Government, to switch them from followers of Christ into followers of the Antichrist, Rome must deceive them. Many are willing to be deceived, but an influential minority need to have the appearances maintained for them while the contents are switched, until such time as even the old appearances can be jettisoned. In this process, it is vital that the people should be persuaded that Catholicism is only what Rome says it is, that no other Catholicism is possible, and that the old Catholicism in particular is dead and gone. Hence the vigor with which Rome stamped it out in the wake of Vatican II.

For if any group of Catholics survives or revives within the Church to demonstrate by their practice of the "old" religion that it is as true as ever, and viable, even vibrant, such a group will be the living proof that Catholicism is not automatically what "Rome" says it is, that another form of Catholicism than that of "Rome" is after all possible, and that the "old" Catholicism is neither dead nor gone. Such a group will accordingly form the major obstacle in the path of the Religious Department of the One World Government. So the more numerically important it is, the more it must be watched for a flaw, circled around for an opening, maybe infiltrated, in any case subverted and above all divided. That is what *Ecclesia Dei* and St. Peter's Fraternity were all about (poor St. Peter's! Let me spare you the latest circle-squaring woes of their Tradition-docile-to-modernism). That is why I simply do not believe Cardinal Oddi when he says Rome is henceforth disregarding the Society. As Churchill might have said, his Eminence is perpetrating a terminological inexactitude (there is a simpler word for it, but a gentleman is not meant to use such words).

Logically, this Rome has to be casting around to find a way of dividing and destroying the Society . . . maybe "unheard of concessions, undreamt of ouvertures," something along the lines of Dmitri Manuilski's famous recipe for the Communists to lull and smash the decadent West . . .

Ah, my dear friends, the Society is a poor affair, humanly speaking quite insignificant, but it is rich in its upholding of the Divine Truth. Until Rome unequivocally returns to upholding that same Truth, there is little or nothing Rome has with which to endow the poor Society, least of all Rome's current version of respectability, so that there is nothing that the Society has to go beg of Rome. In the Catholic Church, and, amongst all human enterprises beneath the moon, in the Catholic Church alone, the Truth is in the driving seat. Read these two blue pages for reassurance as to the at least immediate future of the Society. And keep our Superior General in your prayers, as he dances with foxes and wolves. Dom Putti said of these Romans, "Sono tutti delinquents." Translation upon request!

As for the long-term viability of the Truth, take out your Missal, and see if it includes the wonderful Antiphons of today's Office, the first Sunday in Advent, drawn from the Prophets Joel (3: 18), Zechariah (9: 9; 14: 5) and Isaiah (4: 1,6), and from Deuteronomy (18: 18).

Advent means the coming of the Messiah to rebuild the spiritual Jerusalem (#5) which is the Catholic Church, not the physical Jerusalem which was razed to the ground in 70 A.D. for its crime of deicide. Rejoice and shout for joy, O children of the Church (#2), because no worldly miseries, not even of 1991 or 1992, can stop you from finding the Messiah if you seek him, or from slaking your spiritual thirst in the waters of his Church (#4), and in that day the mountains shall drop down sweetness and the hills shall flow with spiritual milk and honey (#1), collapse of the economy notwithstanding!

Dear benefactors, thank you for keeping the seminary in the black through another calendar year. Have a very merry Christmas to rejoice in the Messiah being amongst us, but please do not send me a Christmas card if you wish to have mercy on my desk!

Join us on the Feast of the Immaculate Conception in making the enclosed Consecration of Russia to the Immaculate Heart of Mary. May she obtain blessing and protection for all of your families, especially for the womenfolk who never wear trou-*!*!* BE QUIET, bishop!

Most . . . most . . . ruefully yours in love of the Messiah.

NO. 101 | JANUARY 1, 1992

Young Mothers, Keep Mothering!

WE AT LAST arrive at January, the month of the Holy Family, Jesus, Mary, and Joseph. In these times, to write every month in defense of the family could not be too much. Of course the family pivots around the mother, so whenever one defends the true woman one is still defending the family, for instance when one attacks women's t*!*!* – "Biiii-SHOOOP!" – don't worry about that howl, that's just the butch ghost from the seminary dungeon – I was going to say, this letter will be written to encourage the young family fathers and mothers.

Young – and not so young – mothers and fathers, yours is not an easy task today of creating a Catholic family. To take a measure of the problem, you need to take a measure of the corruption of Catholicism, which lies centuries deep, and for which you were not responsible. All you are responsible for is resisting the Revolution in your own family when you realize how it works.

Wherever Protestantism prevailed 400 years ago, it dissolved in that part of the world the Catholic Church, or the Mystical Body of Christ, and left man no longer a member of that divine social body, but a lone individual before God; hence modern individualism. Protestantism also "liberated" man's conscience from the authority of the teaching and commanding Church (cf. Mt. 28: 19, 20), leaving him "free"; hence modern liberalism. By the end of the 20th century, even in those parts of the world where Protestantism did not originally prevail, the individualistic liberalism it spawned had deeply penetrated, for instance inside the Catholic Church itself with Vatican II. Hence the entire modern world is soaked in the values of Protestantism, each man free, each man on his own, each man equal in society. But these are profoundly anti-social values. Hence all modern society is breaking down. But the family is a small society. Hence the modern family is breaking down.

For a picture of how, take the spectacle on airports today, or wherever, of one who is obviously a family father with his wife and one or two children, but who dresses, behaves and does his best to look like the Lone Ranger! Poor family! One can watch nature pulling them towards him as his natural dependents, and then his second nature, the individualism he absorbed today from the cradle onwards, pushing them away. However, two can play at the independence game, so one often sees the wife and then the one or two children trying in turn to look as though they do not belong to him, whereupon it is merely a matter of time before each of them goes his or her own way.

Marriage as designed by God is a bond, children are a bind, a family consists of ties, or constraints. But "liberty" means a lack of constraint – "No strings and no connections, no ties and no affections." So "Liberty" destroys the family.

The family as designed by God is a little hierarchical society, with the father as its head, the children under the father and mother, and the servants after them (Eph.

5: 22 – 6: 9, passage including the Epistle of the Catholic Nuptial Mass; cf. Col. 3: 18 – 6: 1). But "equality" means the dissolution of any superiority of rank or position. So "equality" destroys the family.

The family as designed by God is a small society or social body in which each limb or member plays its distinct and complementary part, even mongol children! But individualism means the independence, not the interdependence, of single human beings, and so "individualism" destroys the family.

As an old school teacher of mine used to love quoting, "You pays your money and you takes your choice." Either the modern world continues to glorify liberty, equality, "rugged individualism," revolt against authority, "standing on your own feet," "going it on your own," in which case the family is undermined; or it seeks to defend the family, in which case it must stop glamorizing the anti-social values. It cannot have it both ways. It cannot have its cake and eat it. It cannot love liberalism and family. One of them has got to go. At present it is the family which is going. Decent liberals with the best intentions are, despite themselves, destroying it. The way to hell is paved with good intentions – and bad ideas.

Dear moms and dads! Do you have any sneaking sympathy with the lone rebel who stands up to authority and single-handed makes the true and the good prevail over "them"? Such is the hero of almost every modern film. Beware! Lurking in that values system is the destruction of your family. And the breakdown of the family, God's own framework for making human beings, lets loose an avalanche of evils, unmaking human beings: divorce, contraception, pornography, abortion, euthanasia – need one insist?

Young mother that wrote to me, over 15 years ago, you became a Catholic and a Traditionalist, after growing up in the '60's and '70's somewhat indoctrinated, you told me, in the Women's Liberation Movement, going through college, qualifying as an educator, even working on Capitol Hill, becoming "capable of a great deal," finding "excitement and fulfillment" with other adults in the workplace. Then you married, you decided to listen to your priests, you stayed at home with children, a slew of whom arrived, including by now two teenagers, after you had climbed over a mound of diapers and never caught-up laundry and mess that the family makes, on top of which a few years ago the decision to find Catholic schooling for your children drove you into commuting two hours a day for the three of them while homeschooling two more and raising a toddler. "This has been crazy!!" you say.

Not so crazy, mother! What did you dream of on Capitol Hill? Fighting pornography? I tell you, if your mother's warmth and purity is in the hearts of your boys, you will have done more to immunize them against it from within than all those legislators put together will ever do to protect them from without! Or did you perhaps dream of getting into the interesting fight against abortion? I tell you, if you have put the supernatural Faith first, and stayed at home to raise a slew of kids in that Faith, you have done more in the hearts of your girls to fight abortion than if you and they took part in numberless marches and campaigns and demonstrations.

Mother, you may not think so right now, but you have chosen the better part. Just wait to find how empty the nest is when the slew have flown off! Can't wait? Get back to me in twenty years' time! Meanwhile God bless you richly and may you have all the support you need, because the hand that rocks the cradle rules the world, because the mother's heart is the children's schoolroom, because what you alone can put into your children's hearts and souls today will be the making or unmaking of society for all of us tomorrow.

Husbands, get behind the mothers raising your children! Grampa, gramma, shoulder to the wheel, your kids still need you! Fellow-parishioners, lend a hand with that mound of laundry, one little gesture goes a long way! Catholics, let us get together, the whole world depends on us! And young moms, keep producing a slew more of k*!*!*— "BiiiiSHOOOP!" Oh, folks, I must be going!

God love you all through 1992. Live by your Catholic Faith, and you are building on rock, and no wind or rain or floods can harm you (Mt. 7: 24–25).

NO. 102 | FEBRUARY 1, 1992

Cardinal Oddi's Visit to Ecône

A RUMOR CIRCULATING recently from at least one source in the Northeastern United States has it that "the Society of St. Pius X has turned over all its property to the Vatican. In protest several German seminarians of the Society are said to have left it, and the priest secretary of one of its bishops is said to have resigned."

The only reason for quoting such a rumor is that it provides an opportunity to tell the truth: in April of last year, three seminarians left the Society's German Seminary in Zaitzkofen in Bavaria because the Society will not refuse to recognize John Paul II as Pope of the Catholic Church. For the same reason an Oblate Sister rendering some service as a secretary to Bishop de Galarreta in the Argentine, also severed her connection with the Society over one year ago.

As for the Society turning over its property to the Vatican, one has to guess that last year's summer and autumn contacts between Rome and the Society must be the grounds for this wishful thinking on the part of our adversaries (to our right and to our left), who hope that the Society has surrendered or is about to surrender its position to Rome. Last December you received with this letter the text of an interview between the Society's Superior General, Fr. Franz Schmidberger, and an Italian journalist. That interview hardly showed the Society "giving away the store."

Let me now give you a first-hand account, made public several months ago, of another of these contacts, the September visit of Cardinal Oddi to the Society's now motherhouse in Ecône, Switzerland. Then you can see again how the Superior General reacted. Here is how the Society's French District Superior, Fr. Paul Aulagnier, who was present, described that visit in the French District's bi-monthly magazine, *Fideliter*:

> Cardinal Oddi often used to ring up Archbishop Lefebvre. He had telephoned Ecône in August to say he would be in the area and that he would call by the Seminary. He was told, you are welcome, just give a little advance notice.
>
> Without further notice he turned up on September 18 at lunch-time. He was in a clerical suit, having come in a car driven by his nephew . . . The Seminary Rector hastened to greet the Cardinal and to bring him straight to lunch . . . the meal took place in silence as is usual during the beginning-of-school-year retreat. After the meal we invited him to exchange a few words with us over coffee in an adjoining room of the Seminary. The Seminary Rector and Vice-Rector were present, one of the Seminary professors, a Society priest from Italy and myself.
>
> The Cardinal showed us a good deal of sympathy. He told us how fond of us he was and how much he respected the Archbishop whom he held to be a holy man. He told us he wished there would be an agreement with Rome, that he was ready to do anything to make a solution possible but we would have to hurry up because he and the few cardinals favorable to us

were getting on in age, and once they were gone, he was afraid things would be even more difficult for ourselves. I told him we put our trust in Providence, as did the chaste Suzanna in the book of Daniel, Chapter 13, meaning that God will not abandon those who put their trust in Him.

The conversation was very lively. The Cardinal is a short man, corpulent, old, tired, and not well, but in his eyes one can read profundity, intelligence, sympathy, affability. Our conversation was altogether straightforward, good-natured and peaceful. Above all we convinced him that we were still attached to the Roman Church and ready for any contact or meeting to try to come up with some solutions towards an agreement, provided only Catholic Truth and Tradition be safeguarded. However, he made clear that his visit was on his own initiative, that nothing had been pre-arranged...

He told us: 'I am getting old, I am no longer in any position of importance, I have much less authority.' Nevertheless, he did still seem to have easy access to the Holy Father. He suggested to us a solution along the lines of Opus Dei, with a personal prelature. He admitted that we were in a stronger position with our bishops now consecrated, and that Rome, if we could show a little flexibility, might eventually agree to arrange things. He gave us to understand that Cardinal Ratzinger was also fond of us...

After the conversation ended, the Cardinal went to visit the Archbishop's tomb nearby. He prayed briefly and then said out loud so that everybody could hear, "Merci, Monseigneur" (Thank you, your Grace). Most touching. Who could be so churlish as to doubt the Cardinal's sincere affection for the Society's Founder and for all that he stood for?

However, know that the Society's Superior General replied last month to the Cardinal's beguiling advances (unofficial, of course), with a private letter not due to become public, but the essential contents of which are known: given the doctrinal differences between the Society and Conciliar Rome, differences unchanged by anything proposed by the Cardinal, then for as long as Rome remains Conciliar, a fruitful and open collaboration between the two does not seem possible.

As soon as the Archbishop died in March of last year, a certain churl was predicting that Rome would begin again towards the Society with the routine of carrot and stick. One may speculate that it was carrots for lunch at Ecône last September 18 (not pre-arranged, of course). And if the Superior General's reply to the Cardinal was as straight-forward, good-natured and peaceful as the Cardinal's advances to the Society – and what else would it be? – we can expect a Roman diet of carrots for a little while yet.

Especially carrots which might split the recalcitrant Superior General from any of his subjects, or any of his subjects from their Superior. If I was a Roman prelate today, I would be prowling round and around the Society like a lion, or a wolf, or a fox, seeking a way in, looking for the unguarded sheep or the sleeping shepherd. I could have had enough by now of this confounded Society! And when my supply of carrots (which would be exhaustible!) had run out, I would – weeping, in public, copiously – resort once more to the stick.

And if these donkeys of the Society were too stupid to feel any longer the Church's grand stick of "excommunication," then – then – what would I do? – I have it! – I would turn to the State! After all, the Liberal State clamorously separated itself from the Church, but ever since the Church at Vatican II grasped the wisdom of the Liberal State (*Declaration on Religious Liberty*, #3, #6), Liberal State and Liberal Church have been back in union (#13), and I can rely on the State to get this infernal Society out of my way.

You are shocked? Already in France since 1988 the liberal government has conspired with the liberal Church to block payment of much-needed bequests to the Society; in Canada the liberal State can be seen now preparing its Inquisition to crush any religion laying absolute claim to superiority! Liberals preparing an Inquisition ?? See the story at the end of the enclosed *Verbum*.

Dear friends, the Society does not, humanly speaking, stand a chance. From a variety of angles, it cannot win. But in our divine Faith lies a power which cannot lose. All the cunning and might of Imperial Rome could not overcome the simplicity and Faith of the tender virgin martyrs. Let us be faithful and patient under our daily cross, and with the dear Society, without it if necessary, we too shall go singing to our Eternal Bridegroom. But we shall meanwhile pray for our superiors in the Society and for the Cardinals in Rome, that God give them light and courage. Two or three times a week, an extra decade of the Rosary is prayed at the seminary here for the intentions of the Pope.

Sedevacantism: Too Simplistic, Too Absolute

L ET US GET into another argument (no, not yet Flak III!). A Catholic likes using his mind on his Faith, like burnishing a treasure.

The position taken by the SSPX in today's crisis of the Church has again come under attack. The arguments of the sedevacantists who believe the See (Sedes) of Rome is vacant have been brought forward once more in the first issue of a magazine just launched in the USA which I will call CR. The arguments are not new, but it will do no harm to explain once more why the Society acknowledges the authority of the present Church leaders, despite the damage they are doing, or allowing to be done, to the Catholic Church.

This damage is of course the reason why the so-called sedevacantists cannot accept that the recent Popes (since, say, Paul VI) have really been Popes. How could Christ's own Vicars so betray Christ's own Church? Answer, they cannot be real Vicars! The argument is simple, and notice that it rests on truths of the Faith. If the sedevacantists did not believe in Christ, in his Vicars and in his Church, the present betrayal would be no problem. The sedevacantists believe in Our Lord and in His Church. In this respect they differ from the Liberals and are far superior to them. However, their arguments are too simple. Let us have a look at the latest version of them.

CR says that faced with this crisis of the Church we can take one of three positions, that of *"Ecclesia Dei,"* or that of the "Lefebvrists" (i.e., the SSPX), or that of the sedevacantists. The *Ecclesia Dei* position is at least consistent, says CR, but it means submitting to and siding with the liberals. The "Lefebvrist" position refuses to submit to the liberals, but it is riddled with contradictions. The only non-liberal and non-contradictory position is that of the sedevacantists.

As for the futility of the *Ecclesia Dei* compromise with the official Church, the Society and the sedevacantists are agreed. No chicken with its head still on walks into the fox's den for protection! But how does CR argue that the Society is mired in contradiction? By a triple-barreled argument, or by three parallel arguments based on the Church, on the Faith and on the Papacy.

Firstly, the Catholic Church as instituted by Our Lord must be visible and indefectible. But the presently visible Church , i.e., the official Church, has gravely defected, by liberalism. Therefore either liberalism is acceptable – absurd – or the official Church is not the real Church. But the Society insists on partly treating it as the true Church, partly not treating it as the true Church, so the Society is in contradiction.

Secondly, the Catholic Faith is either integral (i.e., complete in all its elements) or it is not at all. Now the Novus Ordo system of doctrines, moral teachings, worship and discipline pertains to the Catholic Faith. Therefore it is either integrally Catholic and to be accepted entirely, or it is not Catholic at all and it is to be entirely rejected. But the Society insists that for instance the Mass of the Novus Ordo is not automatically invalid, and yet it refuses to let people attend it, so the Society is again in contradiction.

Thirdly, true Catholic Popes even outside of their solemn or extraordinary Magisterium can prescribe nothing harmful to souls in discipline or worship (Denzinger 1578). But the liberal Novus Ordo system was prescribed with the full authority of the recent Popes. Therefore either the Novus Ordo system is not harmful to souls – absurd –or these seeming Popes are not real Popes. But the Society insists on recognizing their authority while refusing their authority! And so once more the Society is caught in impossible contradiction.

Moreover, an extra difficulty for the Society is that since it is caught in contradictions, somebody has to decide what it will accept and what it will refuse. But Archbishop Lefebvre alone had the prestige within the Society to do this work of sifting, so that now that he is gone, the Society must disintegrate.

Leaving aside for the moment the last argument, it will be noticed that each of the three main arguments consists in, an either-or. Since the "either" always results in liberalism while the "or" results in sedevacantism, both rejected by the Society, then obviously the Society believes there is a third possibility which is in each case being excluded by CR. Let us take each argument in turn:

Firstly, the Catholic Church considered in her pure state as Bride of Christ is indeed indefectible. But she is embodied, by Christ's will, in human beings, churchmen, who are, as human beings, defectible. By the CR argument, no churchman should ever defect! But see how the Apostles ran away in the Garden of Gethsemane! What the Church's indefectibility requires is that at no one time should all the churchmen defect, which has not happened, even today. Hence the Society, believing in the Church, sifts the churchmen, as Our Lord told us to do – "beware of wolves in sheep's clothing."

Secondly, the Catholic Faith must indeed be professed integrally in all its parts, and any system defective in any of those parts will not be Catholic, either as a whole or in its defective parts. But nobody can say that any of its Catholic parts, as a Catholic part, is not Catholic. For instance in the third century the Church judged, after a bitter dispute, that baptism administered by the Donatist heretics was valid. This baptism was culpably incorporated in a non-Catholic whole, but that did not invalidate it as a Catholic part. Thus the Society rejects the Novus Ordo Mass both as a whole and in all its non-Catholic parts, but it no more says that the hereticising whole necessarily invalidates all the parts; including for instance the Consecration correctly said, than that the Donatist heresy invalidated the Donatist baptism. Hence the need to sift.

Thirdly, it is true that if the Pope uses the full weight of his Apostolic authority to impose upon souls some measure of discipline or worship, that measure cannot be harmful, but from the very beginning of, for instance, the Novus Ordo Mass, a handful of wholly competent canon lawyers pointed out that Paul VI never, while instituting the New Mass, at the same time strictly abrogated or prohibited the continuation of the Old Mass. Therefore, strictly, the Novus Ordo was an option rather than an obligation. So neither the Society nor anyone else was, or is, obliged to declare Paul VI was only a seeming Pope. Providence in a sense kept him liberal even when he enforced his favorite laws! But neither the Society nor anyone else is obliged to accept those anti-Catholic laws, even if Paul VI was a true Pope. Hence again the need to sift.

Nor is the Society nor any other Catholic essentially dependent upon Archbishop Lefebvre to do the sifting of what to accept and what to refuse amongst the parts of the Novus Ordo religion, always refusing it as a whole. The yardstick is Tradition, which is independent of us all. True, Archbishop Lefebvre proved himself to be an outstanding yardstick of Tradition while he lived, and all true Catholics miss him today, but he would have been the first to say that the documents and monuments of Tradition are as accessible to us now as they ever were to him.

Contrary to what many sedevacantists and liberals may think, the Society did not follow the Archbishop blindly. Had he ever made a major departure from Tradition, I am sure the Society would have split much worse than it ever did. And then, were he so indispensable, how could the Society have lasted already one year without him?

Sedevacantists will not like being told they resemble liberals, but when they, like them, exaggerate the importance of Archbishop Lefebvre's person to the Traditional movement, surely it is because they like them overestimate authority and underestimate objective Truth. That Truth is the whole strength of the so-called Traditional movement. Our Lord said that if all human voices were silenced in his defense, the very stones of the street would cry out in protest. And that is one more statement true not only because of the authority of him who made it, but also because of the very nature of truth. "Fear not, little flock . . . "

However, the interesting thing with the article of CR is to attempt to discern the common pattern or mistake behind its three main arguments. Surely there is a common mistake of sedevacantists, and surely it is this: they fail in general to distinguish between the abstract and the concrete, between abstract principles and concrete people, between abstract errors and the people erring.

Richard N. Williamson

St. Augustine said, "Slay errors but love those who are erring," (which is still neater in Latin: Interficite errores, diligite errantes). Contrariwise, liberals love the errors together with those erring, while sedevacantists slay the erring together with their errors. The Liberals' softness on people extends to softness on principles; the sedevacantists' hardness on principles makes them go hard on people. Only the Catholic in St. Augustine's footsteps keeps his balance by being firm on principles while going easy (not soft) on people.

Thus it is true that the Catholic Church, Catholic belief and the Catholic Papacy are in their abstract state free of all taint, but to save us concrete sinners, Our Lord willed that Church, belief and Papacy be embodied respectively in churchmen, believers and Popes, in which human condition all three are bound to be mixed more or less with human failings and non-Catholic elements. For, underneath the moon, what is more contradictory and mixed up than human beings?

But sedevacantists do not understand mixture. For them everything is either-or. Thus CR cannot understand how the "Conciliar Church" and the Catholic Church can overlap, and indeed as abstract systems concilliarism and Catholicism absolutely exclude one another. But in the concrete, or in real life, what is easier than for conciliar folk still to have something Catholic in them, or for Catholics still to have slack things or something conciliar, about them? To many conciliar folk surely applies Our Lord's own rule: "The bruised reed he shall not break: and the smoking flax he shall not extinguish" (Is. 42: 3; Mt. 12: 20), meaning that so long as there is a glimmer of Catholicism in them, Catholics should make every reasonable effort to restore that glimmer to a bright flame, which is of course why the Society has long reached out to the erring conciliarists, believers and Popes. On the other hand, to all Catholics surely applies Hamlet's saying, "Use each man according to his deserts and who should escape whipping?"

Fortunately Our Lord looks first not upon our weak achievements but upon our good intentions; a man can be mired up to his neck and over in error, in the kingdom of slacks, in contradictions, in filth, but for as long as he still seeks God, or desires the truth, or wants to do his best as he sees it, the Good Shepherd reaches out to him and will not let him go.

Let CR go back over the words and deeds of the Archbishop and the Society. CR is entitled to judge that either of them here or there went astray in the delicate task of discerning between the error and the erring, but CR cannot make the accusation stick that the policy of slaying the error while loving the erring is contradictory. It is the Sacred Heart's own policy, fortunately for us all!

Amongst other flyers enclosed is one for Our Lady of Victory Home School which recently moved from California to Idaho. Last year we recommended Our Lady of the Rosary Home School based in Kentucky. The SSPX in the USA recommends at present both of these Home Schools to Catholic parents, not because it thinks that everything that either of them does is perfect (they do not recommend one another!), but because home-schooling is becoming so important, and our best information is that each of them does much more good than harm. Heaven knows, either of them could at any point cease recommending the Society, but we recommend them.

Dear readers, may the penances of this Lent serve to diminish mightily within us the part of error, and to enable the Truth to shine ever more purely within us. The struggle will be over only when we die, or, as St. Francis de Sales said, a quarter of an hour after we are dead, but it is a sacred struggle. God bless you and keep you.

"JFK"

One week ago was the first anniversary of the death of Archbishop Lefebvre. Before he died, the controllers of the modern world had pushed him as absolutely low as they could push him, but what man has abased, God is exalting. As quietly as he lived, the Archbishop's name is quietly rising, and will go on rising, until his name once again becomes a curse-word under the Antichrist – "Without him we could have had a situation of no opposition," they will then say.

But now he is safely home, nothing can touch his achievement. It is locked into history. His words and his deeds stand like a rock. More and more people are going to read his words, and more and more people are going to write about his deeds, and as the Devil well knows, there is nothing more he can do about it. All the punches in the book he threw at the Archbishop during his life, but after his death all the Devil can do is make the Archbishop prevail. For, the wilder the storm the Devil calls up in the world and Church, the more clearly it will stand out that the Archbishop was right, and the more people will turn to him, especially youngsters.

I pity decent teachers inside the Novus Ordo system recognizing the finest part of the young minds and souls in front of them turning towards "Lefebvrism" like young plants turn to the light, and then being obliged by the system to cut Lefebvre down again, and to keep cutting him down. Then either their decency goes under, or, in a few cases, they break with the system, but murder will out.

For a classic case of murder will out, see the recent film "JFK" by Oliver Stone, now circulating in the English-speaking world. In a world drowning in lies, it is a grand blow for the truth. It is not a religious film, indeed innocent and vulnerable eyes had better watch a videotape edited when it comes out, rather than now see certain scenes in the complete film. Nor was President Kennedy a religious hero, far from it, indeed in God's eyes his assassination may even have been something of a punishment for his sins – we shall know at the Last Judgment.

But in any case he had courage, he was intending to govern as he saw fit, with the increasing support of the American people, he was more and more threatening the powers that be behind the Establishment, particularly with certain moves he was making against the Federal Reserve, and so before he could break them, they used the Establishment to break him, to blow him away in what one might call the crime of the century, right out in public, in Dealey Plaza, Dallas, to demonstrate their power, and to warn any future President never again to take seriously the idea of governing by the people for the people.

This is the story that Oliver Stone begins to tell. He by no means tells the whole story, but whereas some viewers of the film or readers of this letter might be tempted to deny that the government of their democracy could ever be guilty of such a crime, I can assure you from direct Society contacts in Texas and Louisiana that as much as Oliver Stone does tell of the story is substantially true.

But, Excellency, stay out of controversial politics! Keep to religion! Dear readers, my concern is the Fifth, Eighth and above all First Commandments. The Fifth: the assassination in Dealey Plaza could not have been a more flagrant violation of "Thou shalt not kill"; the Eighth: the subsequent cover-up of the truth has been a continual denial of justice, murdering of true witnesses, parading of false witness; the First: it is because many people make an idol of democracy and a false god of their country that they refuse to believe that their leaders, their government, could ever do such a thing. Secularism is a religion of which the State is the Church, its Constitution is the Bible and its politicians are the priests. How could our President dip his hands in blood, or cover over a trail of it?

Catholics should never fall for such idolatry, and many will protest that nothing could be farther from their thoughts than such foolishness. Really? And if the idolatry is skillfully intermingled with love of country? And if their country is founded on a principle of liberty and equality for all religions, in other words on the principle that truth in religion does not matter?

I do not know if Oliver Stone is a Catholic, in fact he has the reputation of being an out-and-out liberal, but in any case "JFK" is the film of a brave man who loves truth. See it, to see beneath the gloss and the glitter of what the 20th century really is. See it, to guess at the controllers of the modern world. See it, to be reminded of the truth in Jeremiah's words (17: 5): "Thus saith the Lord: Cursed be the man that trusteth in man, and maketh flesh his arm, and whose heart departeth from the Lord!"

On the contrary, continues the Prophet (17: 7), "Blessed be the man that trusteth in the Lord, and the Lord shall be his confidence." Such was Archbishop Lefebvre. Had he not trusted profoundly in God, he would have given way to rage and despair at the power of men assassinating the Church, in the same diabolical early 1960's, long before he found the Society. But, putting his trust in God alone, he started over again from nothing, and now his cause is advancing inexorably to its triumph, because it was and is God's cause.

A fitting first anniversary tribute to the Archbishop is the publication of our Superior General's letter to Cardinal Oddi of January 7 of this year within his enclosed letter to Friends and Benefactors. Read it to be assured that the Archbishop's mind continues to govern the Society: respect for Rome but no respect for apostasy; love of the erring but slaying of the error.

Also enclosed is a schema on television. I think its usefulness lies in its division into three parts: on the one hand, the enemies of television cannot deny that as a machine it is, like all machines, usable for good as well as evil (Part 1); on the other hand few even of the friends of television will deny that today's programs include horrors without number (Part 3); but what often escapes notice is that even if the programming of the machine was angelic, still by its nature, once installed in an average modern home, TV's normal effect will be more or less gravely harmful in a variety of ways (Part 2). Like water and fire, TV is a good servant and a bad master, but given modern living conditions and original sin, TV turns much more easily than fire or water from good servant into bad master. Of course if one denies original sin, there is little problem . . . indeed those who have little problem with TV must ask themselves if they believe in original sin. In theory, of course. In practice...?

The Seminary is looking for a chef. A single man or an older couple would be ideal, sharing our beliefs. Accomodation may be available. Major incentive: daily Mass.

NO. 105 | MAY 8, 1992

Reasonableness of Garabandal

How will it all end? Here in the USA the rioting in Los Angeles of one week ago resulting in 58 deaths (and the death toll is still rising) has reminded us of the question – how will it all end? In honor and love of Our Lady for her month of May, let me devote a whole letter to a prophecy coming, I believe, from her, which I will argue fits this situation of the world like a key fits a lock.

Now this particular prophecy, or the framework of apparitions supposedly of Our Lady within which it was made, has not yet received the official approval of the Church as being worthy of belief by Catholics, and to this extent we are on unsure ground. However, Our Lady appeared at Fatima in 1917 in apparitions whose worldwide importance will surely be questioned by no reader of this letter, yet only in 1930 were they officially approved by the Church. Between 1917 and 1930 was nobody to pay any attention? Had everyone shunned them from 1917 as being unapproved, would they have finally been approved in 1930? The message of Fatima had been neglected enough as it is – how much more would it have been neglected had there been no approval in 1930?

Of course the prime responsibility of approving or disapproving an intervention of Heaven lies with the official Church which is Heaven's appointed representative on earth. Nevertheless if Heaven does intervene, it provides evidence which is designed to suffice to persuade us that the intervention was from Heaven, and much of this evidence is made accessible not only to officials of the Church. How would Fatima have ever been approved if everyone had denied themselves access to the evidence so long as it was not approved? And had Fatima not been approved, where would we be now?

Truth to tell, some critics will scorn even Fatima on the grounds that to save our souls we strictly need to believe no truths outside the Deposit of Faith, all of which truths belong to what is called "public Revelation," closed a little after 100 A.D. with the death of the last Apostle, and anything else is "private revelation" which does not matter, including Fatima.

But each thing in its place. Take a comparison: marriage is good, the religious life is better. Marriage being good no more makes it equal to the vocation than the vocation's being better makes marriage bad. Similarly belief in public Revelation's being absolutely necessary to salvation no more makes private revelation useless than does private revelation's being useful make it – for any Catholic with any common sense – anywhere near as important as public Revelation. Each thing in its place.

Down the ages Mother Church has officially approved of numberless private revelations as being believably from Heaven. Shall Heaven be accused of having wasted its time? Obviously not! Obviously such "private revelations" have frequently given souls access precisely to public Revelation. For instance, how many hundreds of thousands of souls suffocating in modern materialism have not reinvigorated or rediscovered their Catholic Faith at or through Lourdes, a "private revelation" of our Lady in 1858? Authentic "private revelation" is the invaluable servant of public Revelation. Public Revelation may well be the one and only launching-pad for Heaven, still it would not be reached by many souls without the stepping-stones leading to it of "private revelations." Can these be reasonably dismissed as unimportant when without them many souls could, but would not, have been saved? Each thing in its place.

For precisely by its closedness, the Deposit of Faith, or public Revelation, can no longer change, whereas the Devil is constantly laying all around it fresh snares and diversions. Then it is to be wondered at that the Mother of God should in all ages obtain from her divine Son permission to lay down fresh stepping-stones? Not that we should open our arms to every new craziness passing itself off as apparitions of Our Lady, but that in St. Paul's words we should "Despise not prophecies. But prove all things; hold fast that which is good" (I Thess. 5: 20–21). If none of Our Lady's apparitions were true, what would the Devil have to imitate, and how could he get his forgeries into circulation?

Of stepping-stones to public Revelation, or to the Gospel, Fatima is a classic example. Just as Satan prepared in late 1917 to launch from Russia upon the whole world the unprecedented plague of Communism to blast or tear men away from the Gospel, so the Mother of God preceded him from May to October of the same year, providing men through her apparitions in Portugal with all they would need by way of special antidote, if only they would use it. Alas, the Consecration of Russia to her Immaculate Heart has still not been done, and because her "private revelation" has been insufficiently heeded, the world is in the trouble it is in today.

Her last gift to mankind at Fatima was the famous "Third Secret," containing surely the antidote for today's even worse plague within the Church of neo-modernism. The Secret was due by her own instructions to be revealed in 1960 at the latest, that is, two years in advance of the opening of the devastating Second Vatican Council. Churchmen, alas, thought they knew better than the Mother of God, and her antidote was locked up in a papal drawer where it has remained ever since. Now is it not reasonable that the Mother of God would at this point, changing not her message but maybe her tactics, try again? And if she tried again, is it not reasonable that the same churchmen would do all they could to smother her voice once more?

This is the background of the officially still unapproved apparitions of Our Lady to four young girls from 1961 to 1965 in the little mountain village of Garabandal in northern central Spain. Let me not here go into the mass of external evidence, accompanying the apparitions, apparently to authenticate them, and upon which the Church will finally pronounce. Let me here merely make a case for the internal reasonableness of Garabandal's double message and triple prophecy, because it is my personal opinion that it is highly unlikely that Garabandal is false, and if it is true, I would like to avoid having people ask at some point in the future – "Did you know about this and not tell us?" With each day that passes more and more people are in agony over the question, "How will it all end?" With each day that passes the answer of Garabandal makes more and more tranquillizing sense. I believe Garabandal is true, but I am not here arguing it is true, still less imposing it on any readers, I am merely proposing that it makes sense of what might seem an otherwise senseless situation of world and Church.

Richard N. Williamson

Whether authentic or not, the two solemn Messages of Garabandal of October 1961 and June 1965 picked up where the Third Secret of Fatima, locked away in 1960, surely left off, namely with the crisis in the Church. In 1961, notice one year before the opening of Vatican II, the lady of Garabandal said, "We must do much penance and make many sacrifices. We must often visit the Blessed Sacrament. But above all, we must be very good for, if we are not, we will be punished. The cup is already filling, and if we do not amend our lives there will come a great chastisement."

In her second longer Message, given a few months before the closing of Vatican II, she was more insistent, saying amongst other things, "...Previously, the cup was being filled. Now it is overflowing. Many Cardinals, Bishops and priests are on the road to perdition and are taking many souls with them..." So much for Vatican II! Small wonder if the cardinals, bishops and priests were not in a hurry to approve of the lady of Garabandal!

Her triple prophecy made in the course of the same four years was of three great coming events: a Warning, a Miracle and, if mankind is not converted by these, a Chastisement to which the first two events point. Let us then begin with the Chastisement, spoken of in both Messages.

What it will consist in, the girls were not allowed to say, but they were shown it: on two successive nights they had of it a vision so horrifying that they let out such cries of horror that all the villagers within earshot went at the first opportunity to Confession. Said one of the girls, "It will be a result of the direct intervention of God, which makes it more terrible and fearful than anything we can imagine."

We look at the sins of the turn of the century, chastised by World War I. We look at the greater sins of the 1920's and 1930's, proportionately chastised by World War II. We look at the far greater sins of the 1960's to

1990's – is it not reasonable that a merely human World War III would not be enough by way of chastisement for mankind in its present state? Of course mankind can convert, but does that look likely? God exists, He cares, He is not powerless to intervene, He is just, so how could He not chastise? But he is also merciful, which is why it is reasonable – not obligatory on His part – that He provide beforehand a proportionately great Warning.

For indeed people today are so confused, all over the world, that like the inhabitants of Niniveh in Scripture, they cannot tell their left hand from their right (Jonah 4: 11). Now for this stupidity men have nobody to blame but themselves, but how far can for instance the youngsters today be blamed when they are fed synchronized lies by their schools, politicians, universities, media, even churches and parents, in brief by everyone meant to know what life is about? Stop for a moment and think how deep the confusion is in people's minds and lives around us. Could not many of them almost go before God's judgement seat and plead ignorance? And where today is His true Church to guarantee them His existence, His love and His law? In which case does not the Warning as told of by the lady of Garabandal to the four girls fit, like a key fits a lock? –

> The Warning will come directly from God, like a fire from heaven visible to the whole world and from any place where anyone may happen to be. Immediately it will be transmitted into the interior of our souls where by its light everyone, believer and unbeliever alike, irrespective of whatever religion he may belong to, will see the state of his soul with complete clearness. He will experience what it is to lose God; he will feel the purifying action of the cleansing flame. Briefly it will be like having the Particular Judgement in one's very soul while still alive. It will last for a very little time, but it will seem a very long time because of its effect within us.

Does not such a warning fit? For a few (long) moments absolutely everybody without exception will see the complete truth about their soul and its state before God. Within a few hours, days, months, the enemies of God will no doubt be doing everything with their media to bend people's minds all out of shape once more, but everyone will have had a clear chance to know the truth and to choose it. What a grace! However, the lady of Garabandal told of God's mercy reaching still further.

At Fatima, the Second Secret had consisted of a great warning of what Russia would do (by 1992, has largely done) to the world, if the instructions of Our Lady were not carried out, and this warning, originally given in July of 1917, was solemnly ratified and confirmed by the miraculous dance of the sun which took place three months later before an awe-struck crowd of 70,000 people.

However, the sins and incredulity of this end of the 20th century far surpass those of its beginning. If then a miracle is provided to overcome disbelief in a warning, might one not expect from Garabandal, if it is true, a Miracle far surpassing even the dance of the sun at Fatima? That is exactly what the girls were told of by the Lady of Garabandal:

> Within one year of the Great Warning, on a Thursday evening at 8:30 p.m., on a feast of a Saint devoted to the Holy Eucharist, lasting for about a quarter of an hour and coinciding with a great event in the Church, will take place a Great Miracle visible to everyone in the village of Garabandal and in the surrounding mountain arena. It will be the greatest miracle that Jesus has ever worked for the world. There will not remain the slightest doubt that it comes from God and is for the good of mankind. It will take place at the site of the clump of pine trees overlooking the village, where it will leave a permanent sign that will remain until the end of time.

This sign it will be possible to film or televise, but not to touch. All unbelievers present at the Miracle will be converted, and all invalids will be cured.

Now if one visits Fatima today, one finds of course no trace of the miraculous dance of the sun which did so much to help people believe in Fatima. The miracle came and went. But given the vastly greater disbelief of our own day, is it not, once more, entirely reasonable that, if Garabandal be true, greater help should be given to overcome disbelief in it? Modern men believe in their television? They will go nowhere without their video camera? What could be more reasonable than to provide televisual man with a permanent televisible sign? "I will not believe until I can photograph it with my own video camera!" – catch an aeroplane and go ahead!

There are various objections to the authenticity of the apparitions of Our Lady at Garabandal which I will not go into now, although I am sure they can all be answered without great difficulty. The official Church has made no final pronunciation upon Garabandal, as it has made upon Fatima to approve or upon Medjugorje to disapprove. The SSPX has no official position either. For myself, I believe in it. All I have tried to do above is to make the case that if anyone has difficulty in fitting together in his head the insane facts of the modern world and the sane truth of his Catholic Faith, the lady of Garabandal provides an admirable solution. And if one day she were proved beyond doubt not to have been Our Lady, our Faith in public Revelation would not be shaken one bit, we should merely have to renounce one set of stepping-stones towards it. Meanwhile may Our Lady accept as homage offered to her this presentation of the triple prophecy of Garabandal. Our only intention has been to serve her and help her save souls.

Richard N. Williamson

Make note in your calendars of the coming tour of Society Chapels in the U.S. Midwest and East by Fr. Fernando Rifan from the Diocese of Campos, Brazil. He will be giving a slide lecture on the heroic rescue of Catholic Tradition within the diocese, firstly at the seminary here on the evening of the Ordinations, Saturday June 20th; then at each location in the evening, June 21 Chicago; June 22 Detroit; June 23 Pittsburgh; June 24 Philadelphia; June 25 Farmingville, Long Island. Dr. David White's book on Campos is on its way to the printers. He is likely to be accompanying Fr. Rifan.

God bless you, and may Our Lady keep you in her care.

NO. 106 | JUNE 5, 1992

500th Anniversary of Columbus' Landing

To commemorate the Quincentenary or 500th Anniversary of Christopher Columbus' Discovery of America, the seminary is offering you the enclosed *Verbum* in color. If you are tempted to ask how Columbus' feat can be considered seminary news, the answer must be that without what he did, there would be no North American Seminary at all, so we are commemorating the common ancestor of all of us on this side of the Atlantic Ocean.

His feat was stupendous. Today, with satellites spinning round the world in 90 minutes, with telephone calls reaching to the other side of the globe at the speed of light, and with every square yard of the earth both surveyed and lying wide open to aerial surveillance, it is difficult to recreate the sense of what it must have felt like east of the Atlantic. Sailors had ventured no further westward than Portugal's Azores Islands. What lay further west? Nobody knew. Columbus had himself collected all scraps of information from all previous mythical or possible westward voyages, but they amounted to no certainty. It was Columbus and nobody else who unlocked the gates of the ocean and discovered a New World, and made the unknown known.

Surely, it is more than anything else the airplane that has extended our sense of the horizon and diminished our sense of the limitations that always used to hem in explorers. However, in flying today over the Caribbean, one can still recapture a sense of the magic of the world into which Columbus sailed for the first time: the bright blue sea, the scattered islands, the lush vegetation, the balmy climate. Columbus himself was enchanted, as are today millions of – holidaymakers!

But the Caribbean is much more than just a playground. Starting with Columbus, it has been the geographic hinge of North and South America, and the cockpit of the continent's history down to this day. Following the Spaniards who came with Columbus, there have been, down the 500 years, incursions of the French (still in Martinique and Guadaloupe where the Society of St. Pius X has large and growing parishes) the Dutch (ever heard of Curacao liqueur?), the British (British and French fleets used to play hide and seek in the Caribbean), the Americans (to whom Puerto Rico fell in 1898) and finally the Russians – President Kennedy tussled with Khrushchev over Cuba in the 1960's and President Reagan had to deal with their latest effort in the 1980's to spread their errors from the island of Grenada.

Grenada! The very name is like a bell, to toll us back to Spain. The other European and world powers may have followed Columbus in and out of the Caribbean to play politics, but to Spain and Portugal alone fell the honor and the glory of following Columbus in planting the Cross and Catholic civilization throughout Central and Southern America. As shown in the Verbum centerfold, a Rosary of Catholic nations sprang up from the profound Catholic piety that impelled Queen Isabella of Castile to sponsor Christopher Columbus to cross the ocean. To this day, more than half of the world's Catholics inhabit the countries to which these two incredibly great souls gave rise. Their role is duly acknowledged by the numerous statues, especially of Columbus, erected in Latin American cities, but as these countries today are losing their Catholic Faith in the worldwide apostasy, so Columbus and Isabella are losing their places of honor. In Bogota, Columbia, the pair of then statues have been moved out of the city center towards the airport, and they are due to be moved further out still, I recall being told.

For indeed, the modem world is more and more estranged from everything Columbus and Isabella stood for. They were godly, it is secularized; they embodied a Catholic monarchy, it believes in pluralist democracy; they believed in hierarchy and obedience, it believes in equality and independence; they believed in spreading the Faith, it believes in religious liberty; they believed in missionaries, it believes in liberation theology. And so today throughout the Continent engendered by Columbus and Isabella, tens of thousands of Protestant vultures are feeding on the carcass of its decaying Catholicism, and the vile media rejoice in Isabella's successors apologizing for her cornerstone policies.

But the chickens are coming home to roost. Catholic order is not an optional extra. Catholic order is not overthrown with impunity. Nations cannot rest on Protestant foundations. They can only rest on what still remains, or has been re-injected, of Catholic foundations, and when the vile media will have completed their work of uprooting those foundations, then chaos will come again.

Over one hundred and fifty years ago the missionary impulse of Columbus and Isabella was still expanding from Mexico up the western coast of North America, and in a line of Catholic mission-stations founded to evangelize the local Indians in what is today California, one was called "Nuestra Senora la Reina de los Angeles de Porciuncula." Within one hundred years the little mission-station was swamped within the modern megalopolis seething around it, to which it bequeathed its religious name, The Angels, but which was founded no longer upon Columbus' ancient religion but upon man's new-found religious liberty, enshrined in a Constitution guaranteeing freedom and equal rights for all. Unfortunately, by the beginning of our own decade the freedom had untied bonds of family, the equality had undermined school and authority, and the religious liberty, by equally protecting all churches contradicting one another, even churches of Satan, had made every church in effect look foolish. With family, school and church undermined, the delinquents began to roam the streets.

Now this was grave, but much graver was the national media's ability so to play on liberty, equality and rights, on the public's veneration of citizens' liberty, racial equality and the individual's rights, that when the Los Angeles police force in the course of their duty to arrest a particularly menacing delinquent resisting arrest, used a measure of force judged to be reasonable by a jury exposed to all the facts and not just to the media's selection of them, nevertheless 83% of the public as measured in one poll judged that the jury had made a mistake. Actually, given the weight of the media onslaught, the astonishing thing is not that 83 % of the public were deceived, but that as many as 17% still kept their common sense about them. So the delinquent emerged a hero, the police were discredited and demoralized, and the media and professional agitators are free to plot their next – they no doubt hope, final – assault upon law and order.

"Excellency, when will you stop mixing our sublime religion with your contentious opinions on politics?" My dear friends, the exclusion of Catholicism, or of Christ the King, from ideas of how to run a nation is exactly the problem. The problem is neither delinquents nor the big cities nor even the media, but deeply anti-Catholic ideals being rooted in the mass of the people. The solution is not the Constitution. In fact the Constitution, especially when treated as the solution, is the problem.

Columbus was not a great sailor who happened to be a Catholic, but a great Catholic who happened to be a sailor. In 1992 we are commemorating his name but despising his ideas. America owes him its very existence, yet treats him as though he had no idea what he was really doing – his religion uniting State and Church was as quaint as his little ships whose replicas we parade up and down the coast!

My dear friends, if chaos is upon us we have only ourselves to blame. By integrating Faith and politics, Columbus founded America. Whoever separates them, is disintegrating America. Let this be the real lesson of the 500th anniversary. I wish you enjoyment of the Verbum, and a riot-free summer.

NO. 107 | AUGUST 1, 1992

The Slaughter-Fields of Verdun

IN THE COURSE of a five-week tour of centers of the SSPX in Germany, Austria and France, I was able two weeks ago to visit a fascinating historical site not apparently religious but without doubt designed by the Lord God to teach us all an immense lesson: the battlefield of Verdun. Alas, the lesson is not being learned.

Verdun is a little garrison town in Northeastern France tucked close under the southern frontier of Belgium and Luxemburg, and only 50 miles from the present Southwestern frontier of Germany. When France lost the Franco-Prussian war of 1870–1871, the cession to Germany of Alsace and part of Lorraine brought the German frontier much closer to Verdun, which is why over the next forty years the French built a ring of underground forts amidst the hills to the west, north and east of Verdun. When the next war between France and Germany broke out in 1914, World War I, the powerful German armies broke into France (the French had hoped to invade Germany) but were stopped at the Battle of the Marne (with the help of an intervention of the

—242—

Mother of God). Both armies dug in, so that a long line of trenches reached from the North Sea to the northern frontier of Switzerland. Trench warfare began, waged mainly by infantry on the ground being continually exposed to enemy shells from overhead.

Through the year 1915, Verdun held for the French. However, the Germans had pressed hard both to the Northwest of Verdun and to the Southeast, so that it formed like a salient or bulge in the frontline. In 1916 the Germans decided on an all-out attack to carry Verdun, as being the centerpiece of French resistance on the whole front.

The attack was launched on February 21, 1916, with an extraordinarily heavy artillery onslaught designed to wipe out the French frontline. Thanks to their far superior organization and war-supplies, the Germans did succeed in advancing some miles in a few days, but thanks to some heroic fighting by the French soldiers, the Germans failed to make the decisive breakthrough they had hoped for.

So from March to December of 1916, as the Germans refused to back off while the French refused to give way, both great nations funneled the wealth of their resources and the cream of their manpower into the 75-square mile battlefield. Estimates vary as to the number of casualties in those ten months, but one estimate is of 420,000 men dead, and another 800,000 gassed or wounded. In any case the monumental Ossuary of Douaumont, built on the battlefield after the war was over by the Catholic bishop of Verdun to give decent housing to the anonymous bones of the thousands of corpses being continually discovered on the battlefield after the war, presently houses the bones, visible through the Ossuary's ground level windows in heaps stacked by sectors of the battlefield, of 130,000 soldiers, and bones are still being disinterred.

Richard N. Williamson

Twentieth century wars may by now have hardened us to such statistics, but not even the 20th century has any other such concentrated carnage to compare with the Battle of Verdun. For if the First World War in general saw warfare become horrible as never before with the deployment for the first time in war of the full might and ingenuity of modern industrialism, e.g., aerial bombardment, flame-throwers, poison gas, etc., nevertheless these new horrors were particularly concentrated by the ferocity of the fighting at Verdun.

An estimated 60 million shells, grenades, mines and bombs so thrashed and whipped and poisoned the 75 square miles of battlefield that for tens of years after the battle nothing would grow on the desolate lunar landscape, littered with all kinds of military scrap iron. Nature is now reclaiming her rights, and today green woods have mostly covered over the horror of desolation, but still today a glance amidst the trees in any direction for miles upon miles shows the tortured ground pockmarked with hillocks and pits and mounds and shell holes for as far as the eye can see. Nine inhabited villages were wiped off the map, leaving not even ghost villages behind, the village of Fleury having been taken and retaken fourteen times. They will not be rebuilt. There are too many unexploded shells remaining in the ground.

Upon the men who survived the fighting, the horrors of Verdun had a profound effect. The savagery of the industrialized weapons, the weight of slaughter and mutilation, and the littleness of the results achieved – by the end of the ten-month battle the frontline was much where it had been at the beginning – left the soldiers with a deep sense of futility and discouragement. The French army was never the same again – in 1917 it suffered from grave mutinies within its ranks and the German army was also fought to a standstill at Verdun. True, the French had held Verdun, but at what cost! In 1917 the

British had to take over the weight of the counterattack, and when the Battle of the Somme also became a relatively fruitless mutual slaughterhouse, then both French and British had to wait for the arrival of fresh armies from the USA before the war could be brought to an end.

To an end? The Treaty of Versailles concluding in 1919 "the war to end all wars" was, as clear-sighted observers immediately saw, so designed as to make sure there would be another war. It broke out in 1939 as "the crusade for democracy," and resulted mainly in the great advance of Communism, enslaving Eastern Europe!

But in that case, one might ask, the senselessness is not confined to the slaughter of Verdun, but extends to World War I as a whole, and to World War II? Then was it really in vain that all those young men filled the Ossuary of Douaumont with their bones? Yes, if one leaves God out of the picture. And that is why the horrors of World War I drove many a young man without God to despair, and blew all lingering pleasantness of the Edwardian age to smithereens. The world was never the same again.

But as soon as one brings God into the picture, everything comes into clear focus. Firstly, as to the individuals, many of the young men who died amidst the heroism and sacrifice of war will have saved their souls which they could easily have lost if they had lived on into the corruption of the interwar peace (lesson to be borne in mind for tomorrow's Chastisement). Secondly, as to the nations, to mention only the combatants at Verdun, France had ever since the 1789 Revolution been more and more defying God with her Freemasons and their secularism, while Germany had likewise been persecuting the Catholic Church with Bismarck's "Kulturkampf." Both nations, before God, thoroughly deserved to be punished, and He would not have loved them had He left them unpunished (Heb. 12: 6). As it was, He tried twice in mid-war to mitigate the punishment, firstly by His Vicar Benedict XV offering to all the warring nations to mediate between them, an offer which they united in turning down; secondly by a special messenger, Claire Ferchaud, requesting France in particular to put the Sacred Heart on its flag, request likewise turned down but which, if accepted, would have brought a speedy end to the war, with Catholic justice instead of the treachery of Versailles.

Thus the godless nations had only themselves to blame for the false peace of 1919, for the ensuing hot war of 1939 to 1945, for the ensuing Cold War of the next several decades, for its sham resolution of a few years ago, and for its real resolution which we still await. On one thing the nations are all agreed – they want nothing to do with God.

Thus the battlefield exhibits at Verdun, well done though they are, hardly mention Him. His wrath alone makes sense of them, but He is the Great Absentee. Instead, the exhibits are made to teach the lesson of internationalism: Let us just get rid of the patriotism which set the French at the Germans' throats and vice versa, let nationalism and national borders vanish, let us on the basis of economic union establish political unity and thus we will build an international paradise, with peace and plenty for all!

Fond illusion! Godless internationalism will not solve, but will only compound, the problems of godless nationalism. Frenchmen and Germans fought so bitterly at Verdun not because they loved their country, but because they loved their country unwisely, with a love not moderated by a superior love of God and of His one true Church. The problem was not patriotism, but an unwise patriotism. For as long as all Europeans were Catholic, Christendom (that was its name) was essentially united, and wars within it were relatively minor affairs, at least when compared with modern wars. Had France and Germany in 1917 been more Catholic, they would have stopped the slaughter by accepting Benedict XV's offer, in fact they could have avoided war all together by asking Pope Pius X to mediate between them in 1914, before war broke out. As it was, they declared war, whereupon the British Foreign Secretary made his famous quote: "The lights are going out all over Europe and we shall not see them lit again in our generation." Within days Pope Pius X died of a broken heart. And by way of a solution to scorning our God, we are now being prepared and instructed to scorn also our country!

How blind men are when they do not have Jesus Christ and the light of the Catholic Faith! "I am the light of the world; whosoever followeth me walketh not in darkness but shall have the light of life" (Jn. 8: 12).What illumination in these few words of Our Lord! –Those who do not follow him walk in darkness, and will not have the light of life. Poor Europe!

But be consoled, the lights have not gone out entirely over Europe, a very few have been lit again in our generation, I mean at least the centers in France and Germany and Austria of the SSPX, and in other countries of Europe which I did not this time visit, but which are all growing, not in spectacular fashion, but slowly and quietly.

For instance in Stuttgart, Germany, the Society's German District Headquarters is replacing its present allelujah-garage (German expression!) with, if you please, in a typical grey suburban-industrial area of a modern big city, hemmed in on all sides – with a brand-new pre-fabricated baroque church! Pre-fabricated baroque! Have you ever heard of such a thing? Well, go and see it in Stuttgart! And you may see up on the scaffolding young workmen – not workpersons but workmen – with dinkum blond pigtails, happily painting baroque, with their ghetto-blaster on one side of them and a coca-cola bottle on the other!

Ah, dear readers, not all is lost. Pray hard, and we might even make seminarians out of young men with pigtails and ghetto-blasters!

Have happy summer days, but do not take a vacation from loving God. He takes no vacations in looking after us!

The Cardinal Lienart Question

IF ONE LOOKS around one today for examples of insanity, there is not exactly a poverty of choice, but one of the choicest specimens within our ken must be the notion that Archbishop Lefebvre was invalidly ordained as a priest, and/or invalidly consecrated as a bishop.

It is an old piece of insanity which has been around for several years. It first appeared soon after the Archbishop rose to prominence in defense of Catholic Tradition. It has been firmly refuted, but every now and again it still gets wheeled out on stage by enemies of the Archbishop on the right, like an old cardboard cannon, to be fired off amidst theatrical effects with a tremendous pop of a bang, whereupon it disappears backstage, waiting to be trundled out again for its next dramatic appearance.

Now people who love pops and bangs are thoroughly entitled to a bang for their buck. The only thing is that too many bangs are liable to damage the eardrums so that one can no longer listen to reason. However, since there are interesting points of doctrine involved in this case, then for all those whose hearing is not too impaired, here are some arguments, drawn in large part from an article written on the question by Michael Davies in *Approaches* #71, November 1, 1980.

Archbishop Lefebvre is supposed to have been an invalid priest and/or bishop because he was both ordained priest and consecrated bishop by Cardinal Lienart, who was a Freemason, and who therefore cannot have had the sacramental intention necessary to perform validly the ordination or consecration of Marcel Lefebvre.

Michael Davies replies, firstly, it is not proved beyond doubt that Cardinal Lienart was a Freemason. Secondly, even if he was a Mason, he did not necessarily have an invalid sacramental intention in confecting a sacrament. Thirdly, every time he externally used the proper sacramental rite in a normal way, he may and must be presumed to have had internally the intention necessary for validity. Fourthly, even if the Cardinal both at the ordination in 1927 and at the consecration in 1947, secretly withheld the necessary sacramental intention, nevertheless Marcel Lefebvre became a valid bishop and priest by either or both of the two bishops co-consecrating him in 1947 with the Cardinal. Let us take each of these points in turn.

Firstly, it is not proved Cardinal Lienart was a Freemason. Michael Davies says that when he wrote his book on Pope John's Council, he would have liked to show key figures of the Council, like Cardinal Lienart, to have been Masons, but when he examined the evidence, he found it insufficient: one French writer's allegation in one book, without supporting documentation. Whoever affirms Lienart to have been a Mason must bring his proof.

However, secondly, let us assume Lienart was a Mason. In that case, say the anti-Lefebvrists, Lienart cannot as a Mason have validly received and/or bestowed the sacrament of Holy Orders. Such a statement betrays a grave ignorance of Catholic doctrine of the sacraments. To receive or bestow a Catholic sacrament validly, the right sacramental intention suffices, an upright moral intention is not necessary. Just as, in the eating of an apple, whether I morally bought it or immorally stole it makes no difference to the validity of eating it – it fills my stomach just the same – so in the giving or receiving of a sacrament: whether my moral intention is lawful or unlawful makes no difference to the validity of my giving or receiving it so long as I fulfill the necessary sacramental conditions.

Thus as far as intention goes, to receive validly the empowering character of Baptism or Holy Orders, I need only intend in undergoing the rite to receive the sacrament; to bestow validly the character I need only (as a qualified minister) intend in putting together the requisite words and acts to do what the Church does. This is because the sacraments' primary cause is God, and the human minister need only do the minimum necessary to make himself God's instrument.

Thus immorality of intention need not invalidate the sacrament. Thus an unbeliever can validly baptize, an apostate priest can validly say Mass, and a Freemason can validly ordain or consecrate. Hence even if Lienart was a Freemason, he need not have given invalid Holy Orders to Archbishop Lefebvre.

Ah yes, thirdly, but even if Cardinal Lienart could have validly ordained and consecrated Marcel Lefebvre, still he will not in fact have validly done so, because although in 1927 and 1947 he went through all the correct external motions by saying the necessary words and performing the necessary acts, still, as a Mason who must wish to harm the Church, he will have invalidated the Holy Orders he bestowed by secretly holding back the necessary internal intention to do what the Church does.

Richard N. Williamson

Reply: in theory such a purely internal withholding of the necessary sacramental intention is possible whenever a bishop or priest or minister of a sacrament goes through the correct external motions, and any such withholding would indeed invalidate the sacrament. But since any such withholding can by its nature be known to God alone, then the Catholic Church teaches that whenever a sacramental minister correctly performs the externals, he can and must be presumed to have had the corresponding internal intention unless and until there is clear proof to the contrary.

Now in general nothing proves that all Masons believe that the best way to hurt the Church is by invalidating any Orders they bestow (for instance they may well believe they will hurt her more by gaining higher positions inside the Church by gaining all the Catholics' confidence by the most perfect performance of their sacramental functions); and in particular, it is certain that Cardinal Lienart in 1927 and 1947 correctly used the proper external rite. Therefore the burden of proof is on the anti-Lefebvrists to prove that this Cardinal on these occasions withheld the necessary intention. What evidence do they have? None. They cannot even prove he was a Mason, let alone that he withheld an intention on this or that occasion.

But again, fourthly, let us assume that Lienart was a Mason and let us assume that he deliberately invalidated the Orders he conferred on Marcel Lefebvre. The Anti-Lefebvrists have still not won their point, because, as Michael Davies quite correctly argues, Marcel Lefebvre would still have become bishop and priest in 1947 at the hands of either or both of the two bishops co-consecrating him then with Cardinal Lienart: he would have become bishop, because out of the three bishops performing the rite of his consecration, one alone needs to have had the correct intention for the sacrament to have been valid, and the odds against all three having secretly withheld their intention are simply astronomical; he would have become a priest because as the greater contains the lesser, so bishopric contains priesthood. For to receive higher Orders without first receiving the preceding lower Orders is in the Catholic Church today unlawful, but as Michael Davies learnedly argues, the position of some theologians and canonists that it is also invalid is having to be abandoned. For instance, St. Cyprian was made a bishop without first being made a priest.

Now this fourth point, always assuming that Cardinal Lienart was a Mason and that he withheld the sacramental intention in 1927, does leave open the possibility that Archbishop Lefebvre was not a priest until 1947.

To which one can only reply, fifthly, that the most elementary Catholic common sense, going by the fruits as our Savior commanded us to do, observes the marvelous fruits of Fr. Lefebvre's priestly ministry in French Central Africa and concludes that these could not have come from a non-priest. Still less could the fruits of the Archbishop's episcopal ministry in all French Africa, and then his defense of Tradition throughout the world, have come from a non-bishop.

But our cardboard canonists stand this argument on its head: since Archbishop Lefebvre's so-called defense of Tradition is in fact a sham and a sellout to Rome, they say, then he cannot be a real bishop, and this is why they grasp after the Lienart argument. To which the only reply left is that they may not be sedevacantists, but they surely are mentevacantists!

Archbishop Lefebvre's work continues to bear fruit. Fourteen new candidates for this seminary are due by the end of this month to join 34 seminarians from last year. We enclose a SCSF card, which if you fill it out and send it back to us, will make it easier for you to contribute regularly to the seminary, because each month you will receive with the Seminary Newsletter a return envelope, and as your incentive or reward within the United States you will receive the letter by first class instead of by bulk mail. That is why some people receive the Newsletter ahead of others. All you need do is sign up to contribute!

We are steadily grateful to our regular contributors. The SCSF each month provides a substantial part of the seminary's income. We are especially grateful when we think that the increasing difficulties of the economy in the USA must be making it less easy for many to contribute. But what happens to the USA – and to the world – if there are no priests? Also we must pray for vocations. What would the material seminary be if no young men came forward? Thank God for a steady flow of vocations here at Winona, but if this flow were twice the size, how many more of you would be happy in a few years' time!

Enclosed too is a flyer on praying the Rosary. Please God all of you readers know how to pray the Rosary, but keep the flyer to pass on to somebody else at the right moment, especially to a soul of good will that has never prayed the Rosary before. When the bombs start flying, Our Lady will be recruiting! Prepare to be her recruiting agent!

NO. 109 | OCTOBER 6, 1992

Schism, By Shifted Goal Posts

A VERY INTERESTING article appeared recently in a twice-monthly paper out of Italy called *Si Si, No No*, in its August edition, Anno XVIII, #14, pp. 4–6. The article itself is a little technical, dealing with matters of Church law, but perhaps it can be explained in not too difficult terms.

The anonymous author, signing himself "Churchman" (all articles in S.S.N.N. are under pseudonyms), is defending Archbishop Lefebvre against the accusation of schism which was leveled at him when he consecrated four bishops on June 30, 1988. "Churchman" admits that JP2 was right in calling the consecrations "a schismatic act" if those consecrations be judged by the New Code of Canon Law promulgated in 1983 in the wake of Vatican II; but he demonstrates that that Council and that Code, in order to condemn the Archbishop, have to depart from Catholic Truth and Tradition, and so the Archbishop is innocent of any real accusation: he may be in schism with that Code and that Council, but only in a matter in which they are themselves in schism with Catholicism. As he always used to say, "They have only thrown me out of their Conciliar Church to which I never belonged!" Let us go into detail.

By consecrating bishops against the Pope's orders, the Archbishop committed an act of disobedience, which if it was justified by the crisis of the Church was not real (or formal) disobedience but only apparent (or material) disobedience. In any case Catholic doctrine is, in the words of the great Dominican theologian Cajetan, that "however obstinate disobedience may be, it does not become schism so long as it involves no revolt against the function of the Pope or the Church." Now the Archbishop made it abundantly clear at the time that he was in no way revolting against the Papacy or the Church, so JP2 in *Ecclesia Dei* needed to back up his condemnation of the Archbishop's act as being schismatic. This the Pope did by saying that the Archbishop was in fact rejecting the primacy of the Pope because "the consecration of a bishop is the sacramental perpetuation of the apostolic succession." Hence the Pope's condemnation rests upon an episcopal consecration done against his orders being not only an act of disobedience, but also necessarily a rejection of his primacy. Is it?

Here is where the new doctrine diverges from Tradition. We must first explain a classic Catholic distinction, between power of orders and power of jurisdiction. A bishop or priest may have both powers, but they are quite distinct nevertheless. His power of orders is the sacramental spiritual power he received at his own consecration or ordination to confect the sacraments, for instance to ordain priests or to hear confessions. His jurisdictional power is his quite different power or authority to say what goes, in a given diocese or parish to which he is appointed. This power he received not necessarily when he was consecrated or ordained, but when he was put in charge of that diocese or parish. That at any rate is the Traditional teaching.

Now the Pope's primacy is not a sacramental primacy, or primacy of orders, because as Bishop of Rome he is, purely as a bishop, no more or less a bishop than any other bishop. If then as Bishop of Rome he has primacy over all other bishops in the world, as he does, it is a primacy of jurisdiction, meaning the Pope has the authority to say what goes throughout the Universal Church.

Clearly then, according to Tradition, there is no clash between a "disobedient" consecration, which confers the sacramental orders but no jurisdiction, and the Pope's primacy which is one of jurisdiction. That is why Archbishop Lefebvre, following Tradition, emphasized that he was, in consecrating, conferring Orders but no ordinary jurisdiction. That is why the Society bishops go out of their way to avoid even the appearance of taking up any such jurisdiction. That is why Traditionalists cannot understand the Pope accusing Archbishop Lefebvre of schism. Disobedience, if you wish to call it that. Schism, never. But the Pope in *Ecclesia Dei* is proceeding from a brand new doctrine.

At Vatican II, in accordance with that Council's drive to democratize the Church, the document *Lumen Gentium* introduced the famous doctrine of "collegiality." It declared that "the order of bishops is the subject of supreme and full power over the universal Church" (#22), in other words the Pope shares with the "college" of bishops his supreme jurisdiction over the Church. Moreover their sharing in his jurisdiction is conferred on them by their mere consecration as bishops! Text of *Lumen Gentium*, #21: "Episcopal consecration, together with the office of sanctifying" (power of orders), "also confers the offices of teaching and of governing" (power of jurisdiction)!

This astonishing departure from Catholic Tradition (Our Lord never said "You (plural) are Peter," but "Thou (singular) art Peter," etc.) raised a storm of protest from the Traditionalists at the Council, and a corrective Note was affixed by Paul VI to *Lumen Gentium*, but that did not prevent the democratic novelty from being carried over into the new Code of Canon Law: Canon 330: "The Roman Pontiff, successor of Peter, and the bishops, successors of the Apostles, are joined together." Canon 336: "The college of bishops, whose head is the Supreme Pontiff... is also the subject of supreme and full power over the universal Church." And for consecration conferring jurisdiction, Canon 375, n. 2: "By the fact of their episcopal consecration bishops receive along with the function of sanctifying" (power of orders) "also the functions of teaching and of ruling..." (power of jurisdiction).

In fact the new Code of Canon Law goes further yet: Canon 331: "The bishop of the Church of Rome... is" (notice, firstly) "head of the college of bishops," (notice, secondly) "the Vicar of Christ and Pastor of the universal Church on earth;" (notice) "therefore, in virtue of his office he enjoys supreme, full, immediate and universal ordinary power in the Church...," as though it is being head of the bishops' college which confers on him his power, as though not the Pope empowers the bishops, but the bishops empower the Pope!

On the basis of this new anti-Traditional doctrine, small wonder JP2 condemned the Archbishop as schismatic! Firstly, by the mere fact of consecrating bishops the Archbishop was impinging on matters of jurisdiction, and he could not be, as he claimed in accordance with Tradition, merely conferring the fullness of Holy Orders. And secondly, by consecrating uncollegial and undemocratic bishops he was putting himself and them right outside the Spirit of Vatican II and the spirit of the new Canon Law, proudly codified by JP2 in the wake of his beloved Vatican II (see his preface to the New Code). At least nobody can ever accuse him of being unfaithful to Vatican II!

But Paul VI with his Vatican II and JP2 with his New Code can be accused of having, in that marvelous modern expression, moved the goal posts. According to the old goal posts, it is the Archbishop who scores, but according to the new goal posts, it is the liberal Popes who score.

But cannot the Popes change the Church's goal posts? Answer, not those that were put in place by Our Lord Jesus Christ himself. Now it is Our Lord who instituted the Catholic Church not as a democracy but as a monarchy, in which the Pope governs the bishops: Mt. 16: 16: "Thou art Peter . . . "; Lk. 22: 32: "[A]nd thou, being once converted, confirm thy brethren" (fellow-Apostles, fellow-bishops); Jn. 21: 15–17: "Feed my lambs" (laity), "[F]eed my lambs" (priests) "[F]eed my sheep" (bishops). And nearly two thousand years of Church history faithfully continued Christ's monarchy down to Vatican II, after which Archbishop Lefebvre was its outstanding defender. Therefore it is the Liberalism of these Popes which is in schism, and not the Archbishop.

Poor JP2! When he finds somebody resisting his Church democracy, then he comes down on them like a Church monarch! A tyrannical imposition of democracy! But that is your liberal's deep-down contradiction: "Freedom for everyone – except for the enemies of freedom"! We continue to pray regularly and sincerely for the Pope here at the seminary.

He is in fact coming to the New World any day now to commemorate the 500th anniversary of the dawning of the Light of Christ in a whole hemisphere of our globe, an event which he genuinely appreciates. Let us hope his visit is not too disrupted by the revolutionaries spawned by his own liberal democratism.

May Our Lord Jesus Christ reign over the nations, may he reign over the New World in particular. Christopher Columbus, Queen Isabella, we thank you for 500 years of a continent's Faith. Pray for us!

NO. 110 | NOVEMBER 5, 1992

Columbus Commemoration in Argentina

ENCLOSED IS A *Verbum* dated from last spring when we published the Columbus *Verbum* instead. That was to tell some of the truth about Christopher Columbus in advance of much untruth that might be told about him around October 12, the day itself of the Discovery of America 500 years ago.

In the Superior General's Letter #43, also enclosed, there is a brief description of the Society's Commemorative Congress held in the Argentine from October 9 to 12. This Congress was a great success. On the Friday afternoon and all day Saturday a series of conferences was given in a hall in central Buenos Aires before an audience of a few hundred people including visitors from all countries of South America except Ecuador and Venezuela. The conferences ranged over a variety of aspects of the Discovery of America, and were well received. Your servant's conference on "Columbus and the Millennia" should be appearing in the December *Angelus*. It surveys the providential role of Columban Christendom over the last quarter of Christianity's 2,000 years.

On Sunday October 11 a large number of participants in the Congress traveled out of Buenos Aires the 30 odd miles to the Society's Seminary in La Reja, where in the morning there was a ceremony of receiving the cassock, Tonsure, and Minor Orders for younger seminarians. This was followed by the traditional Argentinian "asado," or roast, chunks of beef roasted on an open fire from an animal or animals slaughtered for the occasion. At La Reja as at Winona, not all guests for lunch could be brought inside, but in the afternoon everyone was outside for the Argentinian sports, a small-scale rodeo and soccer.

Sunday evening, coming close to 2 a.m. Monday which was the very hour of Columbus' ships sighting land 500 years ago, the seminarians and their professors put on stage scenes from a French play on Columbus from the beginning of this century by Paul Claudel. The seminarians acquitted themselves well, but the star of the evening was no doubt the Rector, Fr. Dominique Lagneau, who displayed remarkable talent as a kind of combined Impresario, Commentator and Master of Ceremonies.

The seminary had few materials and can have had little time to put together a theatrical production, but if one has a real story to tell and conviction with which to tell it, it is astonishing how any material deficiencies drop out of view. When Marshall McLuhan said in the 1960's, "The medium is the message," surely he meant that in today's world the message is so non-existent that the medium has to try to replace it, hence today's obsession with the means or paraphernalia of communication. However, put back a real message, like the epic of Columbus, and believe in it, and all problems of the means of communicating resolve themselves. "Seek ye first the Kingdom of God, and his justice, and all these things shall be added unto you." (Mt. 6: 33)

On the day of the 12th itself, the Quincentennial celebrations ended with a pilgrimage on foot from the seminary in the morning to arrive at the famous Argentinian shrine of Our Lady of Lujan in the evening. Hundreds of footsore but happy pilgrims, mostly youngsters, covered the 20 miles in time for a Solemn Mass celebrated not of course in the Basilica but under pine trees in the nearby garden of a friend. The Superior General gave the sermon, and after Mass the District Superior, Fr. Xavier Beauvais, said a few words of encouragement to the pilgrims before leading them on a brief incursion into the Basilica, where the "Lefebvrites" were not welcome, but where Fr. Beauvais nevertheless managed to make the intended Consecration of the Society's South American District to the Mother of God. Then the pilgrims dispersed.

"If thou knewest the gift of God . . . " The Society had commemorated God's immense gift to souls and to the Church, of the Catholic Discovery of America. Two more thoughts, from before and after the Discovery –

Before, Christopher Columbus had no extraordinary feats to his credit, and had he not persevered in crossing the Atlantic, or had he not succeeded in returning, surely he would have remained unknown to history. For the great part of his life, he had quietly done his professional and religious duties, making himself a devout Catholic and a highly competent sailor. To that devotion and competence, the subsequent fame was like accidental, indeed he died abandoned and disregarded. Moral of the story: to imitate Columbus, we cannot do better than our daily duty. The rest is in God's hands. He may well be arranging heroic fame for a number of souls today quietly pursuing devotion and competence, but the fame is not the point.

Notice similarly after the Discovery that it would have been nothing if after Columbus himself there had not been a host of soldiers, priests, administrators to follow in his wake and construct a Catholic empire for the salvation of millions of souls. The overwhelming majority of these soldiers, priests and administrators are unknown to history, their perseverance, achievements and sufferings are unsung, yet without them Columbus would merely have made an interesting sight-seeing trip . . . Like a series of zeroes which are nothing in themselves but put behind the figure one of a Columbus, make ten or a hundred or a thousand million, the one without the zeroes is insignificant, the zeroes without the one even more so. Moral of the story? The substance of the Discovery lay in countless unknown Catholics quietly doing the daily task laid by Providence before them.

So the Quincentennial has reminded us of a great human achievement, a heroic Catholic exploit, an unparalleled feat of God and man, yet at its heart lies something beyond none of us, but within our daily reach: our daily duty.

Of course that duty alone is set fair to become each day more heroic if the newly elected American President lives up to his campaign promises, for instance to allow (read, to force) homosexuals into the armed forces. Or to allow (read, to force) federally funded clinics to promote abortion as a means of birth control. Poor pro-lifers!

In Maryland on November 3rd, straight abortion, yes or no, was on the ballot, and Marylanders voted 61% in favor to 39% against! We cannot deceive ourselves any longer: democracy, the ballot box, public opinion, the Constitution, decent Americans, even the Supreme Court after 12 years of "conservatives" in control, are not going to get rid of abortion. The people have spoken. The people want abortion. The people want a President who will make the rafters ring with defiance of any supposed limitation upon their liberties, a President who will show the world that man can dodge any drafts. With the election of Bill Clinton, the liberal dream has taken another significant step forward towards the Brave New World "I have a dream" – we have a dream – yes, indeed you have a dream!

Richard N. Williamson

And the Lord God? With a divine patience He is not missing one gram of our wickedness but He is respecting our free will, leaving us to our own devices, and relying on events to prove to us how foolish these devices are. Alas, only a minority will let themselves be woken from their dream. And when the Lord God is finally reduced to cleaning out, with fire and brimstone, there will be many shaking their fist at Him and crying out, "You dare do this to ME? You think you have the right to tell ME what to do? Who do you think YOU are? God Almighty?" (Apoc. 16: 21)

So where did the American dream go wrong? Catholics should be able to grasp the argument, hinted at in the enclosed Verbum, that the trouble with the Puritans' City on the Hill goes back to King Henry VIII in a poor land darkened by heresy almost one century before the shores of North America were a gleam in a Puritan sailor's eye. After all, if the true Faith is important, then heresy contradicting it is important; whereas if heresy is not important because religious liberty is the ideal, then religious liberty and not Catholicism is the real religion.

"Ah, but without religious liberty the nation could never have been unified!" Grand, but the price to be paid was that religious liberty was bound to become the real religion of that land, that is to say, the ideological basis on which the land would be built, more important than any one religion in that land, including Catholicism. But not even the Catholic Church can be built on religious liberty, witness how great sections of the Church have crumbled since Vatican II proclaimed religious liberty through the ecclesiastical land with the Decree Dignitatis Humanae. It is not possible at one and the same time to cast adrift from rock and to build on rock.

May He bless you and keep you through this month of the Holy Souls, for whom remember to pray.

NO. 111 | DECEMBER 1, 1992

The Sadness of Johannes Brahms

A DVENT IS HERE again, a new Church year has begun, summer is approaching fast, the years spin by and "now is the hour for us to rise from sleep," "denn alles Fleisch es ist wie Gras," "for all flesh is as grass, and all the glory of men as the flower of grass. The grass withereth, and the flower thereof falleth away."

These words of Scripture (I Pet. 1: 24) were chosen by the famous classical composer, Brahms, for the second chorus of his "German Requiem," written in the 1860's to commemorate the death of his master and friend, Robert Schumann. The chorus is a mighty piece, with the melody for these words expressing a mighty sadness. It was well chosen as background music for a videotape recently made on the desolation of the battle of Verdun, where in 1916 hundreds of thousands of the bravest young Frenchmen and Germans slaughtered one another to no apparent purpose. The desolation within one musician's breast in 1866 had become the desolation of half a million soldier's lives fifty years later. Thus life follows art. Why? Because both follow religion. In his "German Requiem"

Richard N. Williamson

Brahms deliberately omitted any mention of Our Lord Jesus Christ. Thereby hangs the tale.

The music of Brahms may be unknown to many of you. Generally it is liked or disliked for a similar reason, because of its autumnal cast. Always solid and well-carpentered, often somber, like a late Victorian house of the same period, it appeals to those who, like the poet Keats, enjoy the

> Season of mists and mellow fruitfulness,
> Close bosom-friend of the maturing sun . . .

but whoever resents the season of the dying of the year will prefer less dark-hued music, music that maybe ripples with spring or pretends that life is an endless summer's morning, or prattles of an endless beautiful feeling that everything's going my way.

There is no such superficiality in Brahms who in his Requiem squarely confronts the great problem of life and death by means of a series of texts chosen by the composer himself from Holy Scripture. Indeed the Requiem contains some of his darkest music, and yet the climax comes in the sixth chorus with the setting of I Corinthians 15: 52–55: "For the trumpet shall sound, and the dead shall rise incorruptible: and we shall be changed . . . then shall come to pass the saying that is written, 'Death is swallowed up in victory, O death, where is thy sting?'" And the music is full of heart, with melodies of warmth and consolation – then did Brahms believe in the Resurrection, and if he did, how could his music at other moments be so dark?

Interesting question. Asked once about his choice of texts, Brahms replied that it was meant to be a human, not a Christian, Requiem. How, then, texts of the Resurrection? – "I have selected many things because I am a musician, because I needed them, because I can't argue with the venerable writers or cross out their 'hereafter'. I say no more . . . " However, at the end of his life he said the more: "Neither when I wrote my Requiem (1866) did I, nor now (1896) do I, believe in the immortality of the soul." The quotation from Corinthians referring to the resurrection of body and soul had merely "made a deep impression" on him, "as a symbol that could be set to music."

Clearly, by his own testimony, Brahms was a humanist with no faith in the Light of the World, which explains the darkness in his music, and Scripture was for him not a book of real truth but a quarry of texts to serve as vehicle for noble sentiments in music. On the other hand equally clear from the music is that his sentiments were noble. When death cuts men down like the grass of the field, Brahms presents no facile solution – how he would have despised the Novus Ordo with its white-vested funerals! Death is as tragic as life is grand, but the music feels their meaning: grief and desolation, consolation and calm.

"Oh, Brahms," said his fellow composer Auton Dvorak, "What a great man, and he does not believe!" Dvorak might have said, what a warm heart for such coldness in the head. In Brahms' head is the darkness of unbelief, but carrying over from his heart into his music is the after-glow of the light and warmth of the belief of preceding generations.

However, the heart is not designed to stay warm indefinitely when the head is in darkness. That is why Brahms has been well called, as far as classical music is concerned, the last of the Caesars. Directly after him come Schoenberg and moderns, empty heads and empty hearts, because "the fish rots from the head," says the proverb, and as the head is today, so the heart is tomorrow. Disbelieved Scripture could still tell the sentiments of Brahms, but not those of his successors. Where a head would no longer lead, the feelings were bound to run out. Unless Germany returned to believing, the emptiness and coldness were bound to come out in something like the battlefield of Verdun. Life follows art follows religion.

Thus war and peace, politics and music, all activities of man as man and not just as an animal, are governed by man's faith or his lack of it, and that does not mean, just any faith. It is an insult to man to hold that just so long as he fills his head with some nice convincing delusion, then everything will come out fine. Yet how many people think that just so long as one believes in something, or Someone, it matters little what or who one believes in. All such people have a low opinion of men. No. Men need the truth. They can recognize it. They may refuse it. But it is what it is, independently of them, it is what they need and upon it they flourish, whereas upon a diet of lies, however flattering and cozy, men wither.

Now there are certainly truths within the reach of man's reason, which he needs and cannot live without, for instance water is not gasoline and gasoline is not water. But if it turns out to be true also that the main truths are above the reach of his reason – not contrary to it, but above it – then he will have to reach for them with something more than just reason, but they will still have to be truths and not just withering delusions.

Now Catholics know by their reason that there is one Supreme Being, God, just as they know by their Faith, with an absolute certainty of possessing the truth, that he is three Persons in one Being, that the second of these Persons took flesh, that he founded one Church (not two, let alone two thousand), and that within that Catholic Church the divine condescension to men that began with his Incarnation continues in the most incredible manner in the sacraments, so that for instance he who in his human life handed himself over once into his enemies' hands in the Garden of Gethsemane, now in his sacramental life puts himself – now literally! – into their hands times without number every day whenever he is for instance mistreated in the Holy Eucharist.

Nor is this view of the Master of the Universe a comforting delusion, kidology, feel-goodery or sentimentality. It is rock-solid supernatural fact. Whoever denies it, Protestant or Jew or Communist or atheist or Hindu or whoever, the Catholic knows with an absolute certainty that they are wrong, and he prays to be ready to shed his blood, if necessary, to witness to the truth, for their sake. Upon no less solid a foundation of truth was built the musical tradition and the noble culture to which Brahms was heir. The tradition and the nobility he in turn handed down, but no longer with their foundation, like the grin of the Cheshire cat without the cat, of the same period. It could not last. It did not last. To think that it could have lasted is to insult man. That it did not last is a testimony to man, to his need of truth. Wreckers like Schoenberg were bound to arise who would pull the house down for its lack of foundation. Today's world is full of such wreckers who at least testify to the demand for truth and to the refusal of illusion.

So what are the wreckers clamoring for? Clear. The foundational Truth, fully and clearly professed. They need witnesses to the fullness of the Faith. Blood-witnesses may be the only ones that can convince them, because there are too many words out there already, most of them lies. It will take blood to coagulate such a hemorrhaging of the truth.

Brahms did not return to the foundation of the warmth of which and off which he composed. Nor did his countrymen, in general. They were given a terrible lesson at Verdun, but instead of returning to God, they turned to national socialism, only to be given an even more terrible lesson in World War II. Chastened for a while, under Catholic Chancellor Adenauer the Germans rebuilt, but misled like everyone else by Vatican II they mostly gave up the Faith and Church of Adenauer and so they are now again rending one another in search of the solution on which they turned their backs – the situation comes daily closer to a cosmic re-run of Verdun. Cosmic, because of course the problem is not confined to the country of Brahms (but maybe some readers needed to see some other country than theirs coming under fire!) – the problem is universal. Dear, dear Catholic readers, the solution is in our hands, as Catholics. It is in nobody else's.

Here is Advent again, the season to prepare for the coming of the Light into the world. He must have entry into our hearts and lives, into our music and politics. How can he solve their problems if we shut him out? He belongs in our homes, in our schools, in our hospitals, in our music, in our politics. We say no to the separation of Catholic Church and State, no to the promotion of filth in the arts, no to that hypocritical refusal of censorship which vigorously censors and cuts out any thought of God, let alone mention of the divine name.

The latest election in the USA surely shifts the program of the wreckers from forward to fast forward. It is up to every one of us that has the true Catholic Faith to put back into circulation by our example that truth, purity and transcendence of Jesus Christ which alone can persuade the wreckers that they are making a mistake, and if it has to be with our blood, so be it! They have the prison camps ready for us in the Dakotas? So help us God, we will be ready for them. Today's music is in our hearts, and tomorrow's is in the Faith in our minds.

With all good wishes and blessings for Christmas and a Happy New Year, with our unusual Christmas card enclosed, a summary of the Epistle to the Romans.

… NO. 112 | JANUARY 1, 1993

Accompanying Slacks III

A NEW YEAR brings us January once again, month of the Holy Family. The family is so important to human beings, and so threatened, that as I think I said last year, to write once a year in its defense is surely not too often. It has powerful forces for its enemy, and the Catholic Church for its best friend, because the God who instituted the family from the beginning of the human race, is the same God who instituted the Catholic Church to redeem that race, and so there is no way in which His true Church can be anti-family.

That is why Our Lord fortified the family by strengthening the bond which is at the root of the family, by raising natural marriage to the level of a supernatural sacrament, so that the practice of a lawful sacramental marriage is a source of sanctifying grace. Repeat: the practice of a lawful sacramental marriage is a source of sanctifying grace.

That is why in modern times the Popes have again and again defended the sacramentality of the marriage bond, as one sees in their encyclicals of the last century. The sacramentality of marriage is like the top stitch in the seam of society, such that once it is undone, all society begins to unravel – from the secularizing of marriage, to its becoming a contract makable or unmakable at the will of the parties, to divorce, to contraception, to abortion, to homosexuality, to euthanasia, to the break-up of the home, to the irresponsibility of men and the denaturing of women, to countless ills of which even 1992 has not yet seen the end – the chain of woes has an inexorable logic – "God is not mocked."

That is why on throw-away brown paper, recognizable in advance, is enclosed... is enclosed... ladies, I did not write these pages, you wrote them to me yourselves – they rhyme with "backs free . . . " I promise, word of honor, they have been enclosed with not a breath of malice towards the wonderful ladies that wear trousers, but in order to give encouragement to the even more wonderful ladies that do not wear them (because Heaven knows how little encouragement they may get from anywhere else!), but ladies, you are all wonderful, you are all wonderful, have mercy, have mercy – if you believe in genes, have that compassion which genetically belongs to your gender! I too have good intentions! I too mean well! – I only want to defend the family!

Interesting that such a slack subject can make people go so tight! In nearly ten years that I have now been writing this letter, no other subject has caused remotely such a reaction on the part of readers. The question has to be very important to people, especially of course to the tender sex whose wear is in question. The quotations selected for enclosure demonstrate that by no means all members of that sex go along with the wearing of what until recently was worn only by men, even if it is now worn almost universally also by women ...

Maybe the ancient Aristotle was right after all to rank clothing alongside quality, quantity, time, place, etc., as a category of being, modifying the very substance of things. People are then different according to the clothing they wear, and a change of style in clothing both is caused by and causes, both represents and promotes, a change of style of life. In this respect women's fashion is particularly sensitive, because many a man's dreams and much of his love and attention center around his woman, and so how she dresses to please him will correspond not only to her ideas on the shape and meaning of life, but also to his.

Common sense says that the main significance of women's wearing trousers lies in their resembling the men. Modern life may have increased the number of situations for women in which trousers are more – or much more – convenient than a skirt, but nevertheless if the men did not want their women in trousers, the women would not take long to find a way round those situations. As extract #29 says, it was Adam whom God held primarily responsible in the Garden of Eden, and it is the men who are primarily responsible for wanting the way of life represented and promoted by the ladies being in trousers: "I can't help thinking that if today's Adam became a prodigal son and returned to God, he would soon find Eve returning to her proper place too." Ladies, please, the writer of this letter is not getting at you. Men, the writer of this letter is getting at you!

Think! Was it God that designed the difference between the sexes? And if He designed it, do you think He meant for it to be blurred? And if the difference is being blurred, would it not follow that "an enemy hath done this"? Is it not an enemy of mankind that is for instance tearing babies out of their mothers' arms to send the mothers into military combat, in the brute force necessary for which they are necessarily and hopelessly inferior, thus betraying the babies abandoned, the mothers displaced and the soldiers weakened? Alas, any woman ashamed of being less brutish than her man is liable in brutishness to leave him well behind! When men totter, the roof shakes, but when women totter, the earth quakes. The sexes are different – Good Heavens! – that it needs to be said! In any sane society, the old men and schoolboys would rather take up arms than let any of their womenfolk anywhere near combat. Has anyone ever heard of the Nazis enlisting women in combat? To call the feminists "feminazis" is at least on this point an insult to the Nazis.

What deep-laid insanity can have impelled and be continuing to impel the men of England for example and of the United States to so dishonor themselves as to be letting or pushing their womenfolk towards combat? In one word, godlessness, spelled out in the East as Communism (flagrant or disguised), spelled out in the West as Liberalism: Liberty, from any laws of God inscribed in male and female nature; equality to level down all the inequalities out of which God composed those natures; the rights of man, to do as he likes, regardless of the slaughter of the innocents, the babies abandoned while the woman gets in the way of the fighting man. Thank God for the grandmother, or the aunt, or even the day-care lady, or whatever woman stays at home to mother the children. She alone saves the situation, because no man can mother, and no child can do without a mother.

Motherhood is as sacred as life. All men know this by instinct. Nothing is more natural than the sublime honoring by Catholics of the Mother and Child. Listen to a priest's sermon reported in the Society's *Tradition Catholique* from Belgium:

> It was holiday-time. The family had guests to dinner. The children had not yet gone to bed. As soon as the meal was over, mother got up from table, as it was late, she left the guests with her husband and went upstairs to put the children to bed. All together, kneeling around their mother, they began to recite their daily rosary. The littlest, a two year-old, was in

bed. Propped up against the pillow, he had made the Sign of the Cross. But from then on he watched his mother. Kneeling upright, eyes closed, hands folded together, she was praying the "Hail-Marys," absorbed in the inner life of her soul. Quietly, the two-year old got out of bed. Going up to his mother, he drew her hands apart, pressed his back against her and slipped his little hands into hers, which gently closed together again, and the prayer went on.

Men, this is the family, this is the Catholic family, this is the life of the family in prayer which alone can save the world and create human as opposed to inhuman beings, this is the life of the family which it is your responsibility to let the Mother of God help you to recreate. It is not your business to be tender. It is absolutely your business to honor and to protect tenderness in women and children, instead of dishonoring and profaning it. Good women are willing to follow in this direction, but it no more behooves them to lead their menfolk than it behooves you to follow your womenfolk.

Take heart! The task is not impossible. Turn in manly fashion to the Lord your God with all your heart, with all your soul, with all your strength and with all your mind, and the rest will be added unto you. It may be a journey of a thousand miles, but it still begins with the first step. It begins with nothing else. Across the United States and no doubt many other countries, there are numerous young families to be seen at the Society's Mass centers for instance, attending the true Mass, practicing the true Faith, growing in happiness and holiness as the Lord God blesses them with one child after another. Have no fear. The family protected by the Mother of God is stronger than a hydrogen bomb.

As for this month's other enclosure, it has a handsome title, "Lefebvre was right," but not so inspiring contents. Friend of Pope Paul VI from before World War II, Jean Guitton was like him inspired by hopes of a great renewal of the Catholic Church to come out of the Second Vatican Council but, like him again, he has found himself mysteriously disappointed by the results, a disappointment obviously not diminished in the 14 years by which he has outlived his friend.

Why the mystery? Because liberals cannot conceive of their basic principles such as dialogue and religious liberty being wrong. They are such loving and caring persons, they are so sincere, they so love and care for modern man, they are so full of luv, luv, luv, they mean so well, they have such good intentions, that they go out to embrace modern man, then they embrace his principles diametrically opposed to the Faith – and then they are astonished when the Church collapses around them!

How can intelligent men be so blind? Answer, by an operation of error that has built up over centuries for those that have not loved the truth (II Thess. 2). Objection: but look at the third quotation of Guitton, he recognizes that truth cannot change! Reply: Yes, but look at the end of the same quotation: if he loved the truth he recognizes, he would never reproach Archbishop Lefebvre for his manner of having defended it, even had the Archbishop been ten times less diplomatic and more clumsy than he supposedly was. By the side of the Truth, the spokesman and his mode are insignificant. But Guitton loves the world, and that is his downfall – "Love not the world, nor the things which are in the world. If any man love the world, the charity of the Father is not in him. For all that is in the world, is the concupiscence of the flesh, and the concupiscence of the eyes, and the pride of life, which is not of the Father, but is of the world. And the world passeth away, and the concupiscence thereof: but he that doth the will of God, abideth for ever." (I Jn. 2: 15–17)

Truth to tell, "Lefebvre was right" is a misleading caption for the interview, because it is clear from the interview as a whole that Guitton does not really think that the Archbishop was right to round the circle, he is still convinced the Archbishop should have squared the circle. After all, a square is so nice, and a circle is so nice, it would be so nice to combine them!

My dear friends, can you think of any other time in the world when it was heroic merit for girls to wear a skirt or for boys to say that circles are round? Long live the 20th century! Long live 1993! Happy New Year!

NO. 113 | FEBRUARY 4, 1993

The American Patriot's Catechism

THE ENCLOSED *VERBUM* is hardly controversial, but its predecessor, headlined "Discovering America's Roots," presented a picture of the Founding Fathers of the United States which did not gain everyone's approval. In particular, a long-standing friend of the Society here in the USA – who has rendered the Society great service – made a series of reasonable objections which deserve a reply. Let me attempt the "Catechism of a Patriot"...

Patriot: By concerning themselves with questions like the founding of the USA, don't priests risk being diverted or distracted from the saving of souls?

Reply: If any man had two heads, he might keep his religion in one and his politics in the other, but inside any one head at any one time, the two things necessarily interact on one another. A man cannot be liberal in politics without more or less contaminating his Catholic Faith and so endangering his soul.

Patriot: But Archbishop Lefebvre wisely left such worldly matters alone, and kept to the Doctrine of the Faith.

Reply: Archbishop Lefebvre may not have explicitly questioned the founding of the American Republic, perhaps because he was never permanently stationed in the USA, but the ideas of American churchmen he had to fight hard against at Vatican II, in particular, religious liberty. Michael Davies' latest book, *The Second Vatican Council and Religious Liberty*, shows clearly the part played by the compatriots of the Founding Fathers in the fatal establishing of the principle of religious liberty within the Catholic Church at that Council. Its *Declaration on Religious Liberty* is Americanism infecting the Universal Church. The result is that to defend the Faith anywhere in the world today, a priest must fight the ideas of the Founding Fathers.

Patriot: But Pope Leo XIII about 100 years ago, with reservations, commended the USA political system. Why should SSPX priests be more demanding than the Pope?

Reply: Pope Leo XIII came before Vatican II; Society priests all come after. The full devastating effect of Americanism (as the Pope called it) upon Catholicism that he then feared, we now know. In Leo's time, the American churchmen could pretend that the Americanism he condemned did not even exist, but by the time of Vatican II, they were positively proud of having "converted" the Catholic Church to the American way – see Michael Davies' book.

Patriot: But the Founding Fathers were decent, God-fearing men.

Reply: By no means all of them believed Jesus Christ is God, but let us suppose they were all, as the world goes, honorable men. That does not change the principles on which they built their Republic, which are Freemasonic principles, profoundly harmful to Religion.

Patriot: But not all the Founding Fathers were Masons, and those that were, were Masons only in name, not in wickedness like the French Masons who caused the blood-drenched French Revolution.

Reply: Firstly, the Catholic Popes have never distinguished a benevolent Anglo-Saxon Masonry from a malevolent Masonry of the countries of Latin origin. They have always condemned Masonry without distinction, as a whole, and many times. Secondly, Benjamin Franklin, an American Mason, was a close friend and colleague of the French Masons when they were preparing the French Revolution. Thirdly, however many or few American Revolutionaries were Masons, the founding principle of their new Republic – religious liberty – is a key Masonic principle.

Patriot: But the Founding Fathers' idea of liberty was the Catholic idea of liberty, only they left out the authority of the Catholic Church. How can you blame Protestants for that?

Reply: Firstly, their subjective innocence or ignorance God alone can ultimately judge. Here we are questioning their objective achievement. Secondly the opposition between true liberty, centered on God, and Masonic liberty, centered on man, is radical. The difference is not "only" the omission of the Catholic Church (quite an omission!) but two wholly different concepts of God, man, life and law, as Leo XIII makes clear in his Encyclical *Angelus*, freely quoted in Michael Davies' book.

Patriot: Well, the religious liberty established in the First Amendment has given a marvelous freedom for the Catholic Church to thrive in the USA, ever since the founding of the Republic.

Reply: Freedom, yes, as Leo XIII acknowledges, but a marvelous freedom, no. The problem, in a few words, is that when men found a republic (as they do today all over the world) not just on the practice but on a principle of religious freedom, they are obviously putting the interests of their republic above the interests of any one religion, otherwise that religion would have primacy in their republic, as today Islam has primacy in Mohammedan republics. Now men are social as well as individual animals. Hence in a republic of religious liberty, a man may be a pious Catholic individually, but all the social institutions of his interreligious State are preaching to him that his Catholicism is of secondary importance. At this point he may try to split his politics from his religion, but that is no more possible than to split man from God. So one of two things must happen: either his liberal politics contaminate his Catholic religion, which is how the American bishops at Vatican II ended up "converting" the Catholic Church to the American way, and which is why USA freedom is after all not so good for the Faith: or by the light of his one true Faith he condemns his country's religious liberty and sets out seriously to convert his fellow countrymen.

Patriot: But given the mixed religions of the inhabitants of the thirteen Colonies, how could the Founding Fathers have founded their republic on any other principle than religious liberty? Impossible!

Reply: No intelligent engineer builds a bridge on sand, but if, for whatever reason, he is forced to do so, at least he does not glorify his bridge. On the contrary, he puts up a notice: "DANGER: YOU CROSS THIS BRIDGE AT YOUR PERIL." No intelligent Catholic glorifies a republic built on religious liberty, even if it is his own country. Otherwise politics are going to become his real religion, i.e., what he first believes in for the welfare of mankind.

Patriot: But the Founding Fathers had no intention of excluding God, or of making liberty into their religion.

Reply: "The way to hell is paved with good intentions." You cannot, however good your intentions, lay down certain principles and not expect their consequences. You cannot establish religious liberty in politics and not expect to undermine all religion wherever those politics apply, at which point religious liberty becomes your real religion.

Patriot: Well, the Founding Fathers may have wanted no State Church, but they did want a country based on Christian principles. The country was Christian, and they assumed it would remain so.

Reply: In that case their right hand did not know what their left hand was doing, which is typical of decent liberals: their decency is at war with their liberalism and their liberalism with their decency. Poor pro-lifers! Many of them seem still to believe in democracy, petitions, letters to editors, etc., etc., but in fact President Clinton's sweeping away the Reagan-Bush roadblocks to abortion within two days of becoming President was not in defiance of, but in radical compliance with, democracy, petitions, etc., etc. Where religious liberty takes social precedence over the Catholic Faith or any faith, then implicitly my country's way takes precedence over any law of God, then my countrymen's votes entitle the President that they elect to do as he wishes, and any minority that still objects to abortion, for instance, should graciously admit defeat and stop raising the issue, because the people have spoken. And if such a minority insists, the State must be turned loose on it!

Patriot: But the Founding Fathers would be aghast at the present-day development of their Republic.

Reply: No doubt the large majority of them, but that merely shows that, like the Council Fathers of Vatican II who voted for the documents that would serve to destroy the Church, they did not know what they were doing. Liberals are blinded by their illusions. When it comes to building bridges, or republics, no amount of good intentions will make up for ignorance of the laws of engineering.

Patriot: But the situation is no worse in the USA than in many European countries, so the problem is not the Founding Fathers of the USA.

Reply: It is most true that the situation is in significant ways worse in Europe than in the USA. The problem everywhere is liberalism, or the shaking off of God's truth and God's law. So, true, the problem in the United States is not the Founding Fathers as founding fathers, a task to which they brought many good qualities, but the Founding Fathers as liberals. In establishing religious liberty, they laid the cornerstone of their Republic in liberalism.

Patriot: But what else could they do?

Reply: You may appeal to historical circumstances, but if these forced the engineers to build on sand, sand is still sand.

Patriot: Are you claiming all Americans are Americanists?

Reply: By no means. Michael Davies' book is dedicated to the American churchman, Msgr. Joseph Clifford Fenton, editor of the *American Ecclesiastical Review* from 1944 to 1963, "whose clear, consistent and courageous defense of Papal Teaching on Church and State must once again be vindicated as the authentic Catholic position."

Patriot: Then the only reason why President Clinton has prevailed over the Catholics is because time ran out for the Catholics before they could convert the Republic.

Reply: No. The reason is because too many American Catholics aligned themselves with the Masonic principles of the Republic instead of condemning them, which is why their bishops "converted" Vatican II. God bless American pro-lifers – the movement is stronger in the USA than in any other country – but let them throw the best of their talents and energies into purely supernatural action because it is only by the purity of their Catholic Faith, not by any human means, that they can prevail.

Patriot: Do you love America?

Reply: Whoever loves Americans will tell them the truth. Whoever would flatter them with pleasing lies, scorns them.

Patriot: I still think Society priests would do better to leave all such questions alone.

Reply: Any Catholic priest must ask St Paul's question: "Do I now persuade men, or God? Or do I seek to please men? If I yet pleased men, I should not be the servant of Christ" (Gal. 1: 10). May God bless the America needing and waiting to be converted to the fullness of the Catholic Faith!

NO. 114 | MARCH 1, 1993

Pope John Paul II's Voodoo Scandal

INSANITY OF THE mind is like vice in morals: if it is not denounced, it becomes normal, and as it becomes normal, so more and more people are liable to be infected without even realizing it. Here is how Alexander Pope said it 250 years ago:

> Vice is a monster of so frightful mien, (i.e., appearance)
> As to be hated, needs but to be seen;
> Yet seen too oft, familiar with her face,
> We first endure, then pity, then embrace.

This letter will denounce a particularly shocking piece of insanity, but after cursing the darkness will point to a lighted candle.

According to the *Encyclopedia Americana*, 1953 edition, Vol. 28 page 184, Voodoo is

> certain superstitious rites and beliefs current among negroes in some islands of the West Indies, particularly Haiti. Brought originally from West Africa; it was characterized by worship of the green snake, incoherent dances, and, sometimes, by human sacrifices. The

secret ritual, which took place at night, was performed by a priest or priestess possessed of sufficient devilish skill to render them objects of wholesome dread. Their services were more often invoked in destructive than in curative offices. If a Negro desired to destroy an enemy, he sought the aid of voodoo, and in many cases the victim died from sheer fright.

From the *Catholic Encyclopedia*, 1913 edition, Vol. 6 page 57:

> Voodooism is simply African fetishism transplanted to American soil. Authentic records are procurable of midnight meetings held in Haiti, as late as 1888, at which human beings, especially children, were killed and eaten at the secret feasts. European governments in Africa have put down the practice of the black art, yet so deeply is it implanted in the belief of the natives that Dr. Norris does not hesitate to say it would revive if the whites were to withdraw.

The same Encyclopedia, on fetishism in Africa, says on the previous page:

> The fetish is used not only as a preventive of or defense against evil (i.e., "white art"), but also as a means of offence, i.e., "black art" or witchcraft in the full sense, which always connotes a possible taking of life... Those who practice the black art are all "wizards" or "witches" – names never given to practitioners of the white art. The user of the white art uses no concealment; a practitioner of the black art denies it, and carries on its practice secretly. The black art is supposed to consist of evil practices to cause sickness and death... Only a wizard can cause sickness or death. Hence witchcraft belief includes witchcraft murder.

Now listen to a believer in Vatican II addressing adherents of Voodooism in West Africa a few weeks ago:

> The Catholic Church looks favorably upon dialogue... The Second Vatican Council recognized that in the diverse religious traditions there is something true and good, the seeds of the Word... Everywhere our attitude is one of respect, respect for true values, wherever they may be found; respect especially for the person who seeks to love these values, helping to banish fear.
>
> You have a strong attachment to the traditions handed on by your ancestors. It is legitimate to be grateful to your forebears who passed on this sense of the sacred, belief in a single God who is good, a sense of celebration, esteem for the moral life and for harmony in society...

Now go back and read the three quotations from the Encyclopedia, slowly, and read again the two quotations of the believer in Vatican II, slowly. Who is that believer in Vatican II? Pope John Paul II. You do not believe it? After this letter, there is a word-for-word reproduction of the bottom half of page 7 of the *L'Osservatore Romano*, English weekly edition of February 10, 1993, including the official Vatican newspaper's sanitized account of voodooism! The mind can hardly cope with such a scandal.

The Vicar of Christ on earth shaking hands with, and paying homage to, the servants of Satan, and praising their good qualities? Over the years since Vatican II there may have been intrinsically worse scandals, but have any been so flagrant? The mind reels. Is the Pope in his right mind? Apparently, yes. He has been steadily treating the enemies of Christ like this for years. No wonder some Catholics have concluded he cannot really be Pope, and they solve the problem by "sedevacantism," i.e. by taking the position that the See of Peter is vacant. However, a far greater number of Catholics watches their Pope continually saying and doing these things, and draws the natural conclusion that the enemies of God cannot be so bad after all, which is what the Pope steadily seems to teach, in word and deed. Thus insanity becomes normal, and normal Catholics become insane. Or else, Satan is a good fellow. Logically, what would – or could – this Pope say to condemn Satan, if he met him?

The mind reels. It may turn away from the problem, but the problem will not go away. In the next issue of the *L'Osservatore Romano*, or the issue after that, there will continue to be such pictures and such speeches. Is there any solution between denying that the Pope is Pope on the one hand, and joining in the Satanic love-fest on the other hand?

The SSPX believes so, and acts upon that belief, and with the grace of God bears fruits of Catholic sanity. Following Archbishop Lefebvre, it has always held the position that unless and until clear proof emerges that the apparent Pope is not really Pope, one must at least act as though he is. On the other hand, no Catholic can follow him in insanity like this homage to black magicians. To attempt to explain the fact of such insanity, various members of the Society may have various explanations.

From the standpoint of the Lord God, the insanity is surely a blindness which is a punishment of the persistent refusal of the Church's leaders to do His will instead of theirs, for instance to perform the Consecration of Russia to the Immaculate Heart of Mary in the way she has requested for the last sixty years. If you have still not read the Third Volume of Brother Michael's *The Whole Truth About Fatima*, get it and read it to obtain a flood of light on the present situation of the Church.

From the standpoint of men, the insanity may be seen as the logical conclusion of the mind-rot of liberalism which "liberates" the mind from its submission to reality.

In religion, the key step is the acceptance of the principle of Religious Liberty, which unhooks the mind from any objective God and results in the meltdown of Catholicism. See the enclosed pink flyer which is designed to be an appetizer for Michael Davies' recent book, which is an excellent introduction to the whole subject. Notice in the Pope's address to the voodooists, section #4, how he rests his whole action and address upon the "inalienable right" of "freedom of religion." How weak his appeal to the black magicians to convert to Christianity! How sincere his handshake for them! With the principle of religious liberty, that is completely logical. He is following out sanely an insane principle. He is not clinically, but ideologically, insane. So he is melting down the Catholic Church.

But if you are still in doubt as to the ideological insanity of religious liberty, gift of Americanism to the Council as Michael Davies shows with all references to prove it, then see the enclosed yellow flyer, and if you are a man, come on one of the Doctrinal Sessions to be held at Winona this summer in order really to get under the hood of liberalism, Americanism, and modernism. With the help of God and never without, the SSPX is lighting a candle in the darkness.

And what does it get for its pains? This Rome is intent upon breaking up the Society, a quite logical intention, because the Society is fitting into neither Rome's program nor its timetable. Rome's program is perfectly coherent: "We do want the fundamental views of Christianity and the liberal values dominant in today's world to be able to meet and make one another mutually fruitful," said Cardinal Ratzinger in November of last year in a remark quoted in both the *Catholic World Report* and *30 Days* of January of this year (read either magazine if you must, but trust neither). To achieve this blend of Catholicism and liberalism the same Cardinal is ready to envisage remolding the Papacy. *The National Catholic Reporter* of Feb. 26th last quotes him as saying, "The ministry of unity entrusted to Peter and his successors can be realized in very different ways. History offers examples of different styles. But they do not have to be repeated. Today we have to respond to different situations. But I wouldn't dare for a moment to say what the future possible practical realizations of the papacy might be."

On the contrary, the Chancellor of the United Nations University for Peace, Professor Robert Muller, quoted in the *Fatima Crusader* of winter 1993, does not hesitate to project such possible realizations: "Ecumenism is outmoded now. We must now move towards universal government, which will soon see the light of day, and under the impetus of John Paul II, who would be honored if he gave the Church this program."

Thus Catholicism having blended with liberalism under a remolded Papacy is to integrate under a one world government into a universal religion which leaves ecumenism behind. This centuries-old plan of the secret societies is coming at last close to fulfillment.

As for the timetable of Rome, the one-worlders may be hurrying Rome on. Firstly, the prize of world dominion is coming very close, and they are eager to grasp it. Next, this Pope may have a cancer leaving him less than a year and a half to live, and a successor like the Jewish Cardinal Lustiger of Paris might be much less able to draw the old-fashioned Catholics after him. Besides, a dying Pope could promise them the moon which a successor could immediately take away again. Finally, it might be feared in Rome that the SSPX will harden its position within a year or so.

Altogether, if Rome is to advance in comfort towards the Brave New World, now is the time to take out that dangerous pocket of resistance in its rear, the SSPX. For if there were no Society, then all the decent Catholic souls presently made anxious at the Church's march towards the New World Order would have no alternative but to follow, whereas if the Society continues to show forth a Catholicism of Petrine Rock coming under no secular government, then souls have an alternative, and if Rome lurched too far too fast towards the One World, many souls might attach themselves to the alternative and make it altogether more formidable.

It all means the Society must be gotten to, and gotten to quickly. Which would explain some recent moves by Rome sketching out a deal whereby we might lose our excommunications if we would only accept to be more ecumenical, with a church building in Rome thrown in as carrot . . . hence maybe also the recent stick in the USA, or flurry of attacks, or was their close timing just a coincidence?

The Wanderer and the *Homiletic and Pastoral Review* have accused the Society again of schism . . . Gentlemen of *The Wanderer*, Fathers of the Review, must you see in the *L'Osservatore Romano* a picture of the Pope shaking hands with Satan himself before you will admit that there is an emergency in the Church justifying obedience to God before obedience to men? Would you admit it even then?

And other adversaries of ours in the USA, wishing to accuse us of unfaithfulness, put forward a case to present fidelity as they see it. Bless him, Michael Davies wrote a long open letter in reply so utterly demolishing their case as to enable any reader to see fidelity for what it really is.

However, let nobody accuse Michael Davies of being in the Society's pocket! When I wrote recently to congratulate him on his book, he took the opportunity to relate with glee that he had just seen Wales defeat England in the Rugby International and he had seen it on television, to boot! Harumph! No doubt he was wearing slacks at the time! Mr. Davies, England must let Wales win sometimes, but thank you for your article and for your book! You must now be offending a number of your conservative friends, but the eyes of some may be opened by no amount of disaster. Long may the Society continue to have your support.

Lastly, a sweet little attack – a gentle lady writes two and a half plaintive pages to complain of being taken to task in somebody's Letters when she does not feel she should be – surely no need to specify. She concludes, "Though I know it means little to you, I do want to say I still like you in spite of differences and think highly of you in most respects, even if you are a bit bonkers." Don't tell her, anybody, the writer of the Letters went into bonkership years ago!

Dear friends, pray for the Pope, pray for the Holy Father, pray that he consecrate Russia to the Immaculate Heart of Mary. Most likely we have much more to live through yet, but prayer is our invisible strength and our unfailing consolation. Lord, let us lose all, but not you!

May He bless you and keep you.

Death of Fr. Barrielle

BESIDES MARKING THE second anniversary of the death of Archbishop Lefebvre, last month also included the tenth anniversary of the death of Father Ludovic-Marie Barrielle, probably the second most important figure in the founding of Ecône and of the SSPX.

He died within the walls of Ecône seminary (surely a special reward for the seminary's faithful servant) on March 1, 1983, in his 86th year, having been born in the South of France in August of 1897. What could such an old man from the end of the 19th century have had to give to young seminarians of the latter part of the 20th century? Answer: a very great deal, and thereby hangs a tale.

Look around you for a few moments, and think – is not our late 20th century littered with hulks of youth no doubt well filled with homogenized milk and hygienic vaccines, but morally, intellectually and spiritually dying, or dead? Beneath the glossy surface, so well showered, so well prinked up, is there not an inner chaos of confusion and distress? Still, small souls, crying for attention and guidance, desperate for truth and discipline, yet habitually repelling anything that resembles either? Jarring contradiction, expressed in their grinding and jarring music, rock, which is for many of them the only passionate attachment in their lives.

Whence comes such dereliction of the youngsters? Certainly from the oldsters. The youngsters may not be without sin, but they are surely more sinned against than sinning. While materially cosseted as never before, they have been spiritually abandoned because for generations back there has been building up in their so-called civilization the aversion from things of the spirit and recourse to the consolations of matter. As each generation made by God for God comes of age in surroundings more and more excluding God, so the contradiction and abandonment have grown sharper and sharper in a process now piling up the young suicides and due to terminate in a frenzy of self-destruction, symptomized by Clintonitis.

Of course when each generation gave up on the idea of fighting the materialism and decided to join it instead, it was immediately praised for its "maturity" and for "leading a well-adjusted life" – the hippie had put on a dark suit and gone to Wall Street – but that was often the very same moment when the abandonment of the following generation became final. Looking around us today we would have to say the process is close to its end. One cannot materialize youth without destroying all future.

Such dark thoughts from our darkening scene are the backdrop for understanding how an old man like Fr. Barrielle could do so much for the youngsters of Ecône. Firstly, he never abandoned the old, old truths and discipline to which he remained passionately faithful; secondly, he gave himself heart and soul to passing these down to the young generation of seminarians, who loved him for it.

His own vocation had begun, he used to tell us, in his mother's arms, when at the age of one and a half as the priest came by in a procession of the Blessed Sacrament he uttered his first words – "Me pwiest!" Seminarian in the First World War, ordained priest in 1924, he joined the diocesan clergy in Marseilles where he rose to being the parish priest of a large city parish.

He loved the work and he was good at it, but he realized that he was missing something, something to get religion really into the bloodstream of his big city parishioners. During the Second World War, some of the men in his parish fascinated him with tales of the five-day Ignatian Retreat they had done with a Spanish priest, Fr. Vallet, the fame of whose Exercises was spreading. Fr. Barrielle went himself to do these with Fr. Vallet, and there he was "like hit over the head" with his second vocation – to abandon his beloved parish, to drop all and enter as a Novice into Fr. Vallet's new little Congregation for the purpose of giving the Spiritual Exercises.

In these Exercises of St. Ignatius, at the school of Fr. Vallet who had absorbed the true Ignatian spirit through – or, alas, despite? – being a former Jesuit, Fr. Barrielle discovered the something missing from his parish work, the literally heaven-sent instrument to pull modern men out of their distracting merry-go-round and to set them, by several days' serious prayer and penance, firmly on the road once more to saving their souls. Not that Fr. Barrielle's parish experience was useless; on the contrary, it all turned out to have been a marvelous preparation for the understanding and counseling and instructing of men within the grace-filled framework of the Retreat.

There followed many happy and fruitful years of preaching the Exercises in the post-war period, but then came Vatican II (1962–1965). The modernists who took over the Church in the wake of the Council could not tolerate the old Faith being so strongly conveyed by the old-fashioned method of Ignatius, so Fr. Vallet's little Congregation came under severe pressure to update, meaning water down, the Exercises. Since Fr. Barrielle was unwilling, he was relegated from the central Retreat House to a distant house in the North of France, and there he might have remained for the rest of his days, hugging to himself the Ignatian treasure that Fr. Vallet had rescued from the Jesuits, but which risked being cast aside again because nobody wanted it, had not at this point, obviously Providential, come Fr. Barrielle's third vocation.

Another veteran of God's wars, driven in the late 1960's into an amply deserved but nevertheless early retirement because he too would not abandon the old-time religion, had been called back into service by a group of youngsters seeking-bless them! – the old-time religion. For the love of God and of seminarians, Archbishop Lefebvre had responded to their call. In 1970 he had founded for them the Priestly Fraternity, or Society, of St. Pius X, and at about the same time he had opened a house for them in the now famous location of Ecône. But while he had some young priests coming forward to help him form the youngsters presenting themselves at his new seminary, he was lacking an older man for their spiritual direction. The Archbishop thought of an old war-horse put out to grass in the north... he blew on his trumpet. The old horse, now in his 74th year, pricked up his eyes – yes, it was the right trumpet again! – he snorted, he whinnied, he set off at a trot, soon the old legs were galloping to the aid of the Archbishop, and by the Archbishop's side he remained to the end of his days.

From 1971 to 1983 Fr. Barrielle spent at Ecône an astonishing eleven, nearly twelve years, more fruitful than ever, because he had been faithful to St. Ignatius, and now he was faithful to the Society. When first he arrived at Ecône, he had dreamt of reviving Fr. Vallet's little Congregation to give the Exercises, but it had not worked out. However, when old retreatants invited him out of the seminary to give them the Exercises during seminary vacations, why not take a seminarian along with him to act as Brother Assistant? And, goodness gracious, why not let Brother Assistant begin to learn to give the Exercises as well? And that is how the Society's seminarians wound into giving the powerful Ignatian Retreats which are now a vital part of their apostolate as priests all over the world.

But Fr. Barrielle was not only faithful to the Exercises, he was also faithful to the SSPX. In the course of the 1970's, a number of older priests came to the Archbishop's aid at Ecône, out of sympathy for what he was trying to do, but few could take the heat and the pressure that came on the Archbishop as he was attacked by Rome on the one side, by the sedevacantists on the other, and so most of them left again. Not Fr. Barrielle. He was wholly convinced that it was God who had raised up Archbishop Lefebvre to defend the Faith, the Church, the Mass and the Priesthood, and this conviction he strove with might and main to impart to seminarians. Worthy of note is that the seminarians he directed are those who in general seem best to have kept their balance within the Society since then.

Fr. Barrielle was a great personality. Warm-hearted, direct, explosive, intuitive, with a great Faith and a great love of the Sacred Heart, of Our Lady and of St. Joseph, he poured himself out in his priesthood. He was both full of God and full of humanity. He had a great impact on the seminary, where the gap he left has still not been filled ten years later, and he left his mark on the entire SSPX. Any of you that have profited by the Exercises preached by Society priests are indebted to him. Physical infirmities might have slowed him down towards the end of his days, but his spirit was lively, humorous and ardent to the end. So full of life was he that it seemed to take several years after his death for one to realize that he was actually dead. God rest his soul, though I can hardly believe he was long in purgatory. He must now be enjoying a grand reward.

The moral of the story? Oldsters (and middlesters), if you know the old, old truths and discipline, you have something of priceless value to give to today's abandoned (not materially) youngsters, something which they desperately need. Even if you are 74 years old, think if there is not some way in which you can hand down that treasure. Easier said than done, I know, and obviously Providence made smooth the circumstances for Fr. Barrielle. But at least never betray the old truths, never denigrate them, nor dilute them, nor let them slip, but stand firm by them, and damn the torpedoes! Youngsters do not need oldsters to pretend to be teenagers, they do need them to point out by example the road to heaven and by word the road to hell.

"'Generation Gap'? Whassat, my boy, whassat?" old Fr. Barrielle would have sputtered. "Never such nonsense! Now are you saying your prayers, my boy? How good God is! Courage! Patience! What do you expect?" For those who knew and loved him, it warms the heart just to think of him. Shall we see his like again? We shall, if we turn from things material back to things spiritual. Children matter more than money, and it is never too late to tell and to teach adolescents to pray. Let God, Rock of Ages, be the passionate attachment of our lives and all these other things shall be added unto us.

God bless you and keep you, especially those of you spiritually succoring the young.

NO. 116 | MAY 4, 1993

Importance of the Family Rosary

F OR THE MONTH of Mary, and for St. Monica's Day in particular, let me allow a mother (and grandmother) to write most of this letter for you. It is an article entitled "Reflections on the Family Rosary."

"The rosary shall be a powerful armor against hell, it will destroy vice, decrease sin, and defeat heresies." This is one of the 15 promises given to St. Dominic and Blessed Alan by the Mother of God, Our Lady of the Rosary.

> For close to twenty years, we have been saying the family rosary with children and now grandchildren. This wonderful practice is not part of my heritage (I converted at thirty). Therefore, it was a practice undertaken without convictions fostered by fruitful experience or observation, but only out of obedience to Our Lady of Fatima's request for families to pray together daily the holy rosary.
>
> During these twenty years, the observable 15-minute picture of the family at prayer has been almost invariably far different from the traditional, beautiful, calm portrayal of the family gathered together for rosary. You know the picture I mean: Dad in his suit and

tie, kneeling upright in front of the statue of Our Lady, the picture of the Sacred Heart of Jesus on the mantel over the fireplace, all of the family reverently joining him, each one equally well-dressed and upright, except for grandmother or mother, who is pictured in the rocking chair with the baby quietly sitting on her lap.

The contrast between our family rosary time and this serene picture used to make me wonder, "What have I done wrong? Where have I failed?" Our rosary prayer time through the years has gone more or less like this:

Mom calls, "Rosary time. Time for the rosary." The eight-year-old quickly runs next door. He says he'll be right back. The family gathers and impatiently waits.

Teenager says, "I always say the rosary. I can't today 'cause I've gotta go."

Mom, with a monumental exercise of self-control, says, "Going must wait! Our Heavenly Mother asked us to pray our rosary together." The eight-year-old returns and the rosary begins.

Then, in varying degrees on any one day, the following interruptions without exception take place:

The doorbell rings. The visitor is invited to join us or is quickly dismissed. The baby spits up, or worse, and has to be tended to. The two year-old pitches a tantrum and must be spanked. The phone rings. It's long distance. The eight- and ten-year-olds argue over their placement in the room and shove one another back and forth, each claiming the other has usurped his place, until they are separated. The fifteen-year-old, who is dying to play seven innings of baseball, followed by a quick game of basketball, is overcome by an inexplicable weakness which necessitates his slouching on the sofa or lying down. This necessitates my poking and quietly threatening him until he overcomes this mysterious ailment.

I even remember one family party when all 60 or so guests had courageously gathered together (it does take a certain type of courage to call the teenager from play to pray) in the hot, stuffy front room for the rosary: The windows were open, the babies were quiet, and so the Devil sent the dog from out in the yard to come sit outside the window and howl off and on for the next 20 minutes!

Oh, help, dear Mother. Is this praying the holy rosary, meditating on the mysteries of Our Lord's life as you asked? It seems that it is the best we can do. I'm sorry.

This has been a day by day picture of rosary time; however, now I can see the picture from a long-term cumulative view. The children growing up, marrying, and having families of their own. They have retained the true, traditional Faith through this tumultuous, error-ridden time in the Church. One of them has chosen the religious life. The babies are now teenagers and they are still praying the rosary. Their faces still shine with the beauty of purity and innocence, even if with a slightly rebellious cast at times.

Deo Gratias! Thank you, dear Lord, for the grace of the Faith. Thank you, dear Mother, for the Holy Rosary. One day at a time, the fruits are not observable. We must simply forge ahead and persevere through all of life's distractions and interruptions. From this grandma's vantage point, I see many families who are succeeding in the practice of the true Faith. Almost without exception, I find that they pray the rosary. And the reverse is true. Family after family can be observed who, through the years and generations, have been slipping farther away from the traditional Church teachings, and are found to have either given up or never to have prayed the family rosary.

Young families, do not worry about the normal family chaos at prayer time. That's life, and it is unavoidable. Just do the best you can and, as the children get older, continue to have them join you at rosary time. Do not let up. After all, the request to pray the family rosary does not originate with us. It comes from our Heavenly Mother, and God blesses our intention. The family rosary is the family necessity. The vice, sin, and heresies rampant in the world cannot be fought on an intellectual level alone. We need supernatural help, and we are promised that we will receive it though the daily recitation of the rosary. This is the defense we need in the battle against our adversaries, the powers and principalities, and it is promised us through the simple recitation of Our Lady's rosary. In spite of the doorbells, dissensions, dogs, and distractions, let us unite and stay united under Our Lady's protection as an army of families praying the Holy Rosary. Our Lady of the Rosary, pray for us!

End of article. Explicitly, it pleads eloquently for the rosary in the home, but implicitly it also reminds us of a grand truth: sanctity is a bread-and-butter affair, to the point, one can say, that if sanctity is not a bread-and-butter affair, it is not for real.

In other words, a life pleasing to God is planted, is watered, and grows, in the ordinary day to day occurrences of that life, and not in the extraordinary occurrences. I want to think that those extra prayers, that extra devotion, that extra gooey feeling in my breast make me a saint, but it is not true – how much simpler if it were! Instead the Lord God does surely register the command performance that I put on for His benefit for an hour or so every Sunday morning, but He is also registering Friday night or Monday morning when I may think He is not so concerned, and in fact my score in His books is averaged out over the 168 hours of my week, or over the 8,760 hours of my year. Hence the sanctity of only a few of those hours is a low-scoring sanctity.

But our ordinary lives make up the great number of the hours of our life. Hence sanctity had better be in the ordinary hours of our lives, or it will not be for real. Temptations resisted, day after day; patience practiced, hour by hour; the interests of God preferred, week in, week out; God loved, minute by minute – that is where sanctity is.

It stands to reason. How could God have given us so short a time on earth to merit our place in Heaven (70 years are short, youngsters, do believe me), if Heaven were not to be merited by the ordinary pursuits in which we spend the great part of that time? Let us beware of giving to God the extraordinary moments not over and above the ordinary moments, but instead of the ordinary moments, like a Sunday spent in extra godly fashion to compensate for, instead of to correct, our disregard of God from Monday to Saturday. Or like the immaculate sitting room where we keep all our best furniture and furnishings, but where we hardly ever sit – real life goes on in the kitchen. Sanctity is not perfection under a slight layer of dust. Sanctity is in the kitchen, so to speak, or it is nowhere.

With its wise realization that sanctity lies in ordinary things in general, the article also wisely suggests that God's will comes through mother's daily grind in particular. If a girl goes through a modern education, there is every likelihood she will be instructed to despise material homecraft – "vegetable at the kitchen sink" – and she will learn that instead of giving her children the time they need, she can give them "quality time." But mothers need encouraging exactly here where they are attacked, in the humdrum, repetitive chores, in the daily material duties.

"Matter" and "material" are Latin words derived from "mater," meaning "mother." "Material" is only one letter different from "maternal." Take what makes up "material" out of "maternal" and there is very little left – a single letter! By God's design, human motherhood extends over not only nine months but nine or nineteen years, and it consists in the daily providing of the children's needs over that time, based on their material needs.

Richard N. Williamson

Let no mother scorn the material, nor let anyone scorn mothers for being material. Her love may be her greatest gift, but her continual material caring is the carrier and expression of that love, without which it can wither.

Nor let anyone scorn the repetitiveness of home duties. Why have mothers been so venerated? Because of their genuine selflessness. How was this proved? Like a real love of God, by its ordinariness and steadiness over many years. Insofar as for year after year she gave her love and care, not "quality time" but all the time needed, she is loved as nobody else is loved in many a person's life.

That is why the home she made is the real answer to all kinds of social ills for which there is no substitute answer. Consider this quotation from the repented sinner, A.S., who made a martyr of the 12 year-old Maria Goretti when she refused to sin with him:

> The difficult problem of purity is largely one of assistance, protection, and understanding. The holiness of maternal love purifies and fills a void in the young heart, and satisfies a longing of our nature which if unfulfilled, turns easily to lust . . . Purity in such surroundings as I was in is not easy for a boy. I contracted evil habits. That started me on the downward path. If only I had had my mother.

Priests, sociologists, reformers, politicians, psychologists have all of them tried to construct replacements in modern times for the broken home and the disintegrated family, but none of these replacements are wholly satisfactory. Mother of mothers, pray for us. Our Lady of the Holy Rosary, reconstruct our homes.

NO. 117 | JUNE 4, 1993

Architects of Neo-Modernism

A FASCINATING SERIES of articles is appearing in the Italian periodical *Si Si, No No*. Fascinating, because they take us down into the engine-room of the apostasy devastating the Church.

Engine-room of apostasy? Just as in the great ocean-going liners of the beginning of this century there could be thousands of people on board, and action going on all over the ship, but the real action driving the ship over the ocean went on in the huge engine-rooms deep below decks populated by relatively few men, so in the ship of the Catholic Church, millions of Catholics in all parts of the ship are now being like shaken to pieces by something which started with a handful of men a long way below decks, out of public view.

What drives the Catholic Church forward? The Catholic Faith. What shakes the Catholic Faith to pieces? Heresy. The *Si Si, No No* articles present six architects of the slippery heresy of neo-modernism, of whom this letter will present the first three who are less well-known, but without whom the last three, of whom everyone knows, would never have been. Another letter will cover the last three. As for this letter, it will be long, but we are sure it will repay an attentive reading. It makes some sense out of otherwise confounded nonsense in today's Church.

The first of the six neo-modernists is a French philosopher living from 1861 to 1949 whose name will be known to very few readers, yet without whom there would have been no Vatican II: Maurice Blondel. How can philosophy be so important when everybody with any good sense knows it is all nonsense? Answer, philosophy is the mechanics of the human mind grasping natural reality, in such a way that as every man must relate to that reality in some way or other in order to live at all, so he must, consciously or unconsciously, philosophize. As Aristotle said long ago, even if we refuse philosophy, we still have to philosophize our refusal of philosophy. For instance, even if a man chooses to follow his feelings, his head still has to hand in, and to go on handing in, its resignation. That action of the head, governing or refusing to govern his life, is his explicit or implicit, conscious or unconscious, philosophy.

Now over the last several hundred years, modern man has been more and more turning his back on reality, because it is governed by God, because it comes from God. Modern man prefers the fantasy of which he himself is creator and master. That is why modern philosophy expresses not a grasp of reality, but a hundred different ways of refusing reality, which is why philosophy has justly got itself such a bad name, and why a man with any good sense does far better to live by that.

However, the Catholic Church acknowledges God, adores Him, loves His reality, or creation ("Brother Sun, Sister Moon"), and expresses its submission of centuries to that one reality in, logically, one philosophy worked out also over the centuries, and today best known as Thomism, named after St. Thomas Aquinas. If all men wanted to submit to reality, philosophy would have, instead of the contempt it earns today, an excellent reputation, and all men would be conscious or unconscious Thomists. On the contrary, the modern world being marinated in liberalism and steeped in revolt, it refuses Thomism as it refuses reality. Accordingly, Catholic thinkers too much in love with the modern world want only a way out of the Church's classical Thomistic theology and philosophy; they want a philosophical justification of fantasy. This is what Blondel gave to Fr. Henri de Lubac, S.J., father of the "New Theology," which was the charter of Vatican II.

The first feature of Blondel's writing noted by *Si Si, No No* is its apparent vagueness and imprecision. His enemies could not pin him down, his friends would not pin him down, because in this way while deserving condemnation, he managed to slip out of ever being condemned by the Church. Nevertheless the grand lines of his thought were clear to friend and foe alike . . .

Blondel starts from the desire "to win over modern man" who is unimpressed by objective philosophy, i.e., by a philosophy of submission to the real object. So on the excuse of reaching out to modern man who is subjectivist, Blondel is going to jump into subjectivism! Modern man is drowning, so we must jump in and drown with him!

Accordingly, a man's mind being objective, or made for the object outside a man, while a man's heart is the heart of the subject or the man inside, Blondel's next step is to argue that the Catholic Faith goes rather from heart to head than from head to heart. So where St. Paul says the Faith comes from outside, "from hearing" (Rom. 10: 14–17), which is Catholic common sense, Blondel says it must come from "experience" inside, which is modernism – the Faith is what I feel.

Hence – third step – the supernatural is a need or a demand of human nature within, because "nothing can enter a man which does not come from out of him and correspond in some way to a need he has of expansion" – Blondel's own words. Thus as Blondel's subjectivism undermined all objectivity of the Faith, so his naturalism subverts everything supernatural, and the whole order of grace transcending nature is pulled down within nature! One may ask, what remains of Catholicism? But Blondel's version of the supernatural held de Lubac spellbound, who in turn bewitched the Fathers of Vatican II, so that in its main documents, e.g., *Nostra Aetate* and *Ad Gentes*, the Council avoided all use of the word "supernatural"! It may be that few people read philosophers and theologians, but these have clout!

Finally *Si Si, No No* quotes Blondel changing the very definition of truth. Instead of the classical definition "the matching of mind and reality" which Blondel dismisses as "chimerical," or unreal – presumably Blondel like most moderns held the mind to be incapable of attaining reality – Blondel's definition is "the real matching of mind and life," a definition leaving room for the truth to be in continual movement, with nothing ever determined or fixed. Hence a shifting truth, an evolving Faith, a "living Tradition" which will enable Archbishop Lefebvre's "fixist Tradition" to be condemned. Truth evolves.

Was Blondel in good faith? A prominent Dominican at the time thought not, and his reasons could be applied as a test to all modernists: 1) Blondel so quotes texts of St. Thomas as to make them mean the opposite of what they say; 2) he repeatedly meets well-argued criticisms from his adversaries with a mere categorical denial; 3) he continually claims to be misunderstood; and 4) he is always "explaining" how his thinking is really orthodox, so that it is disputed what he is actually saying.

However, discerning readers dismissed any supposed later change in his thinking as merely cosmetic, and amongst friends he would drop the disguise. Thus in 1932 when Fr. de Lubac accused him of paying too much heed to his Catholic critics, Blondel replied by return of post that back in the old days of "unbending extrinsicism" (i.e., excessive respect for the external reality!), he had had to go slowly and carefully in order not to incur censures which would have slowed everything down and "compromised the whole effort being undertaken, the cause being defended." In other words Blondel knew exactly what he was doing. He was deliberately deceiving the Church authorities as to his real thinking, in order to be able to continue working from within the Church to "reform" it.

Some "reformer"! Some "reform"! But surely Blondel himself sincerely believed in his work of rediscovering "authentic Christianity"? Yes, and the whole modern world lines up to congratulate him on his planting of the mines to blow sky-high the antiquated Church. But did his conscience congratulate him, or did it rebuke him? In any case when Blondel consulted Fr. de Lubac whether his theses were not going a bit too far, the priest reassured the layman that his thinking was "spontaneously Catholic enough to need no timid coverup." Ah, the responsibility of the priest!

Fr. de Lubac, S.J., subject of the fourth of the *Si Si, No No* articles, born around the turn of the century, and who died only two years ago, was from the time of his studies in Jersey (Europe) in the early '20s a passionate reader of Blondel and other dubious modern thinkers, who were only "half-forbidden" by "indulgent" priests within the Jesuit order. Of course Pope Pius X had only fifteen years earlier strictly forbidden the moderns and strictly imposed St. Thomas Aquinas within Church institutes of learning, and the Lord God had given Pius X to work miracles to show that this was a Saint in whom God was well pleased, but no doubt the Jesuit intellectuals regarded Pope Sarto as the backwards parish priest Pope, and the miracles as being good for the Italian peasants... the modern world is full of rot which comes at a man from all angles and has a thousand entries into his mind and heart. What an immense grace it is to appreciate St. Thomas for what he is!

As for Fr. de Lubac and his comrades, they on the contrary found in Blondel the philosophical support for their Faith which they were disappointed not to find in St. Thomas. De Lubac even admired certain authors because they were disapproved of by Rome, but from one of his teachers he learned how to maintain an outward submissiveness towards Rome. Like Blondel, de Lubac would disguise his doctrine, such disguise being a hallmark of the "new theologians" wrote Pius XII in the 1950's, which is why the Catholic world was so shocked to wake up at Vatican II and discover itself modernist.

For as Blondel had abandoned scholastic philosophy, so de Lubac would abandon traditional theology. In 1932 de Lubac told Blondel that he, Blondel, had made possible a new theology of the supernatural. Mother Church teaches that the whole supernatural order of grace is exactly that, i.e., gratuitous, or a sheer gift of God. Nature may be capable of, and well suited to, supernature, but it in no way strictly requires grace, which is of a quite different order, infinitely superior, and given by God, as God wills, in a manner essentially independent of the receiving nature. On the contrary, the "new theology" of Blondel and de Lubac taught that the supernatural is an exigency and necessary perfection of nature, without which nature is frustrated in its essential aspirations. In other words the supernatural is needed to complete nature which remains incomplete without it; in other words the supernatural is not a gratuitous gift but a part of nature owed to nature; in other words the supernatural is not supernatural but natural, and lies within the bounds of nature.

Here is the heart and soul of the New Theology: man, merely by being man, is saved – hence Karl Rahner's "anonymous Christians," i.e., people who are Christians without realizing it, without even being baptized; hence indifferentism, it is indifferent which religion one belongs to; hence ecumenism, hence no need of the Catholic Church for salvation – oh, Vatican II!

Blondel and de Lubac both knew that their "New Theology," especially their new theology of the supernatural, defied the Magisterium of the Catholic Church, but they told one another that theirs was "the authentic Christianity" (Blondel), "the more authentic tradition" (de Lubac), "the old doctrine revitalized" (de Lubac). When in a famous article of 1946 the outstanding Thomist and Dominican, Fr. Garrigou-Lagrange, attacked the "New Theology" as being merely a rehash of modernism, de Lubac responded with insults and mockery of Garrigou-Lagrange's "simplistic views on the absoluteness of truth." De Lubac accused the Thomists of "notorious ignorance of Catholic Tradition," and when in 1950 Pius XII issued the same warning against the New Theology in his Encyclical *Humani Generis*, de Lubac dismissed it as "highly one-sided . . . it doesn't concern me."

Blondel died in 1949, but de Lubac lived to see the triumph of their New Theology during and after Vatican II. However, there was enough Catholic sense left in de Lubac for even him who had fathered the Council's theology to recognize that its aftermath was a disaster for the Church. Towards the end of his days he undertook in a late work "an examination of conscience." He wrote, "This period is as full of error as any . . . maybe I should have concentrated more on essentials . . . for the last seven or eight years I have been paralyzed by the fear of confronting head on, in concrete fashion, the essential problems in their scalding reality. Out of wisdom or weakness? Was I right or wrong? Would it not seem as though, despite myself, I have finished up in the camp of the integrists who horrify me?" Thus de Lubac finished his life where he began it, in horror at the champions of integral or complete Catholic teaching, with only this difference, that whereas at the beginning of his career he no doubt exulted in the prospect of demolishing their work, at the end of his life, after bringing off the demolition, he at least had the decency to drop a few half-tears over the demolished ruins now staring him in the face...

From the Secret of Our Lady of La Salette comes the best comment on such a career:

> Demons... unloosed from hell... will put an end to faith little by little, even in those dedicated to God. They will blind them in such a way, that, unless they are blessed with a special grace, these people will take on the spirit of these angels of hell; several religious institutions will lose all faith and will lose many souls. Evil books will be abundant on earth and the spirits of darkness will spread everywhere a universal slackening in all that concerns the service of God..."

St. Paul said it more briefly: "In the last days... men shall be traitors, stubborn, puffed up, and lovers of pleasures more than of God: having an appearance indeed of godliness, but denying the power thereof." (II Tim. 3: 4–5)

A disciple of de Lubac is the subject of the fifth of the *Si Si, No No* articles, Fr. Hans Urs von Balthasar, who died in 1988 just as he was about to be made a Cardinal of Rome! Trained like de Lubac within the Society of Jesus which he would leave just before making his Solemn Profession in the 1940's, von Balthasar had from the beginning, like de Lubac, a violent aversion for scholastic theology, and a passionate desire to pull it all down. He wrote later,

> All my studies during the years of formation within the Society of Jesus were a furious struggle against the dryness of theology, against what men had done with the glory of Revelation: I could not stand the form they had given to the Word of God; I would have liked to lash out with the fury of a Samson, I would have liked his strength to pull down the temple and bury myself beneath it . . . All of this I told almost nobody. Przywara understood everything, even without being told, otherwise there was nobody who could have understood. I wrote the "Apocalypse" with that fury that sets out to hurl down a world and rebuild it from the foundations up, cost what it may.

A passionate lover of literature and music, von Balthasar wrote that at the end of his studies of philosophy and theology, "I understood what a great help for my conception of theology was to be my knowledge of Goethe, Hoelderlin, Nietzsche, Hofmannsthal and above all the Church Fathers to whom de Lubac had directed me . . . the phenomenon of Jesus and the convergence of New Testament theologies should be viewed from the standpoint of Goethe"! "Phenomenon of Jesus"- What an expression! One may ask, did von Balthasar have the Catholic Faith? In any case Our Lord is to appear before the moderns to have his worth examined!

In 1936 von Balthasar was ordained to the priesthood and soon he was working in Basel, Switzerland, where he met the prominent Protestant thinker, Karl Barth, whose "radical christocentrism" became the next major influence on his own thinking. Putting then Christ rather than the Catholic Church at the center of Christian unity, von Balthasar made some converts to his surely dubious Faith, including a woman called Adrienne von

Speyr, with whom von Balthasar would be "theologically and psychologically" bound close together for the rest of his days. Under his guidance she began having mystical experiences. He founded a publication to publish them, and since his Jesuit Superiors could not see clear what was going on in her case, he left the Jesuits. He then became a house-guest under her (second) husband's roof until 1960, when he was mobilized by the neo-modernists in their frantic work of preparation for the upcoming Council.

As for the experiences or "charisms" of Adrienne von Speyr, had von Balthasar followed the Catholic Church's classical rules, he would have had no difficulty in recognizing how they contradicted Catholic Faith and morals, but instead of correcting Adrienne by Catholicism, he chose to correct Catholicism by Adrienne. *Si Si, No No* quotes two examples of their enormous joint influence on the Modern Church: sexuality and ecumenism.

On the first point Adrienne considered that she had received from Heaven the task of re-thinking "the positive value" of "corporeity," or the human body. Thus she would write that "the prescriptions (for the sexes) to keep their distance and to practice custody of the eyes are in the sphere of the corporeal no longer in force today," as though original sin was henceforth abolished! Her collaboration with von Balthasar she would express in vivid language of the body, thus blazing the trail for that outburst of "corporeity" in religious life which since Vatican II, behind the slogan of "integrating the affections," has devastated thousands of religious vocations. Von Balthasar likewise could not accept that in the religion of God's taking flesh, the significance of the male and female bodies should be downgraded, and he wanted erotic love brought back into the center of theology.

Adrienne's bold novelties he defended on the grounds of "today's theology being not (or not yet) up to comprehending what is presented" (by Adrienne). But in fact Catholic theology comprehends full well! – such writings which deck out fallen nature in the trappings of grace are, in the words of Scripture, of "ungodly men, turning the grace of Our Lord God into riotousness . . . defiling the flesh, despising dominion, blaspheming majesty . . . who separate themselves, sensual men, having not the Spirit . . . " (Epistle of Jude).

Indeed Adrienne and von Balthasar were separating themselves from the Catholic Church, but to cover their withdrawal, they invented a new concept of the true Church which they called "the Catholic," but which for the sake of clarity we will translate as "the Super-Catholic." Here is their vastly influential error on ecumenism . . .

Adrienne once had a vision of the Mother of God (?) in which she wrote that after she and Mary had together pronounced a formula of self-offering, Mary put in her arms the baby (of Adrienne and von Balthasar) for a second, "but it was no longer only the baby, it was the Church in miniature, so it seems to me there is a just unity of everything assigned to us, it is work in God for the Super-Catholic." Converted (?) from Protestantism, Adrienne considered that her "Catholicism" was not confined to any denomination; indeed she attended Mass only at Christmas and Easter. This concept of Catholicism she transmitted to von Balthasar who would write, "As opposed to narrow scholastic theology, the dimension of Catholic reality is as wide as the world." Yet at the same time von Balthasar sharply criticized Karl Rahner for being anti-Roman, and he did not like the way Vatican II Catholics were selling off the Church. How are such contradictions to be explained?

By the influence of the German philosopher, Hegel, says *Si Si, No No*, and back we come to philosophy. In Hegelian logic, instead of opposites (e.g., day and night, round and square) being contradictory and exclusive, they are complementary and inclusive. From the clash of thesis and antithesis, and only from that clash, emerges the fullness of the synthesis which combines them into one. Thus for von Balthasar, inspired by Adrienne, the various Churches, various religions, even various atheisms are to complement and complete one another in the one all-embracing "Super-Catholic," which is the true Church of Christ, and to form which all the opposites must be in play and none are to be excluded. Thus the Super-Catholic is to emerge as the all-inclusive synthesis superior to the present Catholic Church, which for its part must loosen up and enter into fair competition with all rival systems, including even the anonymous Christians who are Christians unknown to themselves, outwardly not Christian at all.

This Hegelian ecumenism of von Balthasar was seen clearly in action at Assisi in 1986, for example, where JP2 denied that he wanted any syncretist blending of the religions but called on them all to be what they are, including the Catholics! This is because the Hegelian synthesis, to be the true synthesis, requires all the theses and antitheses to be what they are.

As for the Papacy of Peter which might seem an insurmountable obstacle in the way of the "Super-Catholic," von Balthasar provides another Hegelian answer: the Catholic Church must be not only Petrine (thesis), but also Pauline, Marian and Johannine (antithesis), leaving a vague primacy of charity. We recognize the exact model of the JP2 Papacy – unceasing travel, an all-round openness, the urging upon all to be diversely what they are, yet at the same time the urging upon all of a millennial unity.

Thus for von Balthasar, the full "Catholicity" of the true "Church" has never yet been realized; rather it is a hope for the future, for the end of time. As for the existing Catholic Church, it represents with its rigidity and exclusivism merely the Roman version of the Super-Catholic, one version amongst many other versions, one fragment amongst other fragments of the whole, one fragment in which, amongst others, the whole – in the famous expression of Vatican II – "subsists," or is in part to be found. Thus Catholics must listen to members of all other religions. Thus conversion must no longer be by individuals but by religious groups as a whole, and their conversion must be not to the present Catholic Church but to the Super-Catholic. Thus Catholics are urged to quit the Catholic Church, and thus von Balthasar has drawn up a charter for apostasy.

It is all frighteningly coherent and true to life, true to the ruins of the Church that are piling up all around us. Mother Church's leaders are not stupid men, nor do they seem to be acting under constraint, nor do they seem to be of ill will – there had to be some explanation of their persevering in demolition when the results were there for all to see that they were demolishing the Church. In the engine-room of thinkers like these three is the answer. "Blind leading the blind," practitioners of deceit, but – God is just – how much more deceived themselves, by the Father of Lies! They wanted to reform Church and world, and all they have done is wreck both! Kyrie Eleison!

It is time to come back above decks into a little sunshine and fresh air! The seminary, thanks to your support, is drawing to the close of another peaceful school year. Four Society seminarians, drilled in Thomism and full of youth and courage, are to be ordained priests on June 19, to step into the frontline for the defense and salvation of your eternal souls. They have the Catholic Faith, and little else, but this is their victory over the world.

Let us join in thanking Almighty God for the immense graces whereby they and we have not lost the Light of the World, Our Lord Jesus Christ, and whereby the Eternal High Priest is ensuring the continuance of his priesthood on earth.

# The New Testament Priesthood

YET ANOTHER SEMINARY school year drew to a magnificent close with the ceremony of ordinations at Winona on June 19, out of which came four new deacons and four new priests for the SSPX.

The weather just held up. It had poured with rain for several days beforehand, it poured with rain the night before, but the morning itself was dry to welcome several hundreds of faithful friends who comfortably filled a spacious tent. The rain picked up again just after the outdoor picnic was over. Altogether we were lucky.

Thanks be to Our Lord, who now has four new stand-ins to ensure the continuity of His Eternal Priesthood and Sacrifice on earth, and to replace the honorable older priests faithful to the Tridentine Mass, the news of whose deaths, one by one, reaches us in the course of a school year at the seminary with a certain regularity.

The stand-in nature of the Catholic priest, standing in for Jesus Christ the Eternal High Priest, was the main theme of the Ordinations sermon, and it is a truth so important for the right understanding and practice of our Faith that it may profitably be laid out here again.

The argument is drawn from the Epistle to the Hebrews, Chapters 7 to 10, in which St. Paul compares and contrasts priesthood and sacrifice in the Old and New Testaments. See the enclosed flyer.

To all outward appearances, the Catholic and Levitical priesthoods (all Old Testament priests came from the family of Aaron in the tribe of Levi) are quite similar: a succession of mortal and sinful men continuously repeat the offering of their sacrifice in vestments and ceremonies also not dissimilar, for indeed the Mosaic Liturgy was designed by the Lord God (e.g., Ex. 35 to 40) to form and train men for the Catholic Liturgy.

But according to St. Paul, these appearances are deceptive. For whereas the Levitical priests were, he says, numerous, mortal, and sinful, the new priest is one, eternal, and sinless:

> And the others (i.e., the Levitical priests) indeed were made many priests, because by reason of death they were not suffered to continue; but this (i.e., Jesus) for that he continueth for ever, hath an everlasting priesthood . . . For the Law (i.e., the Old Testament) maketh men priests who have infirmity; but the word of the oath which was since the law (i.e., the new priesthood) (maketh) the Son (priest), who is perfected for evermore.

(Heb. 7: 23-24, 28)

So here St. Paul says the new priest is one, everlasting, and perfect, yet we observe Catholic priests to be many, mortal, and imperfect! The Protestant solution to this problem is to deny the existence of the Catholic priesthood altogether. The New Testament priesthood, according to the Protestants, belongs to Jesus Christ and to Jesus Christ alone.

Richard N. Williamson

The same problem arises as with the priesthood, so with the sacrifice. In several places the Epistle to the Hebrews affirms the oneness of Christ's sacrifice, e.g., 7: 27; 9: 26, 28; 10: 10; and in 10: 11–12, and 14 that oneness is clearly contrasted with the multiplicity and repetition of the Mosaic or Levitical sacrifices:

> And every (Old Testament) priest indeed standeth daily ministering, and often offering the same sacrifices which can never take away sins. But this man (Jesus), offering one sacrifice for sins, for ever sitteth on the right hand of God ... By one oblation he hath perfected for ever them that are to be sanctified.

Thus, teaches St. Paul, where the Mosaic sacrifices are repetitive, material, and relatively powerless, the new sacrifice is once and for all, spiritual, and all-powerful. Yet the total number of Catholic Masses celebrated over nearly 2,000 years of Church history must dwarf the total number of all Mosaic sacrifices ever offered in the one Temple! The Protestant solution is again to deny that the Mass is a sacrifice. There was Christ's one bloody sacrifice on Calvary, and that is all. Anything else can be no more than a commemoration of Calvary.

What then gives Catholics the right to interpret somehow else these texts of St. Paul clearly affirming the oneness and perfection of the priest and sacrifice of the New Testament? An answer to this question can take its start from another text of Hebrews, 13: 10: "We have an altar whereof they have no power to eat who serve the tabernacle."

St. Paul speaks here of an altar and of a victim being consumed, as in the Mosaic sacrifices, and so of a continuing sacrifice, implying also a priesthood, but from which the Levites serving the Old Temple are, as such, excluded. Clearly then there is a sacrifice and priesthood of the Christians ("we"), continuing well after the death of Christ.

In that case the only possible explanation taking all the texts into account is that while the Catholic priests and Masses outwardly resemble the imperfection and repetition of the Mosaic priests and sacrifices, inwardly they are quite different. Outwardly the Catholic priests are numerous and less than perfect, but their inward reality is none other than that of the one Eternal High Priest, Jesus Christ; outwardly Catholic Masses are numerous and in need of repetition; but their inward reality is none other than that of Calvary. Thus Masses in their celebration are as multiple and diverse as the extension of the Catholic Church in time and space, but as sacrifice they are one with Calvary. Similarly, Catholic priests in their humanity must number in the millions since the Church began, and the variety of their human imperfections let us graciously pass over, nevertheless as priests they are one and identical with Christ the Sovereign High Priest.

From these texts of Hebrews comes Mother Church's extraordinary teaching concerning her priesthood and Mass, but all taken with all, there is no other way that these texts on the oneness of Catholic priest and sacrifice can be understood. The implications are endless.

As a Jew once said, "If only you Catholics knew what you have in your priests." As the Curé of Ars said, "If we could see the priest for what he is, we would die of love." The priesthood being an accident or mode of being of the priest's human substance, then every act of the priest is substantially a human act, so in everything the priest does there is intermingled more or less of the man. However, when he thinks, talks, or acts as a priest, there is also more or less of Jesus Christ intermingled in his words and deeds, and the more purely he acts as a priest, for instance, in administering the sacraments, the more purely it is Jesus Christ speaking and acting through him, the more he is, without ceasing to be the man he is, a stand-in of Christ.

Thus every Catholic priest is a double reality, both treasure of Our Lord, the objective priesthood, and vessel of clay carrying that treasure, the subjective human being. To forget either half of the reality is to ask for trouble. For instance, if I blur the priest into the man, I debase Christ's priesthood to the level of human frailty, e.g., "Hi, folks, I'm Fr. Jones, but call me Joe," or "He may be a priest, but to me he's got to prove himself as a man." Alternately, if I blur the man into the priest, I am riding for disappointment whenever the frail man sooner or later does not live up to the level of his sublime priesthood. An example might be today's sedevacantists who so cannot bear recent Popes' frailty that they deny they are Popes at all. Some Catholics combine both errors by swinging incense at a priest one moment, and then making war on him the next! They are swerving between sentiments, unstabilized by the Faith. It is Our Lord's wisdom and love to entrust such treasure to such vessels of clay, thus reminding us both that the priesthood is not human and that human beings are not divine.

Such reflections will be a useful prelude to a presentation of the next three articles from *Si Si, No No* in the series; "Those Who Think They Have Won." These three concern no longer philosophers or theologians, but churchmen at the summits of the Church. Blessed the robust faith of the Middle Ages which could endure much weakness of the office-holder without calling in question the office! The individualism of our age has lost the sense of institutions, and is obsessed with the persons and personalities.

NO. 119 | SEPTEMBER 1, 1993

Executives of Neo-Modernism

LET NO ONE say that nobody reads any longer! Numbers of you read and appreciated, as I thought you would, the June Newsletter's summary of the *Si Si, No No* analysis of the leaders of the modern Church's "New Theology": Maurice Blondel, Fr. de Lubac and Fr. von Balthasar. Reader reaction may not have been quite as strong as for the question of sla-BEEP!, or the Holo-BEEP!, but it did make clear that the promised second part of the analysis would also interest many of you.

This second part is more delicate because it criticizes three prominent churchmen. The problem is that modern godlessness undermines all authority, which hollows out institutions, which leaves only individuals. If then the individuals prove unworthy of trust, there seems to be nothing left. That is why many Catholics today cling to unworthy churchmen and follow them in their liberalism because the only alternative seems to be to abandon the Church altogether.

On the contrary, as the July letter suggested, when Catholics have a robust faith, as in the Middle Ages, their faith in the Church as an institution remains unshaken by any misbehavior of the individual churchmen, because the institution is that much greater than the individuals. That is why a Catholic today can severely criticize the recent Popes without having to be a sedevacantist, and he should be able to say these Popes have been very bad for Catholicism without his needing to be accused of losing the Faith or of seeking to destroy the Church. In fact *Si Si, No No*'s articles on Pope Paul VI, Cardinal Ratzinger and Pope John Paul II are highly constructive, showing how things should go right by analyzing just how they have been going wrong.

The sixth article in the series deals with Pope Paul VI. *Si Si, No No* quotes an abundance of sources to show that Msgr. Montini, later Paul VI, was an admirer of the naturalistic "New Theology," of de Lubac in particular, and of the truth-dissolving philosophy behind it, especially of Blondel. When Blondel's orthodoxy was being fiercely contested in France in the early 1940's, Msgr. Montini as substitute Secretary of State published in the name of Pope Pius XII a letter to Blondel publicly and authoritatively praising his philosophical speculations as a "valuable contribution" reaching out to modern man.

This letter seemed to give the support of the highest Church authority to doctrinal error, but it can hardly have been Pius XII's own position, given that in 1950 the Pope would issue a classical encyclical, *Humani Generis*, condemning the "New Theology" from start to finish, and ordering superiors to stamp it out! But how capable Msgr. Montini was of betraying Pius XII is well known from his wartime contacts with Stalin behind the Pope's back, contacts forbidden by the Pope and known to him only later through the Swedish secret service. On learning of them Pius XII immediately removed Msgr. Montini from Rome by making him in 1954 Archbishop – but never, as is normal, Cardinal – of Milan, and from then on to the end of his reign in 1958 Pius XII never received him in private audience.

Typically before leaving Rome Msgr. Montini had worked to nullify the effect of Humani Generis, reassuring a liberal friend that the "New Theology" dear to both of them was an opinion worthy of respect and had been condemned by the Pope only as a matter of form. In fact Humani Generis did succeed for a while in discrediting de Lubac and in preventing the open circulation of his writings, but once in Milan Msgr. Montini continued to encourage de Lubac until Pope John XXIII appointed de Lubac to the Preparatory Theological Commission of the upcoming Council. John XXIII of course swiftly made Montini a Cardinal, from where he could become Pope to support the "New Theology."

Sure enough, as Pope from 1963, Montini opened the doors much wider still to the "New Theologians," receiving them in audience, concelebrating with them, praising them. Many bishops at the Second Vatican Council, ignorant of their theology but knowing that the "New Theology" had been condemned, only supported it because of the lead given by Paul VI.

In giving this lead, Paul VI proceeded carefully with a carefulness that gave some observers the impression that he was hesitant or indecisive, like Hamlet in Shakespeare's play. Maybe involuntarily he had moments when his conscience, or what was still Catholic in him, rose up in anguish at his wrenching the Church off her true path, but voluntarily or with his will, he was resolute in changing the Church's direction, and any carefulness he displayed in doing so was in fact to avoid provoking undesirable reactions on the part of the conservatives, as Msgr. Bugnini testifies in his book on that reform of the liturgy which the two of them brought about together. With his will Paul VI knew exactly where he was going, and he was resolute in going there.

Richard N. Williamson

For instance in June of 1963 he had the orthodox Jesuit Rector of the Gregorian University invite de Lubac to address a Thomist Congress on Teilhard de Chardin that autumn! Thus the Pope himself twisted Thomists into Teilhardists. Thus was the door opened to what the great Fr. Garrigou-Lagrange had called "Scepticism, fantasy and heresy."

Steadily Pope Paul VI smashed the conservative resistance, put the levers of power in Rome into the hands of "renewers" and guaranteed their future, for instance by reforming the rules for the election of a Pope. Like de Lubac, Paul VI towards the end of his days seems by moments to have questioned or regretted what he had done, but as with de Lubac it was no real conversion, rather an attempt to disown responsibility for so many ruins. Thus as late as 1976 he was still praising de Lubac on his 80th birthday. Modernists do not convert . . .

Just recently, in 1993, the Liberals in Rome have, logically, begun the canonization process of their champion Paul VI. Wiser friends of Rome urged the liberals not to do so, because disturbing facts of Paul VI's private life, the moral signpost of intellectual disorder, would have to come to light. But what do liberals care for facts? – which is why the Church is now full of such facts! – they went ahead anyway. Pray the process die a discrete death!

In any case by the time Paul VI died in 1978 he had succeeded in breaking down or dissolving that Catholic resistance which had still been significant at the time of the Council, but which was now reduced to a numerically insignificant handful of "Traditionalists" with two old bishops at their head. The only significant clash remaining center stage in the Church from now on was between the extreme neo-modernists who occupied the teaching posts, and the moderate neo-modernists who occupied the governing posts, but this was no longer a clash of principle, merely a disagreement about how fast the "renewal" should go forward.

Joseph Ratzinger, subject of the seventh article in the *Si Si, No No* series, was at the time of the Council a prominent young priest and theologian in his thirties, colleague and disciple of the leading progressive teacher, Karl Rahner. Soon after the Council, in 1968, Ratzinger published a book entitled Introduction to Christianity which by 1986 was in its eighth edition in Italy. Far from disowning this early work, when Ratzinger became the Cardinal Prefect of the Congregation for the Doctrine of Faith he described it as "a kind of classic," because of its being both "Catholic" and "open to the Council." To show how Ratzinger achieved this combination, *Si Si, No No* presents a series of textual quotations, taken here from the English-language edition published by Herder and Herder in 1973.

Page 142: "God comes to pass for men through men, nay, even more concretely through the man (referring to Jesus) in whom the quintessence of humanity appears and who for that very reason is at the same time God himself." (Note especially the "for that very reason.")

Now if words mean anything, this quotation means that for Joseph Ratzinger Jesus is God because in Jesus appears the quintessence, i.e., the very essence, of man. In other words, any man who would show himself completely, absolutely and perfectly man would thereby be God! And to believe that Jesus is God, all I need to believe is that Jesus is perfectly man!, Forget about the Second Person from eternity of the Holy Trinity descending from heaven and becoming incarnate, all that is too difficult for modern man to believe. Clearly, Ratzinger's way of combining Catholicism with Vatican II is to keep the words of Catholicism, like "God," but to empty out their substance – "God" is no more than supremely perfect man. Ratzinger is certainly "renewing" Catholicism!

Richard N. Williamson

In fact his Introduction to Christianity is introducing readers to a brand-new Christianity. There is just one little problem: it has nothing to do with the "old," or true, Christianity! What he is renewing is modernism and heresy.

It might be objected, these are enormous conclusions to build on one little quote, torn out of context. Alas, there are several such quotes in the book, because the context is Ratzinger's overriding concern to get through to unbelieving and uninterested modern man. For the half dozen quotes given by *Si Si, No No* from only one section of the book (pages 142, 156, 163, 168, 170 and 176 in the English edition), see the complete article due to appear eventually in the English language *Si Si, No No*. This letter will have to content itself with two more samples of the book's "renewing" of Christianity, e.g. page 156: "Must we not much rather claim Jesus enthusiastically as a man, and treat Christology (the study of Christ) as humanism and anthropology (the study of man)? Or should the real man, precisely because he is wholly and properly such, be God, and God the real man?"

The early ecumenical councils answered yes to both questions, says Ratzinger a few lines further down! In other words, he is saying it is the Catholic Church's teaching that Jesus the man, because he is fully man, is God, and so God is man! Where the Church in fact teaches that the fullness of God became man by taking flesh in the Virgin Mary's womb, Ratzinger says it teaches that in Jesus the fullness of man became God! One more quotation, page 170:

> Jesus' being is pure actuality of "from" and "for." But precisely because this "being" is no longer separate from its actuality it coincides with God and is at the same time the exemplary man, the man of the future, through whom it becomes evident how very much man

is still the coming creature, a being still, so to speak, waiting to be realized; and what a short distance man has even now progressed towards being himself.

In context, Ratzinger is saying that the man Jesus was so totally selfless, that the service of others ("actuality") was his very being. The human being of Jesus was thus so perfect that this human being was both the being of God and the ultimate being of man, towards which all men are destined to evolve! In other words when all other men attain the perfection of their evolution exemplified for them by Jesus, they too will be God! Between man and God there is essential identity!

In defense of Ratzinger's book of 1968, one might say he really believed all along what the Church teaches about Christ coming down from Heaven at the Incarnation, but he was merely recasting that doctrine in completely human terms in order to get the Gospel through to humanistic modern man. To such a "charitable" interpretation of Ratzinger's humanism, the reply is swift and crushing: firstly, to recast in purely human terms the coming down of God from heaven to save us for an eternity in heaven with God, is as impossible as, in fact infinitely more impossible than, recasting all seven colors of the rainbow in a single one of those colors. Secondly, anyone who had the Catholic Faith would not dream of so diminishing it, however much he loved modern man. Conclusion: Joseph Ratzinger according to his writing in 1968 did not have the Catholic Faith, he had not even a remote idea of the true Faith.

But has Fr. Ratzinger, the theologian of 1968, been disowned by Cardinal Ratzinger, reappointed in 1991 by JP2 for a third five-year term as Prefect of the Congregation for the Doctrine of the Faith? Alas, not at all, replies *Si Si, No No*. His earlier works are being continuously reprinted, and the Prefect continues to write for Communio, the "New Theology" review founded in 1972 by – Ratzinger, de Lubac and von Balthasar. In the wake of these three follow many others, who constitute the "think-tank" of JP2's Church, either ultra-progressives in teaching or moderate progressives in Church government – today's Rome is ever more crowded with "new theologians."

As Prefect of Faith, Cardinal Ratzinger has eulogized von Balthasar and has patronized the opening in Rome of a center of formation inspired by the life and works of Balthasar, de Lubac and Adrienne von Speyr. On the contrary, dogmatic or near-dogmatic statements of the Church from the last century and the beginning of this century he has dismissed as "a sort of temporary measure."

Hence, concludes *Si Si, No No*, the idea that Cardinal Ratzinger will restore the Church is a myth. True, he can, like von Balthasar and Pope Paul VI, make apparently conservative statements because he dislikes the excesses of modernism, but he globally approves of the "New Theology" while he disowns Tradition and the Magisterium. Hence he lays down false principles and then repudiates their logical conclusions. To wild error he opposes merely moderate error, and so his answer to the abuses is no answer at all. Dear friends, short of a miraculous conversion there is no rescue for the Church to be hoped for from Cardinal Ratzinger, however charming, kind, and well-meaning he may be. It is ideas that matter, and judged by the ideas expressed in his words and deeds, he is a Prefect for the Faith without the Faith!

We come to the subject of *Si Si, No No*'s eighth article in the series "Those Who Think They Have Won." This is JP2. If a Cardinal follows the "New Theology," the Church is in great trouble. But if a Pope follows it, his mere example will be devastating. Alas, where Paul VI was an enthusiastic admirer of the "New Theologians,"

JP2 is a personal follower of them. This emerges clearly, says *Si Si, No No*, from a recent book by a German theologian, Fr. Johannes Dörmann, called *John-Paul II's Theological Road to Assisi*. Dörmann is not a so-called Traditionalist, but, puzzled by the events at Assisi in 1986, he undertook a serene and objective study of Pope Wojtyla's speeches and writings. The first volume is due to appear in English from *The Angelus* within the next six months.

Fr. Dörmann says that JP2's fundamental error lies in holding that absolutely all men, consciously or unconsciously, are in a state of effective redemption by Jesus Christ, i.e., all men are saved. The error arises directly from the "New Theology" so glorifying man as to blur nature and grace. Human nature is so wonderful that it is "super." So whoever has human nature, has supernature, i.e., grace. So all men are in a state of grace. So all men are in a state of grace merely by being men and are saved! Hence a new – brand-new! – version of the Church, of Revelation and of the Faith.

As for the Church, if every man at every moment has grace merely by having human nature, then every man belongs in some way to the Church, so the supernatural Church coincides with natural mankind. Once more, the radical blurring of natural and supernatural.

Secondly, since Church and mankind differ then from one another only by their greater or lesser awareness of their "being in Christ" – the Church being more aware of it than the rest of mankind – then all that Christ revealed to man was the fullness of man, i.e., man's natural supernaturalness. However, this revelation of man by Christ to man is an exterior and secondary revelation, not strictly necessary, because all men are present to themselves, have a natural self-awareness, and so have an interior revelation coming before any additional revelation from outside. From which it follows that the various religions are none of them true or false, because all men have a valid self-awareness of which their religion is the expression. Hence JP2's respect for all non-Catholic "religions."

Finally faith is equated in this system of ideas with man's awareness of his "super" state, whether this was revealed to him through Christ or through some other source. Thus all religions contain some revelation of "God," whence the need for dialogue between those religions as the golden highway to religious peace, which is the most important component of universal peace. Hence Assisi, and JP2's continual travels.

Si Si, No No quotes numerous other instances of the present Pope's allegiance to the "New Theology." His first Encyclical in 1978 commemorated the famous (or notorious!) statement from the Council document *Gaudium et Spes* (#22): "By his Incarnation the Son of God has united himself in some fashion with every man." (This text has been called "the key text of the New Catechism"). The statement is true if it means that every man born alive is potentially saved by Christ, but he will have to do something about it if he wants to be actually saved. The sentence is false if it is understood (as by JP2 and the New Catechism) to mean that every man is actually saved by Christ, whether he knows it and wants it, or not.

In 1982 JP2 glorified the centenary of the birth of the arch-heretic Teilhard de Chardin, and he appointed Bishop Ratzinger as Prefect for the Faith. In 1983 he made de Lubac a Cardinal. In 1983 he desired a symposium to be held on von Balthasar and Adrienne von Speyr; it was held in 1985. In 1988 he made von Balthasar a Cardinal. Von Baltasar died just before receiving the honor, but in his funeral sermon Cardinal Ratzinger declared that the gesture remained valid.

In 1991 JP2 sent telegrams of condolence to the Superior of the Jesuits and to the Cardinal of Paris on the death of de Lubac, referring to his "intellectual uprightness" his "long and faithful service" as a "great servant of the Church," guarding "the best of Catholic Tradition"! Early this year, 1993, he glorified the centenary of Blondel's key book Action, proposing Blondel as a model for philosophers and theologians! And last year he commemorated once more de Lubac and von Balthasar as the initiators of the New Theology review Communio. Those who write for this review, says *Si Si, No No*, are called "conservatives," but in reality they are merely slightly more cautious modernists.

Following the Pope's lead, the entire Catholic press now promotes the New Theology.

Si Si, No No concludes this daunting eighth article on JP2 by enouncing elementary Catholic principles that will enable a Catholic to keep his Faith, his head and his balance amidst this devastation of the Lord's vineyard by his own Vicar:

1) The Holy Ghost cannot in the present contradict everything He has inspired in the past.

2) Public Revelation of the Faith was completed and closed with the death of the last of the twelve Apostles. That is the Catholic Faith. It can never more be changed.

3) Church and Pope are helped by God to guard that Faith, not to introduce novelties.

4) No Pope can contradict past Popes, pronouncing on Faith or morals.

5) No Pope can contradict what the Church has taught and believed always, everywhere and universally.

6) In cases of conflict between the universality of Popes in the past and a handful of Popes in the present, Catholics are bound to follow those of the past.

Finally, a Pope acting or teaching purely personally can neither demand nor receive obedience. His privilege of infallibility excludes his formally or strictly imposing error, but not his pretending to impose it, nor his any less than strictly imposing it. If a Pope wished to impose error, Christ's keeping watch over him would prevent him from using his infallibility. Hence the privilege of infallibility would not prevent the Faith from being imperiled by a Pope's negligence, but it would prevent error from being pronounced "ex cathedra." So today's crisis does not call in question the Pope's infallibility, but it does constitute a grave trial for all Catholics!

So we must pray, we must do penance, and we must resist the destruction of the Church, and according to our station in life, we may recall the Holy Father to his duty.

Dear friends, these articles of *Si Si, No No* are daunting, but they are also consoling – we know what we are up against. What is happening in Rome today is perfectly coherent. On the human level, the Church's present leaders have a dream, and everything indicates they will go on pushing that dream through until the whole Church is in ruins. On the divine level, God is purifying His Church, He is allowing a mass of rotten fruit to fall, and when the process is complete, He will raise His indestructible Church in dazzling beauty from the ruins. He is in control, and He does know what he is doing. He is simply saying, "I am the Lord your God, and I will have no other gods before me. This is my Son in whom I am well pleased, and there is no other Way, nor Truth, nor Life. All other solutions are false, and I will let them break to pieces in your hands. I have loved you with an everlasting love. It is never too late to turn back to Me! I am."

It will be a great grace over the next few years to continue being part of God's solution. He calls us to be no less than heroes and heroines. We must pray for a supernatural steadiness, sanity and serenity.

The Humble Rosary

OctobER, MONTH OF the Holy Rosary. There is no problem on earth, Sister Lucy of Fatima has said, that cannot be resolved by devout prayer of the Holy Rosary, and many other Saints have said the same thing. How can the humble beads have such power?

Simply, because God chooses to give them such power. The Lord God could attach eternal salvation to any practice He might choose to impose, for instance walking on our hands for an hour every day, so that if then we were to walk on our hands for an hour every day, we would save our souls, simply because God had said so.

Instead, ever since His Mother taught the Rosary to St. Dominic in the Middle Ages, God has constantly through His Church and through His Mother taught the reciting of the Holy Rosary as the great means of prayer for everybody, and so as the universal means of salvation. That being the case, it is difficult to see how someone could faithfully pray the Rosary and still lose his soul.

Why the Lord God should have chosen to attach so great a power to such little means – a fistful of beads – is not difficult to see. The beads turn around the central

Mysteries of our Catholic Faith; they are perfectly adapted to human nature; they are humble.

Objectively, the fifteen Mysteries on which the Rosary has us meditate contain all the great truths necessary for salvation, from the life of Jesus framed within the life of Mary. St. Dominic had been racking his brains to find a way of rooting the Albigensian heresy, the Communism of its time, out of the hearts and minds of people across South-West France; the Rosary was the heaven-sent way of replanting in their hearts and minds the truths of salvation. How can the mind dwell regularly for fifteen or twenty minutes around the Incarnation, or the Passion, or the Resurrection, or all three, not as abstract arguments but as vivid concrete scenes, without soaking in the Faith? No wonder hardly a Saint since St. Dominic has not recited or recommended the Rosary.

Subjectively, the Rosary is marvelously adapted to human nature. What are the strategic points in the human frame at which a human being most lives and moves? Surely his mind which thinks, his tongue which talks, his hands which handle. The Rosary occupies all three. The meditation on the Mysteries occupies the mind, the telling of the prayers occupies the tongue, and the counting of the beads occupies the hands. So if the mind strays off the Mystery – nothing more human! – the tongue can take over with the telling of the great prayers of the Pater, Ave and Gloria; and if the mind takes the tongue woolgathering with it, then sooner or later the beads filing through the fingers bring back the Mysteries center stage. No mind can stray indefinitely when tongue and fingers are also harnessed, and if the feet be counted as a fourth mobile point of distraction, then it suffices to pray the Rosary walking up and down.

Lastly, the Rosary is humble. It requires no ability even to read, it requires a minimal effort of the memory to recall the Mysteries and the Christian's basic prayers, yet could the loftiest or most learned of souls ever exhaust those Mysteries or these prayers? Everything of the Rosary is so within the reach of the humblest of souls that proud spirits are tempted to despise it. Woe to them if they do! God gives His grace to the humble, He resists the proud (James 4: 6). To souls praying the Rosary like little children admiring the Christmas-time crib, He gives His grace; upon the modernists who cast out His Rosary and trample on its devotees, He turns His back. If pride is the great obstacle to Heaven, the humble Rosary, as simple as it is profound, is one great remover of that obstacle.

Of course the objection is made that continually praying the Hail Mary is repetitious. Catholics reply by asking what mother ever objected to the child in her arms endlessly repeating "Mama." Our Lord warns us that unless we become like little children (child-like, not childish!), we will not enter the Kingdom of Heaven (Mt. 18: 3). Blessed the souls, especially the families, which obey Heaven and obey the Mother of God by praying the Rosary! There is nothing in the wide world today so purely positive, so easily accessible and so absolutely necessary as the praying of the Holy Rosary. Happy the families which store up grace and protection by praying the Rosary now before the bombs start falling, because it will be a little late then!

For bombs will fall. Unless enough families pray the Rosary and the Holy Father solemnly consecrates Russia to the Sorrowful and Immaculate Heart of Mary, surely the Russian military are simply waiting in the wings for the flow of money from the West to stop, before they push everyone else aside and turn Russia into the scourge of the godless West which Our Lady of Fatima warned us it risked becoming. In the United States God has given us advance warning with earthquakes in the West, with extraordinary storms in the East and now this summer with floods in the Midwest, these latter corresponding it seems to some of the highest per capita abortion rates in the country, yet, anyone with any sense of God is aware, "we ain't seen nothin' yet."

It is because we have not seen anything yet, in comparison with the storm coming, that Catholics and any other souls of good will must be taught the full truth as to where the trouble is coming from – liberalism, so embedded in our way of life as to have become a religionless religion.

Religionless, because liberalism professes the absence of any dogma or creed. Nevertheless a religion, because whole nations can base their political life as nations upon it, practising separation of Church and State but union of liberalism and state. So if a Catholic priest attacks liberalism, he is readily accused of mixing religion and politics – but it is not a question of politics at all; or of being unpatriotic – but it is not a question of patriotism at all.

Read the enclosed testimonial of an encounter with liberalism written a few months ago not by a foreign-born cleric arguing his preconceived theories, but by a home-born housewife describing her recent experiences. She believed in the modern system, she abode by its rules, she played the game and extracted from it all she could, but sheer hard facts drove her as a Catholic reluctantly to the conclusion that the famous and beloved system is systematically anti-Catholic. It all comes back to the words of Our Lord, "He that is not with me, is against me: and he that gathereth not with me scattereth." (Mt. 12: 30) Dear friends, the time is far past for playing games, or for anything other than whole-hearted gathering with Christ – my thoughts and deeds be Catholic or be nothing worth.

Not one word of the testimonial has been altered. The writer would gladly release her name, as she "dislikes anonymous letters," but it is principles, not personalities at stake, so we will only give out her name or address in private. Please, let nobody accuse her of giving up the good fight, or of being unpatriotic. She is now a full-time mother, home-rearing with the Rosary the children God has sent her, which is the greatest thing she can do for God or country. Had there only been more like her, her country could have been saved from liberals and so from the bombs.

From homes like hers should come the whole-hearted Catholics of tomorrow, whole-hearted because whole-minded, who may be scorned for being unpatriotic but who will be the backbone of the Catholic Church and so of their country. Include in your family Rosaries through October the seminarians at Winona, that they become such whole-minded Catholic priests each with an unadulterated love of his own country. They are praying for you each evening at Rosary and Benediction.

NO. 121 | NOVEMBER 6, 1993

A Discerning Young Man

THE WORLD IS getting day by day more difficult for Catholics to live in. From the moment they wish to take their Catholic Faith seriously, they find themselves more or less out of line with most everything that anyone else thinks, says or does around them. At which point, as Catholics either they start disarming their Faith with any one of a variety of readily available compromises, or they live in a state of continual – and increasing – tension with their surroundings, with little or no prospect of the tension easing off. What are they to do?

Surely youngsters who get caught in this situation are particularly deserving of sympathy, insofar as they did not create it, they have merely walked into it. It is understandable if many of them turn to false solutions like drugs, or pleasure, or material success, but the problem, which has been around for a long time, still does not go away. Serious questions deserve serious answers.

Let me quote from a letter that I received last month from a university student in the United States. I have slightly adapted his text:

> I am quite disgusted with school and society in general. Utter amazement is the only way I can describe

my reaction to this great chasm that divides the Catholic from modern society. It has drifted so far . . . At times I rage internally against this whole abomination, and begin to wonder if I am slowly turning into a hater of mankind. But however misguided they may be I am still concerned for the souls of my fellow-men, so perhaps I am just frustrated.

I have come to think that this whole crisis in Church and world can only be solved in blood. We are all guilty for the godlessness of today insofar as we are all sinners; we have all, through sins of commission or omission, contributed to the liberal disease. So God is just in making us all suffer, in demanding our blood as well as that of the leading criminals.

I often wonder if a Restoration will be granted, or would we be the end? Could modern man really adapt himself to a renewed social reign of Christ the King? Or would such a Restoration demand the mass expulsion or, sadder, the mass extermination of whole populations as when the Israelites entered into Canaan? Our Lady has warned us of the annihilation of various nations.

It is easy to lose sight of the seriousness of life, to let oneself be drawn into the fantasy which is deceitfully passed off as reality. We wade in Romanticism, the true opiate of the age, for which a just penalty will be exacted. But I know the Truth, which sets me apart from the liberal and romantic crowd in which I am immersed, so if I were to let myself drift with the crowd I would have to pay a severer penalty. May God deliver us from liberalism! I have seen too many people, even friends, devoured by the Beast. How frightening to know the living damned!

Forgive my rantings, but such thoughts can drive one mad if they are not expressed. But to openly express such things can be truly dangerous in most company . . .

End of extracts from student's letter. Now here is a line of reply:—

> My dear boy (he is humble enough to listen even after being addressed like that!), firstly, here and there you may rant, but you are far more on target than you are off target, and let nobody tell you differently. You are quite right in thinking that the mass of people around us are living out a fantasy, a fantasy of Romanticism, of love without God, which is turning into hate, so that there is going to be a terrible day of reckoning. You are right to be amazed, it is indeed an abomination, but be careful with the disgust or the rage. The great mass of people, in Our Lord's words, "know not what they do." They have lost the Truth, they have deserved to have God "send them the operation of error, to believe lying" (II Thes. 2: 10), they need to be very much pitied.
>
> On the contrary you yourself have not lost the Truth, you have the Catholic Faith by which you are taking the measure of the world around you, and you are essentially correct. Make sure you thank God for that, but with no trace of the pride of the pharisee who thought himself better than everyone else, and in order to keep your grasp on the Truth, every day pray the Rosary, to stop "the operation of error" from closing over your mind and soul as it is closing over so many. The situation you are describing is firstly a supernatural war. You must employ firstly supernatural weapons. Lose the Truth, you lose everything. Pray the Rosary, God will give you to hold onto the Truth.
>
> When you think that the abomination in Church and world will have to be washed out in blood, you are surely right. Scripture says, "Without shedding of blood there is no remission" (Heb. 9: 22). Men are committing a flood of sins needing remission, but they are choking off the flow of Christ's atoning Blood at the true Sacrifice of the Mass, therefore it is their own blood that will have to flow, unless there is a sudden wide scale repentance, which does not seem likely. You

are wise to recognize that all of us sinners will justly suffer, but do not be scandalized if one day you see the blood of the innocent also flowing – the greater the innocence, the greater the power of remission. Remember the blood of the Lamb of God: wholly innocent, wholly powerful.

You are right again in asking if modern man could adapt himself to a renewed social reign of Christ the King. With his idolatry of his rights, liberty and independence he surely could not, unless he underwent a serious conversion, at which point the Truth would make him truly free, as Our Lord promised (Jn. 8: 32), whereas now with all his boasted liberties he is a slave of "the operation of error," and a slave of the unseen masters of the world. But he cannot and will not see it. You are right to evoke the corrupt Canaanites upon whom the Lord God passed a decree of extermination. Obviously each Canaanite was offered before being exterminated all the grace he needed to save his soul for the next world, but he was too corrupt to be allowed to continue to live in this world. Similarly a mass of modern Westerners are in the process of forfeiting their right to life in this world.

Will their extermination be the end of the world? One may think not. Many prophecies speak of a great chastisement cleansing mankind to make possible one final glorification of the Catholic Church, a generation of peace ("In the end my Immaculate Heart will Triumph"), before the final corruption leads to the Antichrist. You are young enough to see the Chastisement. You might even be young enough to see the end of the world.

No matter. Those questions need not concern you. What should concern you is how at all costs to avoid being drawn into the fantasy as you call it, which is deceitfully passed off as reality, the "operation of error." Besides the Rosary, remember another great spiritual weapon given by God to his Church at the time when the operation of error began centuries ago with Protestantism: St. Ignatius' Spiritual Exercises.

The Ignatian Retreats are a providential means for Catholics in a distracted and distracting world to plunge themselves again, if necessary once a year, in the truths of their Faith, to regain their spiritual bearings, to discern the things that really matter, to revive their sense and love of God, to steep their souls in prayer. The yellow flyer enclosed tells of three locations in the United States for these retreats, including December 26 to 31 this year as usual in Winona. Last year's Christmas retreat here was a grand success with 40 retreatants.

Finally the other great weapon in all supernatural warfare, next after prayer, is penance. Do penance. But as Our Lady told the children of Fatima at the beginning of our century, no doubt because she knew how difficult life would become for Catholics, sufficient penance today is to do the duty of our state of life. If you are a student, study; if you become a breadwinner, win bread; if you become a father, look after your wife and children. And leave in God's hands all kinds of other details. He wants us to trust Him. My dear boy, you are luckier than you think. You have not lost the Truth. There are all kinds of questions which are secondary. Look after the primary. Love God day by day. Look after God's interests and He will look after yours. As Padre Pio said, entrust the past to His mercy, the present to His love, and the future to His Providence, and God be with you!

End of a bishop's reply to a serious young man.

Remember especially the Holy Souls in Purgatory through this month of November. God bless you.

NO. 122 | DECEMBER 11, 1993

A Trip Through Africa

THE DECEMBER LETTER is so late off the mark this year that its timing may be perfect to wish all readers a Happy Christmas, and some readers it may reach only in time to wish them a Happy New Year! May you then all be filled with the love of Our Lord Jesus Christ, born in an animal's stall in order to save us from our sins, God of God, Light of Light, true God of true God, and, Light of the World, may He fill your minds and hearts through the coming year. Men are turning in all directions for solutions, but there is no other Way, Truth, or Life.

The December letter is certainly also the occasion to thank you for your support of the seminary through the year. Many thanks. For not only has the seminary survived, but thanks to a few bequests and special gifts, we have, for the honor of the United States, been able to pay back to Europe a long outstanding debt of the SSPX in the USA to the motherhouse in Europe. This was a debt rather of the District than of the seminary, but while it was highly fitting that Archbishop Lefebvre should have helped the Society to establish itself over here in the early days, it is a matter of national honor that we should not remain any longer than necessary in debt to our fellow Catholics in Europe. Our thanks go to them for their longstanding help and for their patience.

If the seminary was to receive any more bequests over and above its own present needs, there are several good causes which it could help. One of them is described in one of the enclosed flyers: the Retreat House in Phoenix, Arizona. The Society already has retreat houses for the Ignatian Retreats in Connecticut and California, but these houses specialize in the five- or six-day retreats, because such week-long retreats are irreplaceable.

However, there are many people who find it difficult to disengage themselves from their obligations for a full week. On the other hand, to take off for a weekend conference every now and again is a regular part of many a busy man's schedule. So it makes sense for the Society to make easily available within the United States something like weekend retreats. These are certainly not as powerful as the week-long retreats, but they could be of immense benefit to numbers of souls. A house specializing in them might be able to provide them all year round, time will tell. Such at any rate is the Society's present thinking for the building in Phoenix. It is not far from completion, but, as you may know, for purposes of an occupancy permit, a miss is as good as a mile.

The main reason why this letter is so late is that I only returned on December 6 from a visit of two and a half weeks to Southern Africa. I had hoped to write the letter on the long flight back from Johannesburg to New York, about eighteen hours from take-off to landing, which includes a stop-over in the Cape Verde Islands just off the tip of West Africa. Alas, "the best laid plans of mice and men gang aft agley" – just the night before leaving, the Rhodesian equivalent of Montezuma's Revenge struck, namely that upheaval of the insides with which the King of Mexico, Montezuma, dethroned by Hernan Cortes, is said to have taken his revenge on almost all invaders of

Mexico ever since. Have no fear. It passed. But it did hold up this letter.

They were a most enjoyable and interesting two and a half weeks. They began with a swift visit to Durban, main city of Natal, the most English of the four states composing what used to be the Union of South Africa. Here the Society has no house, but it has a valiant friend, Fr. Eldred Leslie, looking after a congregation of hundreds of souls, blacks and whites, in a handsome church property which he was able to buy recently not far from the center of the city. Forty confirmations, including some thirty Zulus, and then a picnic in Fr. Leslie's garden, in brilliant warm sunshine. Some people think I deliberately pick the winter months in the north to make visits to the southern hemisphere!

The airplane returned swiftly to Johannesburg, industrial and commercial capital of Southern Africa, where the SSPX also has its main center, a 1912 English school building in Roodepoort, a town lying half an hour west of central Jo'burg, as it is usually called. The main hall of this solid building – how solid the British Empire seemed at that time! . . . so passes the world and its glory – makes a grand church. In a dozen years the Society has built up a congregation in Jo' burg of some two hundred souls. There is the usual impression of stagnation, the usual desire that two hundred were twice or three times as many, but the Lord God does not at present seem to be wanting large numbers for his remnant in any part of the world. What matters in Jo'burg as elsewhere is that there is a hard core of souls holding onto the Faith in quality and numbers sufficient to make it difficult to imagine the pilot light being extinguished. What more is required of it?

After ten confirmations on the Sunday, of whites and blacks, with a sermon and conference on the deep-down religious nature of the modern world's problems, of which South Africa currently has more than its fair share, there followed a week's retreat for the handful of

Society priests in southern Africa, only four of them for a whole subcontinent in turmoil! Three of them did their seminary in the United States. Your support of Winona goes around the world!

Then another swift excursion to Capetown, "fairest cape in all the world," said a famous English pirate, at the southwestern tip of the African continent. Here is where the modern nation of South Africa began with the landing in 1652 of Jan Van Riebeck to plant a colony to guarantee fresh provisions to the Dutch ships sailing from Europe to the Far East. The Calvinism of the settlers from Holland, now called Afrikaners or Boers, predominant amongst the white South Africans ever since, has been their strength and their weakness. Only in 1976 did they let television into their country, and only now is western pornography gaining free admittance. On the other hand, the strictness with which they enforced by law the separation of the races was an Achilles' heel enabling the Liberals to turn international opinion against them, so that now the whole country they so well built is on the brink of being turned over to the Communist puppets of the powers of darkness. All in the name of democracy! What a shame! As Pius IX said, "Universal suffrage, universal lie," or, "One man, one vote: one lie." As in the rest of Africa, it is the blacks who will suffer more than anyone. But they will have liberty? What liberty? As in Somalia? Liberty to starve? The Calvinists looked after the blacks so well that, as is well known, blacks from the "independent" neighboring countries flowed into South Africa. Let us see whether the Liberals' beloved Communists do any better!

Liberals are hypocrites, blinded by their own self-righteousness. Democracy is the junk crusade of their junk religion, Liberalism. Calvinism is preferable to Liberalism any day of the week, but the only true solution is Catholicism which, while recognizing the natural inequalities between souls coming from God, at the same time draws them together in supernatural equality in the Mystical Body of Christ going to God. In Catholic colonies where millions of souls were saved, birds of a racial feather naturally flocked together, but they were not forced to do so. Calvinism would force the races apart, Liberalism would force them together (compulsory bussing, etc.). Only in Catholicism is there – liberty!!

Unfortunately there is not yet a large group of Catholics with the Society in Capetown. Surprisingly for such a large city, we do not yet even have a building of our own, partly because real estate is so expensive, because the setting of the city between mountain and sea is so beautiful. However, a building will come with time because the Faith is there.

Next stop was Port Elizabeth, main port at the very foot of Africa, about an hour by air east of Capetown. Another small congregation, with souls that come and go, as usual, but with sufficient resources and determination to have found themselves a church building in the center of the city. Give these P.E. men a few months, and from a stripped Protestant hall, the earth will soon have another temple and altar befitting the Holy Sacrifice. How truly constructive Catholics are!

Back to Jo'burg, from where the next plane took off for a two-day visit to the ex-German colony of South West Africa, now "independent" Namibia, but where German is still so much spoken that one of the Society priests in Southern Africa needs to possess the language. The Catholic groups are again small, in small cities separated by immense distances of semi-desert, but they have come together to purchase a charming little mission church in a little town equidistant from several cities, Omaruru, where they were as grateful as usual for the celebration of the true Mass. Truly scattered in the wilderness, they are well supported by Society Catholics in Germany and they follow keenly what is happening in the Church abroad. Thousands of miles are nothing in the Mystical Body of Christ.

The last hop in and out of Jo'burg, made possible by today's incredible flying machines, was up to Harare (formerly Salisbury) in Zimbabwe (formerly Rhodesia) for three days. Ever since "independence" came in 1980, living conditions in Zimbabwe have grown worse, and paganism is ousting Christianity. The black population, I was reliably told, are more and more discontented. To retain power, the new "democratic" leaders must buy votes. Having squandered the riches they inherited from the competent and beneficial minority government which preceded them, they are being obliged to borrow money from the international financiers, who thus gain control at knock-down prices of one country after another, on the march to their one world government. And their lackey media can sell to the apostate West any betrayal or treachery they like, so long as it is dressed up as the advance of liberty or equality or human rights! "Those whom the gods wish to destroy, they first make mad," said the Romans.

But the SSPX has built a delightful church from ground zero not far from the center of Harare. Here another multi-racial congregation, presently about a hundred souls, continues the practice of the true Faith. It is one more cork on the storm-tossed ocean of this world. Not all the machinations of the international powers of darkness will sink the Catholic Church. *Deo Gratias* and Kyrie Eleison.

My dear friends, neither Calvinism nor – still less – Liberalism-Communism is the answer, but only that Catholicism which it is your privilege and mine to hold. Do not believe in coming months the media's version of events in South Africa. Throw the television out. Read the newspapers only with your fingers. Read with heart, soul, and mind the Old Testament prophets who used to be read by the Calvinists devoutly, who give the true version of events, and whose one hope lay in the coming of the one Savior of the World, in the tribe of Judah, in the royal city of Bethlehem – Our Lord Jesus Christ. Happy Christmas. Happy New Year.

NO. 123 | JANUARY 1, 1994

Slacks IV, or Dinosaur's Delight

JANUARY, MONTH OF the Holy Family, is the first month of each year. Each year has twelve months, and January is the first. Every year begins with January. Unlike some of the other months, January has 31 days, but like each of the other eleven months, it comes round once a year. There is never a year without January to start it. However, every year January comes in the middle of winter, so since winter is cold, the weather in January is usually cold. Because it is cold, it is usually not hot . . .

– Well done, Your Excellency, that's better! At last you are learning not to be controversial! –

. . . However, January's cold weather requires warm clothing, and so each year about this time some women have a difficulty. That difficulty consists, briefly, in SLA . . .

– Oh no, oh no, Bishop, oh no, PLEASE NO! –

. . . in SLA-MMING critics who wish to interfere in women's choice of fashions, and so since this letter always seeks to avoid unnecessary provocation, because surely none of its readers ever deserve to be provoked, for they all have excellent intentions which are in no fashion to be criticized, then let this January letter tiptoe away from the fatal S-word, and rally instead to the support of those wives and mothers and grandmothers and daughters who by their dress and demeanor are so deserving of support.

Nor need I write myself. After all, what does a middle-aged bachelor with ideas from the Middle Ages know about family life being lived in today's world? But if I quote some of your own eloquent letters, nobody can say they are out of touch with real life. You ladies that stay at home, that wear nothing but dresses, that bring into the world and look after the children that God sends, that love and obey your difficult, neglectful, scornful husbands, you have the total support year in, year out, New Year in, Old Year out, of one pre-historic, antediluvian, out-dated, fascist, colonialist, retrograde, backward-looking, old-fashioned, male chauvinist porcine dinosaur – no names!

Here is the first letter, actually a little over two years old.

> Your Excellency,
>
> Thank you so much for your letter of November 3 (1991). You would think it would be obvious, but I think we women should also be told not to go swimming – or at least not in the bathing suits that are popular.
>
> In addition to immodesty, if there's something equally important that our husbands should forbid us doing, it would be working outside the home. How can a mother preserve the sanctity of the home if daily she is in the world with all its perversions and temptations? The first step in filtering, the spirit of the world out of the home is to throw out the television. It seems the second must be the mother's embracing of her vocation – embracing housework, submission to her husband, having babies as God desires, and poverty if need be, in order to stay home.
>
> I am in my late twenties and for most women my age,

the acceptance of motherhood and staying home as a moral responsibility is repugnant if not an ultimate "heresy." The hidden life has joys which the daughters of Eve will never taste, as long as they remain daughters of Eve. They cannot understand the wisdom of David's saying, "It is good for me that Thou hast humbled me ... " (Ps. 118: 71)

 Thank you, Excellency, for humbling us.
 In Christ and Mary,
 Mrs. X, Ohio

Of course, she is wrong in thinking that anyone reasonable would dream of humbling such wise people as adults of the late 20th century, especially if they are women! Hell hath no fury ...

Here is the second letter, undated, but I have the original on file and can send a photocopy if anyone thinks I wrote it myself.

 Dear Bishop Williamson,
 We just received your newsletter and are always so impressed by your descriptions and flowery style of writing while grasping the truth in such a way that we must ponder, "Why didn't I see this before?" But, better see it late than never ... especially while we still have a breath left in our body – we have a soul to save!!
 I'm just a little slow on your issue of skirts, Your Excellency, but you are so, so right. It is oh, so difficult today to tell the men from the women, especially from behind with these men wearing earrings and pony tails! Ugh!! Start little girls out by putting dresses on them and they take it for granted. Our 6-year-old wears them every day without a thought or even a care as to what any other girl has on.
 As for television, I've been around since it was first available in American homes (I'm an old mother with a 6 year-old), and looking back and to today's programming, it has been insidious how the programs have de-

generated, yet hooked the public on their mesmerizing effect. We rid ourselves of the "beast" well over a year ago (it should have been sooner) and good riddance to it. This has been our first year homeschooling a 16, 13, 11, and 6 year-old, and I and my 13 year-old (my husband, too, I pray) just joined the Third Order of the Society. I can't begin to tell you the change in our two boys. They both serve as altar boys for Father Y, who has been a real blessing to them with his patience and kindness teaching them how to do everything correctly. The highlight of their week is Saturday and Sunday when they can serve (as it is the highlight of all of us). Father Y gave us the honor of staying at our home over the Easter weekend and what a busy time for him! Our two boys were there every step he took, even being up until 3:30 A.M. Saturday and up again at 7:00 A.M. the following morning.

It just thrills my husband and I to watch them flourish with the Church in her budding glory since the destructive Vatican II. We would be so, so happy if one or both had a vocation. One thing is certain: it would never happen in public school! That's a whole new story. If only the parents would open their eyes to the rot and lies taught there. Incredible! Poor, poor souls! So misled, so deceived!

Bishop Williamson, keep right on telling us what we need to know!! We were floundering for so many years that we all are tainted with Liberalism. Show us how to cleanse our minds, hearts and souls from that poison! We need to know, whether anyone likes it or not! We must raise our youngsters in the pure Catholic Faith so that, as you so aptly put it, the Church, like the South, may "rahse" again, and it will! What a heritage, what a blessing to be born into the true Catholic Faith. What an even greater blessing to be a convert in later life as my husband is. What graces he has received! God is so good, so patient, so wonderful. We want everyone to know Him. It is so tragic to see the people searching for the truth "in all the wrong places," as the song goes.

Richard N. Williamson

God bless the Archbishop, we are so indebted to him, and God bless the Seminary newsletter. We can't wait for each and every golden word.
Sincerely,
Mrs. Z, New York

Well, folks, what can I say? I'm a little embarrassed... I mean... Oh well... you see... I guess it's nice to have a bit of company in the dinosaur park!

The third letter goes back nearly eleven years. It has lain in my files for years because I suppose I always thought I might quote it one day (I do get some excellent letters). Ladies, you will have to admit that it looks as though I have for years been getting at the men! After listening to a sermon, this third mother wrote:

> I just don't know when I have felt so very grateful (and relieved!) when I listened to you speak of "man's role in the home" last Sunday in our parish, particularly when you said "no matter how pious (not that I am pious – I am nowhere near pious enough) a mother or a woman is – she cannot provide the lead that the man must provide." Like many women today, I have suffered not only for myself, but my children have suffered, and their children are suffering because husbands and fathers have literally and emotionally abandoned responsibilities and obligations, abdicated their roles and lead self-gratifying lives of their own. Women have been abused, really abused, by the treatment and deprivations visited on them and their children. And I, like so many others, felt that no matter how hard I tried, no matter how hard I tried to compensate, it didn't work. There was no emotional support, no respect, no nothing. I've often wondered what happened to moral values, the goals, protection and love that men were supposed to have for their families – and in the name of God, what about conscience?
>
> Whether or not you realized it, your words helped

not a few women who were at Mass – at least five or six that I know of personally. I just want to say Thank You, Father – your words helped to lighten a very heavy burden for me, and I'm sure many others. Although I must assume responsibility in the matter of choice, I can plead only that I really believed with all my heart that people were basically good, and that the man I loved wanted the same things I did, and that of course meant everything that my Catholic Faith stood for. I couldn't have been more wrong. Somewhere along the line, a lot of men believe that if they provide basic necessities of life, their obligations are satisfied; if they make noises like the big boss, no matter how unreasonable, they are the "head of the house," and discipline takes the form of threats, intimidation, verbal abuse, profanity, and obscenity. It is so sad. Heavy drinking, promiscuity, and "me-firsts" are the badges of masculinity. And how the family suffers!

I hope I didn't take too much of your time by writing, and I don't mean to presume, but I felt so grateful for your words last Sunday I felt I had to tell you how much they helped.

God Bless you and all the priests.
Sincerely,
A parishioner, Virginia

I still always maintain that the large part of modern woman's and the modern family's problems come from the man. For instance, is it a reasonable guess that the vicious feminism of a number of today's feminists goes back to the tragic abuse of their innocence and purity in their youth by some uncontrolled male, even within the family? Women are survivors, but there is abuse which wounds so deeply that revenge can become a major motive to survive.

Boys, men, be it books, magazines, or videotapes, shun pornography! To measure the devastation of pornography, get hold from *Focus on the Family* of the

25-minute interview on videotape given to Dr. James Dobson by the serial killer Ted Bundy on the eve of his execution about two years ago. Lucidly and decently the repentant killer explains how despite a good home, he got into soft-core, graduated to hard-core and from the hard-core fantasy was impelled into the hard-core reality. And he says there are multiple Ted Bundys building up this way in every American town. God, have mercy on us!

Positively, the SSPX priests in Australia are producing a monthly magazine called *Catholic Family* which may be warmly recommended, and is available from the Angelus Press office.

Enclosed is a flyer on the various bishops of Catholic Tradition. It was written not by me but by a SSPX priest here in Winona. If we send it out from the seminary, please believe it is less to attack what anyone else is doing than to give friends of the Society the means or arguments to defend what the Society is doing. Heaven knows, in this present crisis of Church and world, any of us can go crazy at quite short notice!

Happy New Year! If God be with us, who can be against us?

Dinoserely yours in Christ.

NO. 124 | FEBRUARY 3, 1994

St. Agnes & St. Emerentiana

ENCLOSED IS A winter Verbum, unusually in color, in order to share with you a little of the beauty of the magnificent but rare ceremony of the solemn consecration of an altar, because probably few of you will ever be able to attend in person such a ceremony.

The seminary's altar was no doubt consecrated by the Dominicans when they originally built in 1950 their Priory which is now our seminary. But when they withdrew from the building in 1970, leaving it to unknown future occupants, they quite correctly took out of the little cavity in the main altar (known as the "sepulchre") the relics of the three Saints, including two martyrs, contained there, which meant that the altar lost its consecration. Hence our ceremony of the reconsecration on All Saints Day last November.

The ceremony was long – some five hours with Pontifical High Mass following, but that is not disproportionately long for the hallowing of an altar on which is to be offered the Sacrifice, the one and only sacrifice that can appease the just wrath of God, and obtain grace and mercy for mankind: the Sacrifice of the Mass. Such a ceremony of sacralizing, or making sacred, is a marvelous antidote to the process of desacralizing, or secularizing, or desecrating, which is going on all around us. Our world does not want God. In His place it will have trash at best, and at worst, the demonic. Interesting how Satan brings back sacrifice! Especially the sacrifice of innocents, of children, as we are reliably told by police forces today. Parents turning their backs on the Sacrifice of the Innocent Victim, Lamb of God, may justly see taken from them the sacrifice of innocent victims, their own children. The desacralisation of Mass by the Novus Ordo rite is the main explanation of today's catastrophic rise of satanism. Hence, by way of antidote, the Verbum in color.

A sacrificed child, or near-child, is one of the three saints whose relics were placed in the sepulchre of the seminary's altar on November 1, together with St. Thomas Aquinas', patron of the seminary, and St. Peter Martyr's, original patron of the Dominicans' priory. She is St. Emerentiana, foster-sister of St. Agnes, both martyred in Rome in 304 A.D. It was in pursuit of a relic of St. Agnes herself that the seminary obtained a relic of her companion in martyrdom instead. Here is how the two girls gave their life for Christ:

St. Agnes, born around 290 A.D., who was perhaps no older than thirteen when she died – thirteen! – of a noble Roman family, noble above all by the Faith in which they brought up their child. However, not only was Agnes beautiful of soul with her deep love of Jesus Christ and of his Passion, she was also beautiful to behold with a beauty which aroused the passionate attention of a young Roman, Procopius, son of the Roman governor. This young man did everything he could with words and gifts to win Agnes' consent to his suit, but she turned him down on all counts: "My soul lives only for the love of one so noble, handsome, wise, rich, good and powerful that you cannot hope to be his rival. I love him better than my own soul, than life itself, and I would be happy to die for him. When I love him I am chaste, when I approach him I am pure, and when I embrace him I remain virgin."

Procopius fell so ill with jealousy that his father Symphronius, the governor, attempted to persuade her in his place. Meeting also with her resolute refusal to prefer anyone to the Bridegroom of her soul, and learning that this rival to his son was no doubt the God of the Christians, he had here the excuse he needed to submit Agnes to all kinds of pressure. He tried threats, he tried promises, to no avail. Finally he told her to make a sacrifice like all Roman girls to the pagan goddess Vesta, or else he would have her taken – fate more dreaded by Christian girls than death itself – to a place of debauchery where she would be forcibly exposed to the licentiousness of all comers. Agnes did not flinch, expressing complete trust in the power of her God to protect her.

Furious, Symphronius carried out his threat. Agnes was first stripped of her clothing, but God protected her with a miracle making the hair of her head grow instantaneously in such abundance as to cover her complete body. (A 20th century reader is tempted to laugh, but if God exists, if He is all-powerful, and if He protects the innocent, where is the absurdity?) Then Agnes was dragged into the place of infamy to be exposed to all violation, but there she met an angel to protect her, with a white dress so dazzling as to illuminate the darkness around her and to convert the young men who came near her. Procopius, in fact, was struck blind when he tried to approach her. Moments later, recovered enough from his blindness to take up again his pursuit of Agnes, Procopius attempted to force his way through the celestial shield surrounding her. He was struck dead at her feet by the angel.

When Symphronius arrived in despair at the news of his son's fate, and violently cursed Agnes as a witch, the saintly girl calmly replied that Procopius had had only himself to blame for seeking to break through her heavenly protection. The governor begged her to prove she was no witch by bringing Procopius back to life. This she did, by her prayers. Procopius went straight out of the house, proclaiming the God of the Christians to be the true God.

When this latest turn of events reached the ears of the high priests of Rome's paganism, they were infuriated, and they so stirred up the populace to demand the death of the young witch that although Symphronius himself would by now have been willing to let Agnes go free, out of cowardice he handed her over to his subordinate, Aspasius, and himself withdrew from the case. Aspasius had a great fire lit, and Agnes thrown into it, but again God protected her, for as her virtue had honored God by extinguishing in herself and in others the flames of lust, so God honored her virtue by shielding her from the flames of the bonfire – they divided around her, leaving her intact, but burning to death a number of the idolaters standing by. As for Agnes, she prayed a prayer of honor and glory to God, like the three young men similarly protected in the burning fiery furnace (Daniel 3), and the fire went out, leaving no trace.

However, since the uproar of the populace only grew worse, Aspasius handed over Agnes to be executed by the sword. When the executioner appointed to dispatch the girl turned pale and trembled as though he were the one condemned to death, Agnes gave him courage: "What are you waiting for? Kill this body that I do not want men to look on, and let the soul live, which God is happy to look on! May the Lord who chose me for his bride and whom I wish to please, out of his goodness receive me in his arms." So saying, she drew her clothing around her, received the fatal blow, and even in death veiled her face in her hands.

Her body was buried by the Christians with great joy at her astounding victory over the world, the flesh and the devil, on a piece of land belonging to her family outside the Numa Gate, where today the Church of St. Agnes stands. The pagans were as furious as ever and attacked these triumphant Christians, including a young catechumen still not baptized, Emerentiana, the companion and foster-sister of Agnes. But Emerentiana would not leave the place of Agnes' burial, and standing up to the pagans out of love and fidelity to Agnes, won in her turn, baptized in her blood, the crown of martyrdom, being stoned by the crowd just two days after Agnes had been killed. Emerentiana's body was buried alongside Agnes', and her feast is celebrated on January 23 in our missals and breviaries, two days after the Feast of St. Agnes. It is a relic from this girl and heroine of the Faith which is now in the seminary's main altar, nearly 1700 years later.

These stories from the history of the early Church are extraordinary. They tell of a different world, difficult for us to imagine, because whereas it was then a world of paganism giving way to an overpowering Faith, now it is the last remains of the Christendom created by that Faith being crushed beneath a seemingly overpowering neo-paganism. Yet from 1700 years ago to today, neither have God, Our Lord or His one true Church changed on the one side, nor have the world, the flesh and the devil essentially changed on the other. Then let us stop and think for a few moments on what it may need for today's Church to engender another Agnes or Emerentiana.

Firstly, the power of example. We know very little about Emerentiana, little more than the few facts related above. Surely these tell us she was the first fruits of Agnes' example. Closely tied to Agnes before she died, Emerentiana could not be torn away from her in death. Agnes had been that most vivid of all lessons, a living example, which a kindred spirit found irresistible. None of us goes to heaven – or to hell! – alone.

Secondly, the power of the Christian family and home. Of Agnes herself, outside of the heroic events leading to her martyrdom, we know next to nothing, except that her parents reared her from a tender age in great piety. There is no other normal explanation for such heroism as Agnes showed while barely a teenager. God might create this kind of heroism by a miraculous intervention, but normally such a single-minded love of God, such a maturity of resolution, such a refusal of anything remotely harmful to purity, such an accurate assessment of anything the world has to offer, as Agnes showed, can only have come from a home through-and-through Catholic, in which without a trace of artificiality or exaggeration the interests of God, and of God alone, counted. No dubious pictures or consideration for religious liberty in this home. The teenager can hardly have thought, or been encouraged to think, of anything other than her Lord Jesus Christ and his Mystical Body, the one true Church, and Heaven.

Thirdly, the power of fidelity. With easily most of the martyrs we know little of their early lives. Their glory flares up at the end of their lives, apparently out of nothing. But such glory cannot come out of nothing. It normally comes out of a long preparation of faithfulness in little things, which as Our Lord Himself says (Mt. 25: 23), He rewards with grace in great things, for instance of being faithful in martyrdom. Thirteen years of little acts, day by day, each noted by God, had brought the grace of Agnes to the point where, in the supreme trial, she never wavered. She inspired Rome then, she has now – despite a recent fire – a handsome church dedicated to her in New York, and she will inspire Christendom to the end.

St. Agnes, St. Emerentiana, pray for us! As Satan knowing his time to be short, redoubles in fury; as the remaining members of Christ are like torn apart limb from limb; as the lies and seductions of the world seem set fair to overwhelm truth forever; obtain for us that single-minded love of Jesus Christ, trust in His protection, and desire to be with Him in Heaven forever, as carried both of yourselves safely out of this world and into eternity!

Dear friends and benefactors, pray that St. Emerentiana's relic in the seminary's altar may help draw down upon seminarians and their teachers the grace never until the day they die to have in view any interests other than those of Our Lord Jesus Christ, the same yesterday, today and forever!

NO. 125 | MARCH 1, 1994

Pope John Paul II's Encyclical *Veritatis Splendor*

Aㅤ NOTHER LONG LETTER, I am afraid, but when it comes to defending our Catholic Faith, there are no short cuts. Our Lord warned us that at the end of the world there would arise false Christs and false prophets insomuch as to deceive, if it were possible, even the elect. The last thirty years have seen hundreds of millions of Catholics being led astray by the Roman Protestantism designed to integrate them into Satan's New World Order. The operation of error continues, more seductive than ever, to judge by the latest Encyclical letter coming from Rome, last year, entitled *Veritatis Splendor*, the splendor of truth! To dismantle the seduction may take us a little time, but Our Lord told us to "Watch and pray." Let us watch *Veritatis Splendor* to help arm us against even greater seductions no doubt being aimed at us, by Satan at any rate . . .

Let us firstly take an overview of the Encyclical's entire content to give it a chance to speak for itself, and to help avoid parts being attacked piecemeal or out of context. Summaries are bound to distort more or less the original, but this one attempts to be fair.

The Encyclical, containing 120 substantial sections, a little book of 147 pages in the Daughters of St. Paul edition most easily available in the USA, aims to teach us the true foundations of Catholic moral theology, or ethics, because these are being questioned and undermined by errors circulating today (paragraphs #4 & 5).

In the first of the Encyclical's three main parts that follow (#6–27), JP2 conducts a meditation on the passage of Scripture, (Mt. 19: 16–21), in which the rich young man asks Jesus what he must do to have eternal life. The Pope presents Jesus' answer as leading the young man to a progressive awareness of the need to submit to God, to obey the natural law or Ten Commandments, and to answer the further call to perfection, which is finally to be found within Christ. This answer Christ entrusted to His Church, the Catholic Church, to carry down the ages, which is what this Encyclical will be doing.

The Encyclical's second and longest part (#28–83) proceeds to tackle current errors, not on minor points of Catholic morals, but on their very basis: it is an excellent thing, says the Pope, for modern man to be so aware of his own dignity and freedom, but freedom must depend on truth (#28–34). Thus firstly, freedom cannot be made into an absolute, because within himself man finds inscribed in his nature the natural law which is the law of his person and which does not change (#35–53). Secondly, conscience cannot be made into an autonomous absolute, i.e., an absolute which gives itself its own laws, because conscience is merely man's in-built applier of God's law to particular here-and-now situations (#59–64) . A third error, the so-called "fundamental option," also disconnects God's law from here-and-now decisions by pretending that mortal sin consists only in a full-scale rejection of God (#65–70). The last error refuted in this part of the Encyclical is that of making a moral act's goodness depend primarily not upon the act's object, but instead either on the intentions behind it (teleologism or proportionalism) or on the results flowing from it (consequentialism) (#71–82) . In condemning all these errors the Church "respects and promotes man in his dignity and vocation" (#83).

The third main part of the Encyclical (#84–117) presents the Church as defending the true morality, in the past, the present and the future. By connecting freedom to truth, and morality to the Faith, Mother Church guarantees genuine freedom (#84–89), as her martyrs in the past have shown with their witness to human dignity and perfect humanity (#90–94). At present only Mother Church's unyielding stand for true morality can ensure men's dignity and freedom in politics, and men's peaceful co-existence, national or international (#95–101). This morality is possible with God's grace and urgently necessary amidst today's corruption (#102–108), so for the future the moral theologians must work with the Church's Magisterium to deepen her moral teaching, and the bishops must watch over sound doctrine in their dioceses and institutions (#109–117).

And the Encyclical concludes with a call on the help of the Mother of God (#118–120).

Well, some of you may be asking, where is the problem? Obedience to God, the unchanging natural law, objective morality and its link with the Faith are merely a few of the Encyclical's wholly Catholic teachings. That is why the Encyclical has met with a deafening silence on the part of leading liberals, and with enthusiastic applause from Catholic conservatives.

Then what is the problem? Let us go back to the summary. If you saw no major problem from the point of view of Catholic doctrine as you read through the summary for the first time, that is how many honorable Catholics have read the Encyclical. Hence the seduction.

It may take a second reading to see that *Veritatis Splendor* is not as Catholic as at first it appears to be.

The problem is that this Pope has studied and been deeply influenced by modern philosophers, especially Immanuel Kant and his followers, for whom the dignity of man consists in man's freedom, and man's freedom consists in his absolute independence and autonomy, i.e., he is under the law of nobody but himself. On the contrary, the Catholic Church teaches that man is absolutely dependent on God and under God's law in every moment and act of his existence. Now these two positions are in themselves completely irreconcilable. That is why a great Saint like Pope Pius X said, "Kantism is the modern heresy."

But the modern world is saturated in the principles of Kant, and people cannot believe that what they themselves are saturated in can be so wrong. Hence if they are Catholics in the modern world, the temptation is strong to reconcile the autonomy of man with the law of God. Hence *Veritatis Splendor*. Look at the summary again: Part One, the rich young man becomes aware of the truth within him; Part Two, the truth of the natural law is inside me, conscience is within me, errors oppose my dignity; Part Three, true morality ensures my freedom, my dignity, my perfection, my rights as a man . . .

Now to reach out to modern man is one thing; but to pander to his errors is quite another. Let us take another look at the Encyclical itself.

The rich young man of Mt. 19 with whom it begins is presented by JP2 not as being commanded by Jesus from without, but as being guided or led by Jesus from his yearnings within (#7), to an inner awareness of himself (#8) and of the will of God. Of course this Gospel passage lends itself to such a presentation, less of God commanding than of man being invited, which is no doubt why the Pope chose it as a launching-pad for this

Encyclical. But is it wise to introduce an authoritative presentation of Catholic morals – or of any law for that matter – in a mode of invitation rather than command? Is hell for real? It gets no mention in *Veritatis Splendor*. From this first part one might suspect that the Pope is going to highlight the appeal of Catholic morals and disguise any element of command or threat.

At the beginning of Part Two this suspicion is confirmed. As soon as the Pope launches into the analysis proper of the errors he wishes to refute (#28–83), he lays down as his point of departure in (#31) the "particularly strong sense of freedom" of people today: "Hence the insistent demand that people be permitted to 'enjoy the use of their own responsible judgment and freedom, and decide on their actions on grounds of duty and conscience, without external pressure or coercion' (quotation from Vatican II Decree on Religious Liberty)." The Pope obviously approves of this distaste for coercion, but it sets him a grave problem – part of the splendor of divine truth is that God coerces with the threat of eternal punishment anyone who disobeys His law. How is the Pope going to make coercion look, or feel, as though it does not coerce?

Go back to the summary of Part Two: first error, the absolutising of freedom. Now the Pope wants to bring man's freedom – meaning the use of his free-will – under God's law. Well and good. But at the same time he cannot bear making modern man feel that he is being coerced by God's law. Therefore JP2 even when he states a truth is liable to use language that suggests a falsehood. Classic example, #41: Man has "autonomy" (truth, man has free will; false suggestion, man is his own law); obedience to God is "no heteronomy" (truth, God's law does not take away man's free will; false suggestion, man comes under no law but his own); obedience to God is a "participated theonomy" (truth, man in a way partakes of God's law when he obeys it; false suggestion, man takes part in laying down God's law). Alas, modern man will heed not the truth, but the sympathy for his error expressed in the Pope's choice of language.

In fact, from the moment the Pope set up his admiration of modern liberty (#31), he is trying to square the circle when it comes to Catholic morals, because how can God tell man what to do (Catholic morals), without man being told what to do (modern liberty)? Modern liberty is the false liberty of the Boeing 747 being "free" from the laws of aerodynamics, with the result that it is unable to fly. Catholic liberty is the true liberty of souls submitting to the law of God so as to be free to fly to heaven. In fact a Boeing must obey an incredible number of laws, all minutely checked pre-flight in the cockpit, before it is free to fly over the ocean. Modern freedom is from, Catholic freedom is to. The Pope deep down (#31) respects the modern notion of freedom, which has the effect of undermining everything he will say about God's law, however splendidly true what he says may otherwise be.

For example when he goes on to refute the absolutisation of conscience (#54–64), he says many good things about conscience being the voice of God and of God's law, but he still cannot help concluding (#64) that "the authority of the Church in no way undermines the Christian's freedom of conscience," and "the Church puts herself always and only at the service of conscience," expressions suggesting that the Church calls the moral shots without calling them, and conscience while not in command is nevertheless in command. Thus *Veritatis Splendor* gives the store away without giving it away! That is what comes of trying to fit God's truth to modern minds instead of modern minds to God's truth.

The next modern error to be refuted by the Pope in this second part of the Encyclical is the error of the so-called "fundamental option," namely, so long as a man basically loves God, then a few particular mortal sins here or there do not matter. Except for a few traces of existentialism in his analysis, the Pope's refutation is good: a basic attitude towards God is not expressed other than in particular acts, so just one mortally wrong act is enough to put enmity between the soul and God (#65–70).

Similarly when he refutes the modern errors that undermine objective morality (#71–83), either teleologism or proportionalism making an act's goodness depend essentially upon the agent's intention, or consequentialism making it depend upon the act's consequences instead of primarily upon its object, then the Pope clearly affirms Catholic doctrine: an act's moral goodness or badness depends primarily upon the act's object, in such a way that some acts (such as artificial contraception) are intrinsically, always and everywhere, wrong. Yet the last paragraph (#83) of Part Two opens a door to undermining everything he has well said: in this question of intrinsically evil acts he says "we find ourselves faced with the question of man himself, of his truth . . . "; by teaching the intrinsic evil of certain acts, "the Church remains faithful to the integral truth about man; she thus respects and promotes man in his dignity and vocation." Modern man replies, "Grand. Now the integral truth about my dignity and the vocation of my wife is that we should stop breeding like rabbits, so since the Church in no way undermines our freedom of conscience, we are going to use the pill." "But children," replies the Pope, "that is not 'the inviting splendor of that truth which is Jesus Christ himself' (#83)." "But, Holy Father, 'In the Truth man can understand fully and live perfectly . . . his vocation to freedom,' right? – #83. That's what we're doing with the pill!" As a Scotsman once said some years ago of some wimpish kerk (Church) that he had spurned on his way into the real Catholic Church, "A kerk without a hell isn't werth a damn!"

The third and last part of *Veritatis Splendor* presents the Church as the promoter and defender of morality – and true freedom (#84). But the Pope is still framing the question in terms of freedom as though freedom were threatened by the laws of aerodynamics: "How can obedience to universal and unchanging moral norms respect the uniqueness and individuality of the person, and not represent a threat to his freedom and dignity?" (#85). The Pope's framing of the problem being thus man-centered, so are his solutions. Thus martyrs have given their lives for Catholic morality, bearing "splendid witness to the holiness of God's law and to the inviolability of the personal dignity of man" (#92), from which it follows that such martyrdom is not confined to Catholics (#94). What a blurring of nature and grace, or of the natural and supernatural orders! Between a pagan dying for natural motives, however moral, and a Catholic dying for supernatural motives, notably his Faith, there is literally no comparison. However, when the perspective, as in this Encyclical, essentially centers not on God, author of grace and nature, but on man, carrier in himself only of nature, then this blurring down of the supernatural into the natural is inevitable, and it is to be found throughout *Veritatis Splendor*.

Objection! In the very next section (#102–108), before teaching the urgent need today for Christian morality (#106–108), the Pope teaches Christian morality is possible, with the grace of God (#102–105). *Reply*: read carefully: "Temptations can be overcome, sins can be avoided, because together with the commandments the Lord gives us the possibility of keeping them . . . " (#102); "Christ has redeemed us! This means that he has given us the possibility of realizing the entire truth of our being; he has set our freedom free" (#103). Now phrases like these can be given a Catholic interpretation, but they can also be read as though Christ's grace lifts nature to its supreme dignity still within, and not above, the order of nature. After all, would it not belittle what is for modern man the supreme dignity of the human person for it to be lifted way above its own order?

I think that the Pope with his deeply ambiguous mind, suspended between Catholicism and modern philosophy, would answer "Yes and no," and he would be convinced of his answer! For a Catholic, the problem is wrongly set to start with, because for the Catholic the human person has no dignity outside of God in the first place. Questions like, "How can liberty and law not clash?" are for Catholics non-questions.

As for the future (#109–117), the Pope urges the Church's moral theologians to work with the Magisterium. This he does after having again and again expressed his admiration for the principles of freedom, human dignity, human rights and democracy, which are the very principles behind the rebellion of so many of these theologians against the Magisterium! As has often been pointed out, a moderate revolutionary (like the Pope) is incapable of stopping radical revolutionaries (like today's dissident theologians) because he deep down respects, even shares, their principles. A tank cannot be stopped with a pea-shooter. It takes the undiluted truth to stop a radical. *Veritatis Splendor* fluffs its own best lines, and that is why when the Pope finally calls the Catholic bishops to order (#114–117), the most terrible sanction he proposes for them to apply is that they should take away the title of "Catholic" from any institution "seriously failing to live up to that title"! But in the name of human dignity, thousands of these institutions still calling themselves Catholic will soon be jettisoning the title on their own anyway!

This poor Pope! He believes in the modern world, and he believes that he believes in the Catholic Faith. But to believe at one and the same time in such contradictories – essential godliness and essential godlessness – shows at the very least that he does not understand the Catholic Faith which he sincerely thinks he believes in. If he really understood the true Faith, there is no way in which he could take so seriously all the modern philosophers' nonsense about the dignity of the human person.

It is not freedom, but reason, that gives to the rational animal (without grace) such intrinsic dignity as he has. The freedom is merely an inalienable feature – not an inalienable right – of beings with reason. It makes as much sense to talk of an inalienable right of men to be free as to talk of an inalienable right of their digestion to digest! The whole question is, what does man use his faculty of freedom for? If he uses it well, then he has dignity, but if he uses it badly, then he has no dignity except the potential dignity that if he started over again he could use it well.

In other words man is not for himself, he is for God. But again and again in *Veritatis Splendor* the accent is displaced towards man being a value in himself. Of course the Encyclical keeps attempting the reconciliation of this self-worship of man with Catholicism by arguing that for man truly to be a value in himself, he must obey God's laws, i.e., the unchanging Catholic morality. Now it is perfectly true that only such obedience will make man the best that man can be, but it is perfectly false that self-value or human dignity is what Catholic morality is for, because from the moment it was for that, a man's every act would be mortal sin. Catholic morality is for the GLORY OF GOD, to which the dignity of man as conceived by the modern philosophers is directly opposed. "Glory to God on high . . . Thou alone art holy, thou alone art Lord, thou alone art most high, Jesus Christ, with God the Father in the unity of the Holy

Ghost, Amen!" And all my poor person, all my poor dignity, all my poor morality are for you, and for you alone, my God and my all!

The seduction of *Veritatis Splendor* (as of the documents of Vatican II) lies in the fact that the author, while inwardly adoring the human person, still knows his Catholic doctrine well enough to keep the outward expression of his adoration just within the bounds of Catholic orthodoxy. That is why even if their letter is still mainly correct, their spirit is certainly not. That is why conservatives defend the letter of Vatican II and *Veritatis Splendor* while liberals claim – truthfully – to follow the spirit. That is why *Veritatis Splendor* will change nothing in today's Church. The appearances go one way, the inner thrust goes another. The Pope has given us not the splendor of truth, but the splendor of the human person, which is a dangerous half-truth. Watch out in years to come for dangerous three-quarter and even seven-eighth truths!

And pray for this Pope, dazzled by the bright lights of the modern world, which is intrinsically godless. Let us pray especially that he perform as soon as possible, with as many bishops as he can get to obey him, the consecration of Russia to the Immaculate Heart of Mary. Nothing else can save the modern world, because that is what God has decreed will save it. But only our prayers can bring the author of *Veritatis Splendor* to see that.

Also profit by the Society's retreat houses and the Seminary's program this summer. Flyer enclosed. The music course last summer was a great success. The doctrinal courses were also much appreciated. Doctrine matters. Today's collapse of the Church is primarily a doctrinal problem. Think of the Ignatian retreats as rock-blasting. Think of the doctrinal courses as picking up the rocks! But be careful. The signs are that Satan has in mind to close down the quarries before too long!

NO. 126 | APRIL 2, 1994

Impressions of Ordinations

GOOD NEWS FROM the Argentine – the SSPX is advancing and consolidating in Latin America. Progress is not spectacular, any more than it is anywhere else, but it is re-assuring: the pilot light looks like staying lit, there as elsewhere, until the gas is turned on again.

At the invitation of the Society's District Superior for Latin America (except Mexico), Fr. Xavier Beauvais, and of the Rector of the Society's Latin American Seminary, Fr. Dominique Lagneau, both based in or near Buenos Aires, capital of perhaps the most Catholic country in Latin America, the Argentine, I was down there from the end of February to the middle of March.

By the end of this February in the American Midwest, I was saying to myself, I am getting too old for these winters, indeed to get to Miami I had to reroute round Chicago, socked in by a major snowstorm. However, having fled to the southern hemisphere, where of course everything is upside down but at least they have summer while winter is going on up here, I ran into what were apparently two of the hottest weeks of the Argentine's summer, and I found myself saying, I am getting too old to take the heat. No comment!

Richard N. Williamson

Firstly there was a retreat for the priests of the Latin American District, about twenty in number, most of them based in the Argentine, but two on the other side of the Andes in Chile, and three in the far north of the South American continent, in Columbia. These last three priests are immensely isolated. Air travel is available between all these countries, but it is rather more expensive than within the United States, and our faithful in Latin America are not rich. However, I knew that Winona's benefactors would not mind helping to sustain some isolated Society priests, so the visiting bishop helped out with some airfares. On the priests' behalf, thank you. I know they were happy to be back for a week amongst old friends and colleagues at the seminary in La Reja which is their "alma mater," or "motherly mother," in the priesthood.

There followed a week's retreat for the old and new seminarians at the seminary, to mark their late summer beginning of the new school year. Thanks to an intensive program of the Spiritual Exercises of St. Ignatius being given in various locations in Latin America by Society priests over the last few summers, priestly vocations have risen so that there are now more than thirty seminarians and five brothers at La Reja, eleven seminarians entering this year. This is no small consolation to the La Reja Seminary priests who went through some lean times following on the Argentine's intra-Society explosion of 1989, when the former Rector marched out at the head of nineteen seminarians! One hopes that the continued preaching of the Ignatian Exercises will maintain the present rate of new vocations, but one must be under no illusions – everything in today's world conspires more and more against Catholic vocations, against youngsters even thinking of giving their lives to God.

What a shame! Little do the youngsters know what happiness they miss. Père Barrielle back in Ecône used to quote the old French saying, "If you want to be happy for three hours, get drunk; if you want to be happy for a month, get married; but if you want to be happy for the rest of your life, get ordained a priest." Several married men have told me the "months" should be replaced by "weeks" (Oops! No male chauvinism around here! I am sure married women say the same thing!). However, that is not how it looks to youngsters today. Actually, by their instability and immaturity, many of them are as unfit to get married as they are to get ordained. And whose fault is that? The liberal adults who by their liberalism pretend that one need never endure unpleasantness nor take any consequences – all crosses are to be rejected because nobody has the right to make me suffer. Yet "In suffering is learning," said the ancient Greek poet, Aeschylus. In suffering is maturing. In the Cross is our salvation, our only salvation. Poor youngsters! How will they learn? How will they mature?

For them to catch a glimpse of a different way of life, bring them to the priestly ordinations at Winona this year. Flyer enclosed. Here are extracts from the letter of a non-Society layman written after attending last year's ordinations:

> I finally found a few minutes to set my thoughts to paper regarding the June 19 ordinations . . . I must tell you that I and many thousands of other traditionalist Catholics agree with and support the positions of the Society – the only impediment to total acceptance for many is the fact that the Holy Father is not 'officially' in the picture. Nevertheless, I saw nothing at the ordinations that indicated that the Society does not recognize the Pope – in fact, I could see nothing of the schismatic attitudes that the mainline Church's powers-that-be keep talking about, and the sermon confirmed those conclusions.
>
> What I did see was surprising in many ways. I shall

Richard N. Williamson

begin with the ceremonies.

I am still in awe of the magnificent solemnity of what I saw in that tent. I cannot understand how the 'mainline' Church could trash such beautiful tradition in favor of the banalities that dominate the modernist liturgical worship in the Church today. It has become increasingly more difficult for me to accept the validity of much of the 'new' liturgy, and my experience on a foggy Saturday in June at Winona has made it still more so. I saw the Mass again celebrated as it should be, and it was wonderful.

As I knelt on my slicker, I chanced to observe the people around me, and I was immediately impressed by the following:

1. The numbers present. I reckoned the head count to have totaled between 550 to 700, in spite of the weather.

2. They were there to worship God, not each other. The reverence and respect for what was going on was reflected in the actions and faces of all, including the children. What a relief to be free of the howdy-and-shake fiasco!

3. The large number of teenagers and young adults, and the exemplary way in which they conducted themselves. It was so good to see beautiful young women adorned with embroidered veils on their heads and flowing long dresses, and young men who looked and acted like gentlemen.

4. The large number of wives in their late 30's and into their 40's that had children under 2 or 3 years old. I was seated in the back in a row where there were 2 or 3 women whom I judged to be near the end of their child-bearing days who nevertheless had beautiful, healthy small children who were well behaved and a distinct pleasure to 'be in church with.'

5. The international flavor and variety of those present. After the ceremonies, I 'met and mingled' with some who came from 'countries far.' One old woman aged over 80 years, came all the way from Winnipeg; she has been coming to the ordinations since the first,

and, "If God is willing, I will be coming again next year!"

I could go on, but I must keep this letter of reasonable length. Suffice it to say in a single sentence: I am glad that I came to see.

We will pray for good weather here on June 25, when Bishop Fellay will perform the ordinations, and we will pray for vocations, many vocations, many good vocations, from amongst the gracious young ladies and the gallant young gentlemen observed here by our visitor last year!

Confusing Human Dignity and Human Liberty

WHEN I GAVE in lecture form in the Argentine two months ago the letter that you read on the Pope's latest Encyclical, *The Splendor of Truth*, I was advised that an introductory explanation might help. Let me offer you part of that explanation now, because it goes to the heart of much of the confusion in Catholics' minds today.

This confusion arises from mixing up two quite different notions of human dignity, and then two quite different notions of human liberty. Let us start with the two notions of human dignity, which are somewhat easier to disentangle.

Take for example a wine bottle. What is the value or worth of a wine-bottle? Answer, that depends on whether it is empty, or full. Empty, maybe 10 cents. Full, maybe 10 dollars, one may use the same word, "value" or "worth," for when the bottle is empty or full, but there is no comparison between the empty value and the full value, and if one was to confuse the two by trying to sell an empty bottle as though it was full, one would have some angry customers, even if the glass, cork and label of the empty bottle were as handsome as could be! In fact the real value of the empty bottle is only its potential one day to be full, and if like most wine bottles it will only be filled once, then once it has been emptied it is thrown away as worthless. Thus when it comes to a wine bottle, nobody dreams of confusing its merely potential worth when empty, and its actual worth when full of wine.

However, when it comes to a human being, plenty of people confuse his merely potential worth or dignity when empty, and his actual worth or dignity when full. This is because by loss of faith they have lost grip on the supernatural wine in question, sanctifying grace, and on its value infinitely higher than that of the whole order of mere nature. A Catholic knows by his faith that sanctifying grace is a partaking in God Himself, such that he is here on earth merely to fill his nature with as much of that grace as possible by the time he dies. He knows that if at death he goes before his Maker with his natural soul empty of supernatural grace, then however handsome he may have made his soul's merely natural accomplishments and adornments, like so many labels on the bottle, his Maker will nevertheless be so angry as to throw him away as worthless into the eternal fires of Hell. The natural dignity of a man, or the dignity of his nature merely potential with regard to its being filled with supernatural grace, is as nothing compared with his supernatural or actual dignity when his nature actually contains that grace.

For as the bottle is for wine, so creation is for the Creator, so nature is for grace. True, as the bottle is of great value to carry the wine, so the order of nature and a human nature are indispensable for a man to receive grace in. Nevertheless, as no wine-lover in his right mind glorifies bottles in themselves, so nobody who understands what man is for glorifies his merely natural or potential dignity, or glorifies man in himself.

Richard N. Williamson

The problem with the modern world is that by loss of faith in God and in his sanctifying grace, or by its positively turning away from them, the modern world has lost all sense of the full or supernatural or actual dignity of man, and so it glorifies his merely potential dignity as though it were actual or full human dignity. Like glorifying empty bottles. In other words man is the supreme value in himself, by his mere nature. Forget about wine, forget about God. Merely by having human nature, I have the supreme dignity! Glorious glass! What does wine matter? Glorious man! What does grace matter?

This – to a Catholic mind – insanity is the implicit teaching of Vatican II. Its *Declaration on Religious Liberty* in its opening sentence (picked up in *Veritatis Splendor*, #31) bases what will be its demand for religious liberty on human dignity, not an man's actual dignity when he is filled with God, but on his potential dignity which he has merely by being man. That the Declaration does here (#1) mean the potential dignity is clear a little later on when the Declaration (#2) says that even when man refuses the truth, he still retains (the dignity that founds) his right to religious liberty. In other words glass is so glorious that the wine bottle has a right to remain empty!

Again, to be able to drink wine does presuppose a bottle or its equivalent, but that does not mean that the glass has the glory of the wine! Once there is no more wine, the glass is trashed. Empty of grace at death, a soul, however naturally dignified, is flung into Hell. This is because as the bottle's real glory is not to be glass but to be capable of holding wine, so human nature's real dignity lies in its potential for containing (knowing and loving) God, a potential which however glorious in itself ("O, what a piece of work is man," says Hamlet), is nevertheless nothing in comparison with the glory and actual dignity of a man actually knowing and loving God.

But now read Vatican II quotable in such a way, and *Veritatis Splendor* so quoting it (*Gaudium et Spes* #17, V.S. #42), as to blur and confuse man's potential and actual dignities:

> Human dignity requires man to act through conscious and free choice, as motivated and prompted personally from within, and not through blind internal impulse or merely external pressure. Man achieves such dignity when he frees himself from subservience to his feelings, and in a free choice of the good, pursues his own end by effectively and assiduously marshalling the appropriate means." The dignity in the first of these two sentences is the natural or potential dignity of man's nature having free will, or the ability to choose freely and not out of instinct or constraint. The dignity in the second of these sentences is the actual dignity that man acquires when he makes a good use of that faculty of free will. These two dignities are quite different realities from one another, even if the second presupposes the first, as wine at table presupposes a bottle. But by the word "such" at the beginning of the second sentence, Vatican II equates the two dignities, which amounts to trashing not the bottle but the wine! This same glorifying of nature to the level of grace, or abasing of grace to the level of nature, this naturalism, is embedded in Vatican II and *Veritatis Splendor*, and what it means is the raising of man to the level of God, humanism, or the abasing of God to the level of man, atheism, or both, i.e., atheistic or secular humanism. Dear Lord, have mercy upon us! Holy Mary, Mother of God, pray for us sinners that your Son's sanctifying grace be found in our souls now and in the hour of our death!

Exactly parallel to the confusion between the two dignities of man is the confusion between his two liberties: on the one hand his natural or potential liberty, or faculty of free will, intrinsic to his rational nature and inalienable from it; on the other hand his moral or actual liberty, or right use of his free will, not intrinsic to his nature but alienable from it by the choosing of any sin. Catholics glorify the second liberty which presupposes the first, but liberals glorify the first liberty regardless of the second, and liberal Catholics by blurring together and confusing the two make themselves much more liberal than they are Catholic.

This confusion between natural and moral liberty, between the faculty and its right use, between free will and "the liberty of the glory of the sons of God" (Rom. 8: 21), is so common and so damaging that it deserves a letter to itself. For instance that liberty which is inalienable, free will, is not a right but a faculty, whereas that liberty which is a right, Christian liberty, is, alas, alienable by sin until the moment we die. Hence to talk of liberty as an "inalienable right" is confusing nonsense, but there is no space left to go into that here.

However, a correct understanding of liberty will be a major part of the two Doctrinal Sessions due to be held this summer at Winona, from June 28 to July 2 and from August 30 to September 3. Participants will be sent one month ahead a small packet to read beforehand, mainly great papal encyclicals refuting modern errors, but also for instance the terrible Vatican II *Declaration on Religious Liberty* which so hopelessly confuses the two dignities and the two liberties. Sign up, if you wish for a real chance to clear up some confusion.

And also, if you have not already done so, make sure that you let us know if you wish to continue receiving the Seminary newsletter and Verbum. Otherwise you risk being dropped from our mailing list. Thank you always for your steady and faithful support of the seminary. You should have six new priests ordained at Winona on June 25, God willing.

NO. 128 | JUNE 7, 1994

The SSPX's General Chapter

AS MANY OF you already know, from July 11 to 13 next month is due to take place in Ecône, Switzerland, the General Chapter of the SSPX. This is an important meeting of some forty representative members of the Society from all over the world, held every twelve years to elect the Society's main officers, including its Superior General for the next twelve years, and to deliberate on Society policy and affairs.

It is called a Chapter because in the Middle Ages the monks in a monastery would meet regularly to hear a chapter or small section of their Rule being read to them, so the word "chapter" came to be transferred from the section of the Rule, to the reading of the section, to the meeting of the monks to hear the reading, to any assembly of the members of a religious congregation to consult on their affairs. It is called General when they consult on affairs of their Society as a whole, and not just part of it.

There is no need to say how important such an event is in the life of the Society, and so we beg the prayers of all our friends for the occasion. "The heart of the king is in the hand of the Lord: whithersoever He will He shall turn it," says Scripture (Prov. 21:1), and the hearts of forty electors are likewise in God's hand to move which way He will. If He holds back from moving them, they will make human choices, as did the bishops assembled in the Second Vatican Council. If on the other hand God steps in to move the human hearts, they will make choices pleasing to Him, as did the bishops of the First Vatican Council, in 1870. What made the difference? Why did God step in the one case and not in the other? No doubt to a great extent because of the prayers of the people.

Hence the need for our friends to pray for the Society's General Chapter, and hence the enclosed prayer card with a picture of Archbishop Lefebvre and Fr. Barrielle, taken at the end of a thirty-day Retreat of Society members in the 1970's, and with on the other side three prayers slightly adapted from the Roman Missal. A novena prior to the General Chapter would run from Saturday July 2 to Sunday July 10 inclusive.

Mother Church is used to praying for such occasions because she knows that it is God who plays the decisive part. Even in an organization where the leader is designated by popular vote, still his authority and the use he makes of his authority come from above. Scripture again (Prov. 8: 14): "Counsel and equity is mine, prudence is mine, strength is mine. By me kings reign, and lawgivers decree just things, by me princes rule, and the mighty decree justice." The influence of leaders over the people they lead is decisive, and the influence for good over the leaders must come from God. That is why when a people prays to Him, He will give them good leaders, but when they turn their backs on Him, He punishes them by letting them have leaders of their own choice, who will lead them to perdition. People cannot lead their leaders, which is why we must pray to God for leaders to lead well.

Take for instance the aftermath of Vatican II. How many faithful Catholics in distress attempted, and are still attempting, to hold their clergy back from the ruinous reforms? Largely in vain. The priests hold from God their sublime authority, and if they are determined to misuse it, there is little the people can do. God could force the free will of His priests, but that is not His way. Is then God without means to intervene, or are the people without recourse? Of course not.

If the people pray in their distress, then God can convert a few of His misleading ministers, and from the rest He can without any injustice hold back the gift of His grace, whereupon left to their own devices they fall further and further away from Him, until numbers of them quit their religious calling and lose their priesthood or sisterhood altogether, as we have seen since Vatican II, at which point they lose their authority and most of their power to harm the people. And if the people continue to pray in their distress, then God as a free gift can grant them a new generation of priests to replace those fallen away, and these priests He is liable to form from the most surprising material, e.g., fishermen in the case of Our Lord, in order to demonstrate that it is His work and not a work of human hands. Thus God turned His back on the Pharisees, and built from scratch His Apostles.

Here is exactly the story of the SSPX, and it is extraordinary to watch the timing! As the Catholic priesthood was being decimated in the aftermath of Vatican II, Archbishop Lefebvre had just enough help from older priests to be able to found a seminary and a Society to form again true priests on the old model, but by 1977, with a few notable exceptions like Fr. Barrielle, those older priests could not stand the heat of disapproval from Rome, and they left the Archbishop. However, by 1977 the Archbishop had just enough help from his own young priests from within his Society to be able to staff his seminary in Ecône and to continue the Society's apostolate. The relief arrived in the nick of time!

Richard N. Williamson

Since 1977, those juveniles of the Archbishop have all been growing older regularly at a rate of one year every 365 days, so there is some senility creeping even into the Society priesthood! Nevertheless, for those who have eyes to see, it is God and God alone who has raised up this new flowering of the true priesthood in the 1970's, 80's and 90's. He has turned His back on the pharisees of neo-modernism, and He has rebuilt priests virtually from scratch.

The moral of the tale is clear. The fortunes of the Society depend to a large extent upon the prayers of the people. As Catholics appreciate or fail to appreciate what God gives them, so the Society will rise or fall. If then you have any love of anything God has given you through the senilizing juveniles of the SSPX, pray for their deliberations and decisions at this General Chapter, which must be a keystone of the Society's future. And may God repay you for the alms of your prayers!

The good news in this connection is that as I have been circulating at this time of year amongst several of the Society's major centers in the United States to give Confirmation, I have been finding everywhere a warm response to the Society's efforts. Our numbers are not growing by leaps and bounds, but all over there are courageous young parents ready to trust God, with children, children, children, so there is certainly a future! There is also quality, insofar as Catholics seem to be learning to trust the Society when it tells them how far liberalism has eaten into their way of life, how far they must repudiate the modern world and its false ideals. This quality of real conversion is what we must look for, and then the quantity or numbers will look after themselves, in God's good time.

The bad news is that the official Church is even accelerating in its downhill plunge. Towards the beginning of last month the Consistory of Cardinals in Rome was due to consider with the Pope a document newly issuing from the Vatican Secretariat of State projecting ways to celebrate the Jubilee Millennial year of 2000. The Pope then broke his hip and the Consistory was at least delayed, but the projects are no less hair-raising from a Catholic point of view, for instance another major ecumenical meeting of Christians, Jews and Mohammedans, this time on Mount Sinai!

The idea is to bring together the three religions that acknowledge Abraham as their ancestor, but in what sense, for instance, are the Jews of today's Synagogue the descendants of Abraham? Talmudic Jews are the spiritual descendants of the Pharisees, to whom already in his own day Our Lord had to say, "If you be the children of Abraham, do the works of Abraham." (Jn. 8: 39) Jews who reject Jesus Christ reject thereby Abraham, yet here are Christ's own Vicar and many Cardinals apparently ready to pretend they are friends of Abraham! On the mountain of the Ten Commandments the one true God, Lord God of Hosts, three in one and one in three, struck holy terror into the hearts of His people (Ex. 19: 20). Just how much further will He allow Himself to be mocked by His own ministers?

Lord, have mercy upon Thy Pope and upon Thy Catholic Church and preserve it from corruption! We thank Thee for the immense gift to us of Thy servant Marcel Lefebvre. We beg Thee to guide the deliberations and counsels of the Society he founded.

NO. 129 | JULY 1, 1994

The Human Frailty of the SSPX

ANOTHER SPLENDID CEREMONY of Ordinations at Winona last week gave seven new priests to Mother Church, four of whom were from the United States, and four of whom (not quite the same four) will be staying to serve in the United States. One of the Americans, Fr. Thomas Blute, is being posted to the Society's seminary in Australia, while an Englishman, already working at District HQ in the USA, Fr. Helmuts Libietis, will stay there. Mother Church rises above all nationalism, but by so doing is the creator of Christian nations!

A picture story of the ceremony will come to you as usual with next month's Verbum. The weather was beautiful, in contrast to last year when Minnesota in late June nearly froze us! In fact this year some of our visitors were so warm that I had to reassure them that I had plenty of cool fans in the seminary, but I regret to say that the visitors knew that those fans blow only hot air.

Be that as it may, the new priests, six for the SSPX, one for the Traditional Dominicans in Avrillé, France, are, as always, an immense gift of God. To Him goes our primary gratitude. Where would we be without priests? – Padre Pio said the world could more easily do without the sun than do without the Mass. But our gratitude also goes each year to the seminarians who work hard and well to put the ceremony together for the greater glory of God. For all such gifts it is wise for us to be grateful, especially in a darkening world:

> How far that little candle throws his beams,
> So shines a good deed in a naughty world.

(*Merchant of Venice*, Act V)

As the world around us grows more and more naughty, with the devil being given, as a punishment for our naughtiness, more and more power to shut down whatever is true, just, holy, of good report, so candles of goodness, without in themselves increasing in power or light, nevertheless stand out more and more, and we should be correspondingly more grateful for their survival. Who can tell how soon they may be extinguished?

Thus when Catholics attending a true Mass run into any of the difficulties surrounding its celebration, they can become impatient, for instance, at lack of unity amongst all the priests celebrating the true Mass. Such impatience may be justified, at least in past, but would not such Catholics be wiser today to be grateful for any and every single true Mass celebrated? We may not yet be in those days when the sacrifice is going to be taken away (Dan. 8: 11), but if things continue on their present course, those days may soon be here, and then with what longing may those Catholics not look back on a single one of those backroom Masses said in however unfavorable circumstances?

It is called being grateful for small mercies, or, counting one's blessings. Similarly wise, in my opinion, is anybody who does not pin too great hopes on the future of

Richard N. Williamson

the SSPX. Through it no doubt immense gifts and graces have come to many of us in the past and are still coming in the present, but nothing gives us the right to count on their continuation in the future. On the contrary, according to all normal expectations, the more powerful the current of apostasy sweeping downstream Church and world to their perdition, the more irresistible the current becomes, and the more likely it is that the still resisting Society will be swept away as well.

Please, these lines are being written before the Society's General Chapter of July 11 to 14, so they have nothing to do with any particular decision that will be taken there. They are based on entirely general considerations, for instance that every Catholic group or organization has a structure of authority, which authority must ultimately derive from the Vicar of Christ, the Pope. When therefore the Pope repudiates a Catholic organization, as Pope Paul VI and Pope John Paul II have effectively repudiated the SSPX, then that organization is submitted to a severe strain...

Here is another dark thought: in the 1950's the Catholic Church was holding out magnificently against the world, conversions were multiplying, the intellectuals were rejecting Communism, the whole world seemed ready to lie down at the feet of the Church, and what happened? In the 1960's it was the Church which at Vatican II collapsed at the feet of the world! Today the SSPX is holding out magnificently against the false Church, intellectuals are rejecting the Novus Ordo, conversions to Tradition are beginning... Let us beware of that moment when all the Church seems about to lay down arms at the feet of the Society! Exile is painful, the combat is wearisome, the world has its attractions...

Now – brighter thoughts! – of course God is God, God is the Lord of Life and death, God can preserve or destroy what He will, God will never abandon His Catholic Church nor leave His sheep without shepherd, so He can easily provide Society members with special graces to ensure the Society's survival until such time as He inspires a Pope not only to give the surviving Society his approval, but also maybe to lean on the Society for support in reconstructing the Church.

Such a scenario is intrinsically possible, even, without any vanity on our part, plausible. For instance Rome no doubt relied on Archbishop Lefebvre's death in 1991 to provoke the disintegration of the Society, but for over three years Rome has been disappointed. Similarly, right now Rome must be hoping that the General Chapter will sow germs of division or disunity between Society members, but you readers have been praying, and the Lord God can all the more easily grant special graces of unity if true fidelity to Himself was the original reason – and it was – for the Papal disapproval putting that unity under strain in the first place.

Nevertheless, while the scenario of special graces of survival for the Society until the recovery of the Pope, is a scenario possible and even plausible, it is neither necessary nor certain, and that is why we need to be wisely grateful. For instance, humanly speaking, it is wholly possible that the devil of discord or even the maneuvers of Rome will get in amongst Society members – Rome is still eagerly angling for individual defections of Society priests. Now may Heaven prevent that any of us should through any fault of his own cause or promote such discord, but regardless of our good will, the pressures are intense, the confusion is great, temptations are multiple, the devil is cunning and human nature by itself remains weak.

So the possibility of the Society stumbling and falling before such time as God brings the Pope back to his Catholic senses remains a possibility which must be kept in mind. What it amounts to is no more than what any Catholic should know: in the Catholic Church itself I have an absolute, faith, hope and trust, because the Catholic Church enjoys Our Lord's own guarantee of survival and protection ("Upon this rock I will build my Church, and the gates of hell will not prevail against it" (Mt. 16: 18); "Going, teach all nations . . . and behold I am with you all days, even to the end of the world" (Mt. 28: 20)). But in all other institutions I have only a relative faith, hope and trust, relative to their fidelity to the Catholic Church, because within that Church there are many institutions like the SSPX that have come with time, and with time have gone. Upon the Catholic Church I absolutely depend to save my soul, upon the SSPX only relatively. So for as long as the Society seems to be the instrument God has given me to serve the Church, I mean to serve the Society with all my heart and soul, but the Society remains in relation to the Church a means to an end.

That is why for each ceremony of ordinations like those of a week ago I am immensely grateful, and for each month that the seminary can continue to prepare young men to be ordained, and for each year that the SSPX is still there to sustain its seminaries, and yet if any or all of these gifts from God were to crack or perish, I would not be entirely surprised nor would my Catholic Faith be weakened. At the beginning of the Church Militant Jesus Christ led His followers through the catacombs and persecution out into the open, and at the end of the Church Militant He may well lead them from the tent in the open field through persecution back to the catacombs. If it comes to that, and if we make it to the catacombs, for many of us it will certainly not have been without the Society but back in the catacombs we may have to do without the Society.

Ah, dear Society! Dear Seminary! Dear seminarians! Regularly I tell them that as SSPX seminarians they are on a hiding to nothing, that they have everything to lose and nothing to gain; that the whole world is against them; that the whole world is going to hell in a handbasket; that the SSPX could easily perish; that the future is dark and where there is no gloom it is full of doom. Do you know, I do believe that if any of my dire forebodings actually came true, seminarians would be pleasantly surprised!

NO. 130 | AUGUST 12, 1994

Bishop Fellay Elected Superior General

AFTER JULY'S LETTER which discouraged some of you with the reminder that members of the SSPX are only human (St. Philip Neri used to pray to Our Lord, "Lord, beware of me, I could turn Turk this afternoon!"), nobody will mind an August letter bringing some good news.

The most important good news is that thanks to your prayers and sacrifices, the SSPX has a new Superior General, Bishop Bernard Fellay, elected by the Society's General Chapter in Switzerland on July 11 for a term of 12 years, until the year 2006.

Not that this General Chapter disowned the previous Superior General, Fr. Franz Schmidberger, who served from 1982 to 1994; on the contrary by electing him First Assistant, the General Chapter chose to place him alongside the new Superior General, an unusual move, but certainly proving the desire of the General Chapter for continuity in the guidance of the Society.

Rather, as Bishop Fellay explains in the enclosed (summarized) Press Conference he gave on July 15, the regulations of Mother Church and her practice for congregations like the SSPX definitely indicate that a superiorate of 24 years – a quarter of a century – is to be the exception rather than the rule, and so the General Chapter, by changing the Superior General, aligned itself on the wisdom of Mother Church.

Some people may object that back in 1988 one reason for Archbishop Lefebvre's not consecrating Fr. Schmidberger as a bishop was that the Archbishop then said that the Society's Superior General should not be a bishop, so why now has the General Chapter elected a bishop?

The answer is that circumstances have changed since 1988. At that time contacts and negotiations with Rome had only recently come to a halt, just before the episcopal consecrations in fact, so if it seemed possible that negotiations might restart, it also seemed wise not to obstruct them by having them headed up on the Society's side by a bishop that Rome might have felt obliged to punish in the meantime (Sure enough, Rome "excommunicated" the bishops).

However, since 1988, negotiations with Rome have not yet reopened, because the Society has refused to abandon the old religion, and Rome has refused to abandon the new religion, and no amount of diplomacy or subjective good will on either side can bridge the widening objective gulf between the two religions. In this situation the Society no longer felt obliged to spare the susceptibilities of Rome, so if the best man it had was one of those "excommunicated" in 1988, it felt free to elect him, which is what happened.

But does that mean that by no longer caring what Rome thinks, and by choosing a bishop for leader, the Society is setting up a parallel Church after all?

By no means! Reread the July letter. Aside from and apart from the Catholic Church, the SSPX is nothing. Therefore what the churchmen in Rome think, is of great importance, but if they insist upon plunging deeper and deeper into apostasy, the Society must take its own steps to defend the Faith, which includes electing the best man it has for Superior General, whether he is "excommunicated" or not.

But does not the choice of a bishop indicate a drift of the Society towards setting up a schismatic Church? No, read Bishop Fellay's Press Conference, where he speaks of his authority as bishop and as Superior General. His authority as bishop he describes as being a delicate and unusual authority coming from the Catholic Church, for our special circumstances, but certainly not an authority over a new Church. His authority as Superior General he describes as being exactly that of his predecessor, no more, no less, namely an authority confined to directing members of the Society, again, no authority to set up a new Church.

So even added together these two authorities do not add up to an intention of schism on the part of the Society or of Bishop Fellay. Back in 1988 the Society was similarly accused of heading for schism, but surely no fairminded observer can point to anything that has happened in the Society over the last six years to justify that accusation. Why then over the next six years? As Bishop Fellay says, the General Chapter manifested a clear desire on the part of Society leaders for the Society to continue along exactly the lines laid down by Archbishop Lefebvre. In brief, thank you for all your prayers for the General Chapter.

The weather at Ecône for that week was unusually warm, and the warm weather continued at least until the end of July. For the last week in July, I found myself at Fanjeaux in the South of France, giving the annual retreat to the Dominican teaching Sisters at their motherhouse. Besides the girl's school in Post Falls, Idaho, these Sisters operate a series of schools all over France, but for the annual retreat they all gather together once a year in Fanjeaux, this year over one hundred of them. They much edified me.

I cannot remember in the United States having seen many fields of sunflowers, but in that part of the world they are common. In the summer across a whole field these huge flowers quietly stand, all lifting their bright faces in one direction, making a sea of yellow. Now the Dominican Sisters are dressed in black and white, but as one hundred of them sat in front of me with their radiant faces all turned in the same direction, I could not help thinking – as I told them! – of the fields of sunflowers all around their convent.

Ah, girls, are you wondering what to do in life? If you want to be happy, throw away home, marriage, husband and family for Our Lord's sake, and as He promises in the Gospel, He will give you one hundredfold in this life and eternal happiness in the next. In Idaho and in France, the Dominican Sisters are doing marvelous work teaching girls how to do God's will in a difficult world. Several American girls have gone to Fanjeaux, and a number are now back in Idaho. They have emptied themselves out, and Our Lord has filled them full – there is the fulfillment that girls look for, alas, in every other direction! O Lord, grant us many maidens to try a religious vocation!

How his children need his teaching Sisters! And how his Dominican Sisters in Idaho need help to build the new school for all the girls coming to them! They only need some half a million dollars! God bless them, and you!

INDEX

A

aborigines, 31
abortion, 88, 99, 190, 209, 263
abortionists, 175-179
absolutisation of conscience, 371
Ad Gentes, 308
adultery, 177
Africa, 29, 42-45, 54, 133, 135, 288, 345-351
Agnes, Sister, 103
AIDS, 66
altar girls, 53
"alternative lifestyle," 198
Americanism, 279, 289
American National Conference of Catholic Bishops, 104
American Patriot's Catechism, 278-284
The Angelus, 1, 7, 42, 44, 84, 166, 170, 180, 183, 260, 280, 331
Anglo-Saxons, 280
anonymous Christians, 311, 316
Anthony, Mark, 114
anti-abortionists, 130
Antichrist, 54, 95, 119, 135, 150, 194, 203, 204, 343
anti-family, 271
Anti-Lefebvrists, 250, 252
anti-liberalism, 2, 80
anti-modernism, 2, 11, 76
Anti-Modernist Oath, 2
anti-religion, 93
apartheid, 30
apostasy, 8, 83, 124, 150, 157, 227, 305, 317, 394, 400
Apostolic authority, of Pope, 220
Apostolic Delegation, in Lisbon, 119
Apostolic See, 107
Approaches, 250
Archbishop of Lyons, 3
Argentina, Argentine, 154, 156
    SSPX's ordinations in
        impressions of, 377-381
Aristotle, 272, 306
Armada, 70, 116
arts
    and morality, 46-51
Asia

Bishop Williamson's tour of, 68–72
Aspasius, 362
Assisi, 332
    International Prayer Meeting, 316
    re-commermoration of, 27
Assyrians, 101
Asuda, Fr. Teiji, 103
Auckland, 32
Aucre, Mrs. (Nime's flood story), 62
Augsburg, 23, 37
Aulagnier, Fr. Paul, 213
Auschwitz, 55
Australia, 31, 32, 358
authority
    Apostolic authority, of Pope, 220
    of clergy, 74

B

Baker, James, 149
baptism
    administered by the Donatist heretics, 220
Barrielle, Father Ludovic-Marie, 173, 293, 378, 388, 389
    death of, 293–298
Barth, Karl, 313
Basel, Switzerland, 54
Battle of the Marne, 242
Beauvais, Fr. Xavier, 262, 377
Belgium, 242
believers' contemplation and study, 20
Benedictine Order, 10
Benediction, 18, 194, 339
Benedict XV, Pope, 246
Birkenau, 55
Bishop of Avignon, 83
bishops' preaching, 20
Bisig, Fr. Josef, 23
Bismarck, Otto von, 245
blasphemy
    films, *see* films
Blondel, Maurice, 306, 307, 323
Blute, Fr. Thomas, 392
Boer War (1899-1902), 30
Bouchex, Bishop, 15
Bourges, 37
Brahms, Johannes, 265–270
Brazil, 157, 171, 180
Bride of Christ, 219
Brisbane, 32

Buchanan, Patrick, 134
Buffalo Diocese, N.Y., 65, 89
Bugnini, Msgr. Annibale, 325
Bush, George, 34, 93

C

Cabrini, St. Frances, 156
Cajetan, 256
Calvinism, 348, 350
Campbell, John Bruce, 78
Canada, 51, 151, 216
Canberra, 32
Canon Law, 258, *see also* Church Law
    breaking, because of an emergency, 6
    New Code, 255, 258
        Canon 330, 258
        Canon 331, 258
        Canon 336, 258
        Canon 375, 258
        Canon 679, 15
        Canon 680, 15
        Canon 1321, #1, 6, 9
        Canon 1323, #4, 6
        Canon 1323, #7, NC, 6
Canons, *see* Church Law
Capetown, 30, 348–349
Carmelites, 23
Casaroli, Cardinal
    in Moscow, 3
catechisms, 12, 37
Catho-liberalism, 40
Catholic Church, 54, 73, 102, 151, 161, 207, *see also* Rome; Vatican II
    visibility of, 75
Catholic dogma, *see* dogma
Catholic Family, 358
Catholic girls, *see also* women
    Catholic boys' style schools for, 79
Catholic hierarchy, 129, 239
Catholic Liberals, *see also* liberalism, liberals
Catholic Liturgy, *see* Liturgy
Catholic media, 34
Catholic schools, 131, 210, *see also* education system
Catholic Tradition, *see* Tradition, Traditionalism
Catholic World Report, 289
celebrets, 65, 118
"Celibacy in East and West," 119
Central America, 92
Chaldeans, 101

charity, 96
Charriere, Bishop, 111, 140
chastisements, 232
Chesterton, G.K., 188
children, 52, *see also* education system; families; girls; motherhood; young mothers
Chile, 154, 155
Christendom, 83, 363, 364
Christian civilization, 85, 95, 96, 137, 156
Christian marriage, *see also* families; Holy Family; marriages
Church Law, 179, *see also* Canon Law
Church Militant Jesus Christ, 396
Church of St. Agnes, 363
Church of Truth, 5
civilization, *see also* Christian civilization
    collapse of, 80
Claudel, Paul, 261
clergy
    authority of, 74
Clinton, Bill, 282, 283
clothing, 271–277, 353, *see also* Slacks I; Slacks II; Slacks III; Slacks IV
co-education system, *see also* Catholic schools; education system
Cold War, 88. 98, 246
collegiality doctrine, 65, 75, 108, 257
Columbia, 154
Columbus, Christopher
    Discovery of America, 500th Anniversary of, 237–241
Columbus Commemoration in Argentina, 260–264
Communism, 29, 34, 69, 84, 92–100, 93, 94, 95, 96, 97, 98, 99, 149, 194, 230, 245, 274, 336, 350, 394
concentration camp, 55
Conciliar Church, 4, 52, 222
Conciliarism, Conciliarists, 54, 222
Conciliar Revolution, 53
Confederation of Benedictine communities, 10
confession, 104
Consecration of Russia to Mary's Immaculate Heart, 1988, 13, 38, 42, 230, 288, 337
    aftermath of, 7–13
    videotape of, 12
consequentialism, 372
conservatism, conservatives, 333
contraception, 209, *see also* abortion
Council for Peace, Justice, and the Saving of Creation, 54
crimes against humanity, 56
Curé of Ars, 321

D

Daewoo cars, 69
Daly, Bishop, 118
David, King, 62
Davies, Michael, 190, 250, 279, 280, 283, 289, 291
de Castro Mayer, Bishop Antonio, 15, 23, 37, 53, 64, 65, 118, 152, 157, 178, 181, 190
    death of, 166–169
    interview in *30 Days,* 23
    on women's dress, 185
de Chardin, Fr. Teilhard, 332
Declaration on Religious Liberty, 279, 384, 386
Decree Dignitatis Humanae, 264
Decree on Religious Liberty, 38
de Galarreta, Bishop Alfonso, 175, 212
de Lubac, Fr. Henri, 307, 308, 310, 323, 330, 332
de Mallerais, Bishop Bernard Tissier, 17, 193
democracy, 177, 348
democratic socialism, 94
democratism, 259
Denmark, 66
Deposit of Faith, 26, 230
dignity, 369, 372
    compared with liberty, 382–386
Discovery of America (by Columbus), Quincentenary, 237–241
disobedience, 27, 39, 256
Divini Redemptoris, 95
divorce, 209, *see also* families
Dobson, James, 358
dogma, 38, 129
Dominican Sisters, 401
Donatist baptism, 220
Dörmann, Fr. Johannes, 331
Dublin, 53
Durban, 30
Dvorak, Auton, 267

E

Eastern Europe, 92, 149, 245
Ecclesia Dei Commission, 16, 51–57, 115, 118, 152, 161, 204, 218, 256
    arguments of, 19–23
    setbacks, 63, 65
    strategy of, 63–68
Ecône, Switzerland, 296, 387, 389
    Oddi's visit to, 212–216
    ordinations at, 58
Ecuador, 7–8
ecumenical prayer meeting at Assisi, *see* Assisi Prayer Meeting 1986
ecumenism, 37, 54, 127, 129, 290, 311, *see also* religious liberty

education system
    Catholic boys' style schools for girls, 79
Episcopal Conferences, 53
equality, 177, 186, 226, 274
    impact on family, 209
Europe, 72, 346
euthanasia, 209
excommunication of SSPX bishops, 1988, 3, 8, 12, 15, 36
    validity, 6
existentialism, 125
extremism, extremists, 14, 16

F

false ecumenism, *see also* Assisi Prayer Meeting 1986; ecumenism
false obedience, 27
false prophets, 12
false religions, 33
families, 271-277, 337, 352-358, *see also* husbands
    children, *see* children
    rosary, importance of, 299-304
Fanjeaux, 400, 401
Far East, 68-72
The Fatima Crusader, 85, 290
Fatimists, 130
Fellay, Bishop Bernard, 17, 42, 116, 180, 381
    as Superior General, 398-401
females, *see* women
feminism, 80, 88, 187, 188
Fenton, Msgr. Joseph Clifford, 283
Ferchaud, Claire, 246
fetishism, 286
Fideliter, 213
Fiji, 32
Filipinos, 70
films, 59, 224-227
    blasphemy, 66
First Amendment of the US Constitution, 280
First Secret, 102
The Flight from Woman (Stern), 189
Focus on the Family, 357
Fontgombault, monastery of, 37
Founding Fathers, 279, 280, 281
France, 55, 66, 83, 89, 216, 401
    Traditional Benedictine Monastery, 15
    Verdun, battlefield of, 242-248
Franco-Prussian war of 1870-1871, 242
Franklin, Benjamin, 280
freedom, *see also* liberty

Freemasonry, Freemasons, 94, 95, 122, 245, 250, 279
free will, 370, 386
French Revolution, 16, 245, 280
Friedrichshafen, 111, 113
FSSP, *see* St. Peter's Fraternity (FSSP)
fundamental option, 367, 372

G

Gagnon, Cardinal Edouard, 118
Galileo, 173
Gantin, Cardinal, 1
Garabandal, Lady of, 102
    reasonableness of, 228–236
    triple prophecy, 90, *see also* three Messages
Garrigou-Lagrange, Fr., 311, 326
Gaudium et Spes, 332
Gaume, Msgr., 97
gays, 198, *see also* homosexuals, homosexuality
Gentili, Fr. Ruben, 32
Gerard, Dom, 2, 10, 11, 15, 16, 23, 83, 114
"German Requiem," 265
Germany, 66, 112, 242, 350
God
    obeying, *see* obedience
    wrath of God, 58–62
godless internationalism, 246
godless nationalism, 246
Gorbachev, Mikhail, 92, 96, 97
    meeting with the Pope, 83
Gramm-Rudmann, 87
Great Apostasy, 124, 193
Gregorian Chant, 116
Gruner, Fr. Nicholas, 84, 85
Guitton, Jean, 276
Gulf War I, 148–153

H

Harare, 31, 350
Hawaii, 33
Heaven
    intervention of, 229
Hegel, Georg Wilhelm Friedrich, 315
Hegelian ecumenism, 316
Henry, Patrick, 105
Henry VIII, King, 264
hereticization, 109–110, 220
heretics, 109, 123

heroes, need for, 87-91
Hispano-American countries, 156
Hollywood, 200
Holocaust, 56
Holy Family, 207-211, 352, see also families
Holy Matrimony, see also marriages
Holy Rosary, 335-339
Holy See, 10
Holy Shroud, 66
Homiletic and Pastoral Review, 291
homosexuals, homosexuality, 118, 198, 263
Hong Kee Koh, 86
Hong Kong, 70
Honolulu, 33
Honorius I, Pope, 22
Huffington, Arianna Stassinopoulos, 46, 49
Humanae Vitae, 108
human dignity, *see* dignity
Humani Generis, 311, 324, 325
humanism, 329
humanitarianism, 96
Hume, Cardinal, 52
husbands
       role in raising child, 211
Hussein, King of Jordan, 150
Hyundai cars, 69

I

iconoclasm, 50
Idaho, 401
Ignatian Spiritual Retreats, *see* Spiritual Exercises of St. Ignatius
       in Connecticut and California, 346
Immaculate Heart of Mary, 150, 230, *see also* Consecration of Russia to Mary's Immaculate Heart, 1988
individualism, 208, 322
       impact on family, 209
Indult Masses, 64, 75, 152, 161
       and Fatima, 82-86
inequality, worldviews, 134
infallibility, 75
       extraordinary infallibility, 22
       ordinary infallibility, 22
insight, growth of, 20
internationalism, internationalists, 246
Interreligious World Prayer Meeting, Assisi, *see* Assisi Prayer Meeting 1986
intimate experience, 20
Introduction to Christianity (Ratzinger), 327

Iraq, 149
Isabella, Queen of Castille, 238, 239
Israel, 150
Italy, 66, 90
Ito, Bishop John Shojiro, 103

J

Janzen, Bernard, 85, 190
Japan, 68
Jesus Christ, 44
Jews, 391
JFK (film), 224–227
Johannesburg, 30, 347, 349
John Paul II, Pope, 16, 27, 54, 63, 64, 93, 94, 106, 107, 110, 119, 124, 129, 130, 180, 255, 256, 258, 259, 316, 324, 332, 333, 394
    Ecclesia Dei, see Ecclesia Dei Commission
    and New Theologians, 331
    The Splendor of Truth, 382
    Veritatis Splendor, 366–376
    Voodoo scandal, 285–292
John-Paul II's Theological Road to Assisi (Dörmann), 331
Johnson, Emily, 58
Johnson, Shane, 32
John XXIII, Pope, 128, 325
Jonas, Fr., 183
Jubilee Mass, Paris, 82
Judas, 101
jurisdiction, 5–6

K

Kant, Immanuel, 369
Kennedy, John F., 225
The Keys of This Blood (Martin), 190
KGB, 92, 122
Kim, Professor, 69
Korea, 69
"Kulturkampf," 245
Kuwait, 149

L

Lagneau, Fr. Dominique, 261, 377
Laguerie, Fr., 16
Lamentabili, 2
La Reja, 261, 378
The Last Temptation of Christ (film), 59
Latin America, 154–159, 377–381
Le Barroux, 16

Lefebvre, Archbishop Marcel, 3, 4, 5, 6, 7, 8, 20, 40, 42, 52, 53, 66, 73, 74, 94, 95, 108, 112, 119, 136, 139, 142, 153, 166, 168, 169, 181, 182, 183, 191, 219, 220, 221, 224, 226, 249, 250, 253, 278, 288, 296, 345, 356, 388, 389, 395, 399
    60th Priestly Jubilee, 111
    accusation
        of schism, 5, 14, 39, 255–259
    act of disobedience, 256
    condemnation of, 20
    consecration by, 1, 13
    death of, 160–165
    excommunication of June '88
        on doctrinal grounds, 14
    first anniversary tribute to, 227
    health of, 9
    letter to Bishop de Castro Mayer, 171
    L'Osservatore Romano, 6, 66, 138, 287, 288
    on political and regligious union, 95
    priestly ordination, 60th anniversary, 82
    public opinion on his Catholic identity, 15
    racism charges, 133
    sermon at Friedrichshafen, 113
    They Have Uncrowned Him, 14
Lefebvrism, 218, 225, 262
Lenin, Vladimir, 30, 92, 97
Lent, 105
Leo XIII, Pope, 7, 279, 280
lesbians, 198, *see also* homosexuals, homosexuality
Leslie, Fr. Eldred, 347
Leuchter, Fred, 55
Liberal Catholicism, 106, 126–127
Liberal Church, 215
liberalism, liberals, 2, 40, 52, 69, 79, 89, 98, 108, 123, 136–139, 143, 151, 162, 177, 218, 259, 274, 282, 283, 288, 290, 326, 338, 348, 350
    characteristics of, 5
Liberal State, 215
Liberius, Pope, 22
Liberolics, 40
liberty, 177, 186, 226, *see also* liberalism, liberals
    compared with dignity, 382–386
Libietis, Fr. Helmuts, 392
Licra (plaintiff in racism case on Archbishop), 132, 133, 135
Lienart, Cardinal, 249–254
Light of Christ, 259
Liturgy, 23, 319
    parallel Liturgies, 82
    Tridentine liturgy of 1962, 10
London, 52
L'Osservatore Romano (Lefebvre), 6, 66, 138, 287, 288

Lucia, Sister, 119
Lumen Gentium, 108, 257, 258
Lustiger, Cardinal, 15, 290
Luther, Martin, 66
Luxemburg, 242

M

machines, *see also* television
Madiran, Jean, 133
Majdanek, 55
Malaysia, 71
Malcolm Muggeridge, death of, 143–147
Mamie, Bishop, 36
Manila, 70
Manuilski, Dmitri, 92, 205
Marehal, Fr. Denis, 23
Marne, Battle of the, 242
marriages, 186, 208, 229, 271, *see also* children; families; husbands
       sacramentality of, 271
Martinez, Fr., 155
Martin, Malachi, 190
martyrs, 373
Marxism, 78
Marx, karl, 97
Mater Ecclesiae, 4
materialism, materialists, 30, 31, 69, 88, 93, 294
McAlvany Intelligence Advisor, 92–93
McLuhan, Marshall, 261
media, *see also* television
       Catholic media, 34
Melbourne, 32
mentevacantists, 253
Mexico, 158
Michael, Brother, 84, 288
Minimum Knowledge Requirement Sheet for Confirmation, 42
miracles
       in the Society, 173
Missouri State Penitentiary gas chamber, 55
Mitchell, Brian, 77, 79
modern artists, 49
modern critics, 49
modernism, modernists, 2, 5, 21, 295, 330
       characteristics of, 5
       as dream, 5
       modernist Church, self-destructing, 117–121
       and sedevacantism, 122–131
modern liberals, 49
       compared with Catholic liberty, 371

modern materialism, 229
Montini, Msgr., 324, 325
morality, 375
Mosaic Liturgy, 319
Moscow, 29
Mother Church, 90, 129, 229, 310, 317, 321, 388, 392, 398
motherhood, 189, 207–211, 274, 304, 354, *see also* women; young mothers
Mother of God, intervention of, 105
Muller, Robert, 290
Mystical Body of Christ, 25, 109, 207, 349, 350, 364

N

Namibia, 349
The National Catholic Reporter, 290
nationalism, 392
National Review, 46
Natterer, Fr., 17
natural truths, 126
Nazi collaborator, 55
Nazi death camps, 55
neo-modernism, neo-modernists, 70, 128, 231, 390, *see also* modernism, modernists
    architects of, 305–317
    executives of, 323–234
neo-paganism, 363
The New American Man, A Call to Arms, 78
New Deal, 99
New Frontiers, 99
New Mass, *see* Novus Ordo Mass (NOM)
New Testament priesthood, 318–322
"New Theology," 310, 323, 324, 325, 330, 331, 333
New World Order, 291, 366
New World Religion, 56
New Year 1990, message, 87–91
New York, 151
New York Archdiocese, 41
New Zealand, 32
Nimes, 58–62
Nominalism, 123
non-Catholic religions, 332
North America, 65
North Dakota, 18
North Korea, 69
Nostra Aetate, 308
Nourrit, Mrs. (Nime's flood story), 62
Novus Ordo Mass (NOM), 22, 36, 43, 64, 75, 83, 89, 108, 118, 120, 130, 151, 161, 167, 218, 220, 224, 360
    mixed with Tradition, 3

"Nuestra Senora la Reina de los Angeles de Porciuncula," 240

O

obedience, 199, 239, 375
    and Tradition, 24–28
O'Connor, Cardinal, 118
Oddi, Cardinal, 114, 203, 204
    visit to Ecône, 212–216
Old Mass, 220, *see also* Tradition, Traditionalism; Tridentine Mass
Omaruru, 349
One World, 203, 204, 291
ordinary moments/things, 303
original sin, 186, 227, 314
Orwell, George, 31
Osaka, 68
Ossuary of Douaumont, 243, 245
Our Lady of Akita, 101–105
Our Lady of Fatima, 98, 102, 119, 150, 229, 230, 231, 299, 337
Our Lady of Guadalupe, 158
Our Lady of Lujan, 262
Our Lady of the Rosary Home School, 223
Our Lady of Victory Home School, 223

P

paganism, 350, 362, 363, 373
Palestine, 150
Papists, 130
parents, *see also* children; families; young mothers
Pascendi, 56
patriotism, 246, 338
Paul, an African Catholic (letter on Consecrations at SSPX), 42–45
Paul VI, Pope, 107, 108, 109, 112, 128, 220, 258, 324, 325, 330, 394
Pax priests, *see* Liturgy
penance, 344
Penk, 17
Perpetual Masses, 76
personalism, 125
Peter, Lovest Thou Me? (Roux), 106–110, 124
Petrine Rock, 291
Pfeiffer, Timothy, 34
Philippines, 70
philosophy, 306
    definition of, 125
Picasso, Creator and Destroyer (Huffington), 47
Picasso, Pablo, 46–51
Pie, Cardinal, 79
Pinochet, General, 155

Pio, Padre, 105, 161, 344, 393
Pius IX, Pope, 139, 348
Pius X, Pope, 56, 124, 128, 247, 309
Pius XI, Pope, 84, 85, 94, 95, 141
Pius XII, Pope, 141, 310, 311, 324
Poland, 94
Poletti, Bishop, 22
political warfare, 92
Pontifical High Mass, 359
Pope, 171, *see also specific popes*
    Apostolic authority of, 220
    infallibility of, 22, 27, 334
    primacy of, 257
Pope, Alexander, 285
pornography, 88, 200, 209–210, 348, 357
Port Elizabeth, 30, 349
Portugal, 230
Possidente, Fr., 183
Post-Jansenist Revolution, 137
power of orders and power of jurisdiction, distinction between, 256
prayers, *see also* Holy Rosary
private revelations, 229, 230
Procopius, 362
proportionalism, 372
Protestantism, 49, 88, 99, 123, 125, 137, 207, 208, 343–344, 366
Protocol of May 5, 39
public Revelation, 229, 230, 235
public school system, 99
Puritanism, Puritans, 264
Putti, Dom, 205

Q

Quanta Cura, 2, 139

R

radical christocentrism, 313
Raffalli, Fr. Maurice, 59, 60, 62
Rahner, Fr. Karl, 311, 315, 327
Rangel, Bishop Licinio
    consecration of, 180–184
Ratzinger, Cardinal Joseph, 2, 9, 14, 15, 23, 39, 53, 64, 66, 114, 115, 119, 137, 214, 289, 324, 327, 328, 329, 332
    and Gerard, 10
Reagan, Ronald, 34, 93
reconciliation with Rome, 75
religionless religion, 338
religious liberty, 264, 280, 281, 283

Requiem Mass, 18, 76
Restoration, 341
Retreat House in Phoenix, Arizona, 346
retreats, 18, *see also* Ignatian Spiritual Retreats
Revolution, *see* Vatican II
Rhodesia, 30
Ridgefield, 18, 56
Rifan, Fr. Fernando, 182, 236
Rios, Michael, 190
rock and roll, 88
Romans, 5
Romanticism, 341, 342
Rome, 118, 173, 179, *see also* Catholic Church
 carrot and stick approach, 162, 215, 291
 divide and rule approach, 11
 excommunications from, 1
 feelers from, 111-116
 and Fraternity of St. Peter, 36-42
 New Code of Canon Law, *see* Canon Law, New Code
 principles, 136-139
 SSPX
  taking out of, 202-206
 and Tradition, irreconcilability, 13-18
Rome and Queen of the Holy Rosary Chapel in Vienna, Ohio, 203
Rosary, 18, 199
 importance ot, 104
 prayer group, 76
Roux, Abbe Daniel le, 106-110
Russia, 29, 84, 102, 149, 150, 234, *see also* Consecration of Russia to Mary's Immaculate Heart, 1988

S

sacramental marriage, 271
Sacred Heart, 45, 223
St. Agnes, 359-365
St. Agnes parish in Manhattan, 41
St. Athanasius, 22
St. Augustine, 222
St. Boniface, 74
St. Cyprian, 253
St. Dominic, 336
St. Emerentiana, 359-365
St. Francis Xavier, 68, 69
St. Ignatius' Spiritual Exercises, *see* Spiritual Exercises of St. Ignatius
St. Madeleine-Sophie Barat, 79
St. Martin, 72
St. Mary's Academy, Kansas, 130
St. Paul, 307, 319, 320

St. Peter
        fraternity of, and Rome, 36–42
St. Peter Martyr Priory, 360
St. Peter's Fraternity (FSSP), 115, 118, 152, 204
St. Peter's Society, 161
St. Pius X, Pope, 21, 127
St. Thomas Aquinas, 309, 360
salvation, 105, 130
sanctifying grace, 271, 383, 384, 385
San Damiano, 90
San Geronimo della Carita, 22
Santa Maria Trastevere, 27
Sardegna family, 58
Sarto, Pope, 310
Satanism, 88
Saudi Arabia, 148–149
Sawyer, Peter, 31
Schmidberger, Fr. Franz, 159, 162, 202, 205, 213, 260, 262, 387, 398
        letter to Cardinal Oddi, 227
school system, *see also* education system; public school system
Schumann, Robert, 265
Scruton, Roger, 46, 48, 49
SCSF, *see* Seminary Continuous Support Fund (SCSF)
Second Secret, 102, 234
Second Vatican Council, *see* Vatican II
The Second Vatican Council and Religious Liberty (Davies), 279
Secretariat for the Unity of Christians, 83
secular humanism, 134, 135
secularism, 226, 245
Sedecias, 101
sedevacantism, sedevacantists, 30, 106–110, 130, 217–223, 287
        and moderninsm, 122–131
See of Peter, 123
See (Sedes) of Rome, 217
self-righteousness, 348
self-worship, 375
Seminary Continuous Support Fund (SCSF), 27, 253
Seoul, South Korea, 54, 69, 70, 95
sexual identity, *see also* homosexuals, homosexuality
sexual revolution of the '60's and '70's, 78
Shakespeare, William, 189
Shuko Nakama, Mrs., 68
sign of the Son, 104
sillonism, 56
Sillon, Pope Pius X's letter on, 56
sin
        original sin, 186, 227, 314
Singapore, 71

Si Si, No No, 84, 255, 305, 307, 308, 309, 312, 314, 315, 322, 323, 324, 327, 328, 329, 330, 332, 333, 334
Sister Lucy of Fatima, 76, 85, 335
Slacks I, 185–190
Slacks II, 196–201
Slacks III, 271–277
Slacks IV, 352–358
slavery, 30
social equality, *see* equality
socialism, 31, 95
Society of Saint Pius X (SSPX), 83, 107, 111, 119, 162, 190, 217, 279, 288, 289, 290, 345, 350, 358, 389
    20th Anniversary, 140–142
    Columbus Commemorative Congress, 260–264
    Dominican building (Winona), *see* Winona seminary
    in Ecône, *see* Ecône, Switzerland
    General Chapter, 387–391, 398, 400
    German seminary in Zaitzkofen in Bavaria, 212
    human frailty of, 392–397
    La Reja seminary, *see* La Reja
    miracles in, 173
    New Testament priesthood, 318–322
    ordination ceremonies at, 18
    as pilot-light, 191–195
    retreats, *see also* Ignatian Spiritual Retreats; Spiritual Exercises of St. Ignatius
    taking out by Rome, 202–206
    in the USA, 223
    Winona, *see* Winona seminary
Society of St. Peter, 39
Society Sisters in Armada, Michigan, 70
Solemn Requiem Mass, 76
Solzhenitsyn, Alexander, 98
South Africa, 29, 31
South America, 156
South Germany, 17
South Korea, 69
Spain, 154
Spiritual Exercises of St. Ignatius, 56, 81, 159, 174, 295, 344, 378
The Splendor of Truth (John Paul II), 382
"Splitting Faith" (TV program), 34
Stalin, Joseph, 97
Stern, Karl, 189
Stone, Oliver, 225
Stuttgart, Germany, 247
subjectivism, 308
Sun Belt, 12
Super-Catholic, 315, 316, 317
supernatural countermeasures, 98, 102

supernatural truths, 126
supernature, 307, 310, 349
Switzerland
    Traditionalists, 90
Sydney, 31, 32
Symphronius, 362
synthesis of all heresies, 21

T

teleologism, 368, 372
television, 199, 227, 350, 354
Ten Commandments, 226, 367, 391
terrorism, 31
Theresa, Mother, 145
They Have Uncrowned Him (Archbishop Lefebvre), 14
Thiandoum, Cardinal, 114, 135
    letter to Madiran, 133
Third Secret, 102, 231, 232
30 Days, 202, 289
Thomas, Clarence, 197
Thomism, 125, 306, 317
three Messages, 103, *see also* First Secret; Second Secret; Third Secret
Tokyo, 68
Touvier, Paul, 55, 56
Traditional Benedictine Monastery, 15
Traditional bishops, 83
    necessity of, 73-76
Traditional Mass, *see also* Old Mass; Tridentine Mass
Traditional movement, 221
Tradition Catholique, 274
Tradition, Traditionalism, 1, 11, 52, 130, 221, 253, 257
    growth of, 4
    and obedience, 24-28
    progress of, 20
    unity and perseverance in, 170-174
Travis, John, 65
Treaty of Versailles, 245
Tridentine liturgy of 1962, 10
Tridentine Mass, 22, 30, 89, 118, 120, 152, 167, 192, 318
    at St. Agnes, 41
Tridentine priests, 16
trousers, as women's dress, 185-190, 196-201, 271-277
True Mass, 11

U

ultra-liberals, 108
United States, 51, 72, 117-121

women, in military, 77-81
Universal Church, 257, 279
universal education, 99
universal Revolution, 134
U.S. Bishops' Liturgy Committee, 118
utopia, utopians, 122

V

Vallet, Fr., 295
Vatican II, 4, 5, 8, 33, 38, 54, 83, 128, 137, 141, 157, 181, 208, 231, 232, 255, 257, 270, 276, 282, 283, 287, 295, 306, 325, 355, 384, 385, 388, 389, *see also* Conciliarism, Conciliarists
    Freemasonry, *see* Freemasonry, Freemasons
Vatican-Moscow agreement, 102
Verbum, 1, 19, 20, 32, 58, 216, 237, 260, 264, 278, 360
Verdun, battlefield of, 242-248, 269
Veritatis Splendor (John Paul II), 366, 385
Veronica, Mother, 156
vocations, 372
von Balthasar, Fr. Hans Urs, 312, 313, 315, 316, 323, 330, 332
von Speyr, Adrienne, 313-314, 314, 315, 316, 330, 332
Voodooism, 285-292

W

The Wanderer, 291
warning, from God, 233, *see also* wrath of God
Washington, D.C., 29
Weak Link: The Feminization of the American Military, 77
Wellington, 32
White, David, 236
The Whole Truth About Fatima (Michael), 84, 288
Wigratzbad seminary, 23, 152
Williamson, Bishop Richard N.
    visit to Africa, 345-351
    visit to Latin America, 154-159
Windhoek, 29
Winona seminary, 12, 18, 41, 56, 116, 153, 159, 254, 318, 379, 392
    renovation of, 6, 24
wisdom, 32
WNBC-TV, 34
Wojtyla, Cardinal Karol, 331
womanliness of women, 188-189, 198-200
women, *see also* feminism
    accompanying men's activities, 199, 200
    clothing, 185-190, 196-201, 271-277, 353
    liberation of, 78
    in military, 77-81

    obedience of, 199
Women's Liberation Movement, 210
Workshop on Modernism, 56
World Council of Churches, 54
World War I, 242, 295
World War II, 148, 149, 189, 232, 269, 295
World War III, 233
wrath of God, 58–62

Y

Yew, Lee Kuan, 71
young mothers, 207–211
young parents, 51
youth, youngsters, 224, 340–344

Z

Zaitzkofen, Bavaria, 17
Zendejas, Fr., 155
Zimbabwe, 30, 31, 350

www.ingramcontent.com/pod-product-compliance
Lightning Source LLC
Chambersburg PA
CBHW071258110526
44591CB00010B/705